The Rigor of Things

The Rigor of Things

Conversations with Dan Arbib

Jean-Luc Marion

Translated by Christina M. Gschwandtner

FORDHAM UNIVERSITY PRESS

New York 2017

This book was first published in French under the title *La rigueur des choses: Entretiens avec Dan Arbib*,

This work, published as part of a program providing publication assistance, received financial support from the French Ministry of Foreign Affairs, the Cultural Services of the French Embassy in the United States and FACE (French American Cultural Exchange). French Voices Logo designed by Serge Bloch.

Library of Congress Cataloging-in-Publication Data available online at http://catalog.loc.gov.

Printed in the United States of America

19 18 17 5 4 3 2 1

First edition

in memory of Maxime Charles

CONTENTS

FOREWORD

David Tracy

It is hardly necessary to introduce Professor Jean-Luc Marion to this audience, since he has become a very important interlocutor in North America for over twenty years. However, the occasion of the English translation of these fascinating interviews is a good time to remind ourselves of some of his accomplishments in philosophy, intellectual history, and, more recently, theology.

First philosophy. There is no doubt that Jean-Luc Marion is the foremost living phenomenologist. Not only has he continued the great tradition of Husserl, Heidegger, Levinas, Henry, Ricoeur, and others, but Marion has advanced that tradition in major ways, especially through his groundbreaking phenomenological work on related phenomena of givenness and gift as well as his analysis of the saturated phenomenon. Along with these original phenomenological contributions, Professor Marion has also written major interpretive essays on such phenomenological predecessors as Edmund Husserl, Martin Heidegger, Emmanuel Levinas, and Michel Henry.

Second, the scholarship of intellectual history. In the field of intellectual history, Professor Marion early became a major interpreter of seventeenth-century philosophy, especially in several volumes on the very founder of modern philosophy, René Descartes. It is no small thing to provide a new and persuasive interpretation of Descartes. Most intellectual historians today no longer follow the interpretation of Descartes given by the standard histories of philosophy, nor even the once-influential readings of Martin Heidegger or Étienne Gilson—today they follow Marion's. His Descartes work alone would have assured him a major place in his second discipline, intellectual history.

Third, theology. In more recent years, Marion has turned explicitly, no longer merely implicitly, to theology. Here he has both followed and advanced the theological program of his teachers, the great (indeed now classic) resourcement thinkers of early and mid-twentieth-century French theology: Henri de Lubac, Jean Daniélou, Yves Congar, Louis Bouyer, and the Swiss theologian Hans Urs von Balthasar. Marion's earlier work in philosophical theology, beginning years ago with his influential book *God Without Being*, has increased in recent years, augmenting his writing for and editorial work in the French edition of the distinguished journal *Communio*. He has also written a major essay on Dionysus the Areopagite and more recently a brilliant book on Augustine. His present and future work at the University of Chicago as well as at the Institut Catholique in Paris will, so he tells his readers, address the history of theological reflection from the second-century Logos theologian Justin Martyr forward through the history of early Christian theology, including Tertullian and Clement of Alexandria.

Jean-Luc Marion's range, his phenomenological acuity, his unusual skill in *explication du texte*, his hermeneutical care in intellectual history, and his originality on givenness, gift, and saturated phenomena have made Marion one of the most important thinkers of our period.

So much is this the case that nine years ago France awarded Professor Marion its highest honor, election to the Académie Française; the next year, Italy elected him to the Accademia dei Lincei; and the year after that Germany awarded him the Karl Jaspers annual prize for philosophy.

These brilliant interviews fill in many personal and intellectual details for Anglophone readers, just as the original French publication performed that service so successfully for his readers in France.

Indeed, in recalling the many intellectual paths—philosophy, intellectual history, theology—to which Professor Marion has contributed in major ways, I began to ask myself how such unrelenting productivity and creativity in these major fields is possible. Well, as the Scholastics rightfully declared, *Ab esse ad posse valet illatio*. These interviews help clarify the range and depth of Jean-Luc Marion's amazing work.

PREFACE

At least two reasons could have kept me from committing to a book of interviews. First, I have always had reservations about this sort of writing. Second, publishers often aim more at popularizing than at paying attention to the complexity of phenomena. This makes it difficult not to get caught between two equally calamitous options: Either one devalues anything really worthwhile that one has taken such trouble to write, or one becomes anecdotal, giving an *apologia pro vita sua* with its accompanying beautiful lies. And, to call on Proverbs, besides these two reasons there is a third: In these kinds of false confessions, the author always says too much or too little. Whether it is because he distrusts the reader or because of a lack of self-confidence or even self-hatred, he runs the risk of tottering into tall tales or only talking to himself.[1]

I would have given in to these reasons and not thwarted my basic laziness had two friends not intervened. The first, Benoît Chantre, waited with a cordial but pitiless persistence for years to bag me, that is to say, to add me finally to his collection. The second, Dan Arbib, who was my student for a long time and is now an established scholar, persuaded me through a great deal of understanding, clear-sightedness, and tact that well-conducted conversations can become properly philosophical exercises. I would not have taken the plunge without him, and if even the smallest good comes of it, I owe it to him more than to anyone else. I thus reassure myself with the thought that the two share with me both the risk and the responsibility for this exercise and its result. Finally, there was Jean and Marie-José Duchesne's hospitality in hosting the meetings with Dan Arbib. Their home

1. [Literally: "foundering and recounting a 'life of Potemkin' or at the very least repeating a dialogue between Jean-Jacques and Rousseau"—References to a Russian prince, lover of Catherine II, who lived in grand style, and to the philosopher Jean-Jacques Rousseau's *Confessions*.]

in Normandy had been the haven for so many other beginnings that even this undertaking found a natural place there. My gratitude goes to them.

Consequently, this won't be a sketch of memories or a parody of a premature final judgment, made blindly and in bad faith. I will not move forward masked,[2] neither to unmask myself nor to unmask others, but in order to uncover a history that greatly exceeds my own. It was the unbelievably good fortune of my generation to have witnessed the group of notable figures that lived through it or gave shape to it and who often were far more than merely professors or thinkers.

It is my first duty to bear witness to them, if only so that my former and current students might know that the desert they are crossing was once inhabited, even if the period's major figures were still obscure. Maybe this will give them new hope for the present. I have only included anecdotes that go beyond me and have current import. While not engaging in useless polemics, I have not refrained from any overly tidy judgments when it is a matter of evidence that has been ignored and must some day come to light.

My second intention was to try to reconstruct the path my work has taken without simplifying too much by bringing together as best I can its various regions—history of philosophy, phenomenology, theology, and prudential judgment. My entire life has consisted of intellectual work, and I cannot take account of it except in those terms: This is the sense in which I should be read. Retrospectively, I am struck today by its overall coherence. Its main theme in the end is the question of the event, the approach of presence starting from the present understood as gift. What really matters always happens. This is the way in which rigor is unleashed, but the rigor of things, not what we impose on them or think we can force on them.

Jean-Luc Marion
Nonancourt, December 2011–Lods, July 2012

Dan Arbib thanks Judith for her proofreading.

2. [A reference to the important theme of "*larvatus pro deo/larvatus prodeo*," which Marion investigates repeatedly in his work on Descartes. He briefly discusses this in Chapter 2.]

TRANSLATOR'S NOTE

As this is a book of interviews, I have taken pains to render it in conversational English, which unfortunately meant at times sacrificing some literal meanings. When it seemed necessary, I have indicated such deviations in the notes. I have also added some additional explanatory notes, beyond the few already in the French text, about aspects of the French educational system or French culture when certain references Marion makes would probably be unfamiliar to the English-speaking reader and when the context requires it. Any such explanations that were added in the translation—whether within the text or in the notes—are indicated by square brackets.

I am most grateful to Stephen Lewis, who helped me unravel quite a few grammatical constructions or idiomatic expressions that gave me grief. Jean-Luc Marion and Dan Arbib also responded most graciously to several questions of clarification. My work on this translation is dedicated to my parents in love and gratitude.

The Rigor of Things

1. My Path

Jean-Luc Marion, what would you say if you had to summarize in a few comments the meaning of the philosophical work that has prompted you along the course of your career?

This question already gives rise to a paradox, for one really carries on a philosophical project without knowing what prompts it, or even precisely because one does not know it. In a sense, I have never had the impression that I knew where I was going, and I have never started a philosophical undertaking, such as a book or an article, being sure of where I was going or even what I was doing. Obviously, I always know the question I have been asked or am asking myself, but I do not know exactly where I am going, and the interest of high-level philosophical work surely lies in the fact that one covers a distance that one only sizes up retrospectively. It is also true that with each book one sees one's aims with less clarity. In this sense, then, I cannot respond to your question. And conversely, even though I am certainly conscious that a certain unity emerges, I don't think I'm the one best positioned to describe it.

I remember one revealing instance. One day, I think I was in the *hypokhâgne*,[1] I was walking with a friend in the Luxembourg Gardens, and out of nowhere the very simple idea suddenly occurred to me that "the question of being" was not the first question but that it is raised, like a reflection—a reflection more than an effect—from a more primordial situation, which we could call, let's say, creation. Being comes *after* an entirely different event; it comes as its trace, its remnant, and its deposit. Even today I still recall having seen *this* at that moment. I don't think I have ever said or written this anywhere else, but assuredly from the very beginning it was *that* which drove me: namely, whether *to be or not to be* is not the first question.

Entry into Philosophy

"That" *struck you, just as Rousseau had the idea of the* First Discourse *when he went to see Diderot locked up in Vincennes?*

Well, I didn't fall into catalepsy, but *that* struck me maybe like Sartre's tree[2]—I was surrounded by trees—and it was an event for me. I have always been profoundly convinced by this obscurely obvious fact. I later realized that I was conscious of it before having formulated it and even before having formed a notion of its meaning. But since then I have not stopped going back to it.

You had this intuition in the hypokhâgne. *But who motivated you to strive for the École normale supérieure? Did you come from a background that pushed you toward such goals?*

Not at all. When I entered the *hypokhâgne*, I didn't even know that the preparatory class led to the École normale supérieure, rue d'Ulm. And I was

1. [Preparatory class leading to the entrance exams for the prestigious École normale supérieure, in Paris. The school's location on the rue d'Ulm is often added to its name, as Marion does below; frequently it is simply called the École. Several important schools in Paris provide these two years of preparatory classes. The *hypokhâgne* is the first year of preparation, and the *khâgne* is the second or final year. Marion went to the Condorcet school for this course of preparatory study.]

2. [Jean-Paul Sartre's existentialist novel *Nausea* contains a famous passage in which the central character is struck by the gnarled roots of a tree. The passage is a turning point in the novel and in the character's self-realization.]

so naive and ignorant that, when we got our schedules, I was surprised that there was no physics or mathematics! I was elated when I was told there would be no more of that. Actually, I come from a family of engineers, and I was thus destined to be an engineer. And I had everything to equip me for that. From earliest adolescence I was steeped in mechanics, walking around in my uncles' factory, then following them in the industrial yards, for example in the coal mines of the North or those in Asturias. The manufacturing of engines, of gearboxes or of reduction gear, the design of suspensions and of the cooling of motorcycles or cars, that was all part of everyday conversation. I have inhaled the acrid smell of the smelting works and the sour smell of castor oil at the Montlhéry racecourses. I have been deafened by the red roar of open blast furnaces and by the howling of Norton 500 engines running at full speed or the acceleration of scooters shifting gears during a race. At the age of ten, or even earlier, I took my first flight in a Stampe, then in a Piper, with my uncle and godfather, who even made me hold the clutch of a Jodel (the first, a two-seater of 60 CV, I believe). With this advice: "Never move it more than the size of a napkin ring." And: "It's easy to take off: Just face the wind and pull the handle when the back goes up." Or: "Landing is difficult, but it is really just a matter of leveling to the ground with the loss of speed." That was good advice, I think, which can easily be applied to the intellectual life. I also marveled at the wood chips flying from the jointer plane, the coils being cut from the steel by the milling machine or the turning tool, the virtuosity of the fitters, artists who worked in tenths of millimeters without electronics. I wondered at seeing an engine dismantled to its crankshaft, then repaired and reassembled under the hood in a half hour. I even knew how to mix mortar with a shovel and without a cement mixer by using the correct proportions of sand and cement with or without gravel, and how to build a wall out of bricks or even of stones that still need cutting. I admired working with wood or plaster (the watercolors of construction). And many other things. This was my early and fascinating experience of technology. I do not regret it, I still feel nostalgic about it, and I have learned from it. As in running, the middle-distance race—the king of athletics—is the perfect initiation to the life of the mind, in all senses, including mastery over suffering one consents to for a result—for oneself.

What was your parents' profession?

My father was a weapons engineer in the Defense Department. He was in charge of combat tanks, first the AMX 13, then the AMX 30, and also of the armor-plated reconnaissance engine, the EBR Panhard, and so forth. My mother first taught as a teacher trained in the traditional way, then as a literature professor; all my uncles were engineers. In theory I was destined to be good at math and to enter an engineering school, like everyone around me with the exception of one grandfather, a retired lawyer and respectable painter, and another grandfather, a mountaineer killed as an Alpine chasseur at Douaumont in 1916. Probably providentially I found myself little by little inclined to literature—I think to the great displeasure of some of my family. My father, who miraculously survived the retaliation camps[3] from 1940 to 1945, was of the opinion that literature, in his words, "is just a lot of hot air." This always seemed strange to me because he had Corneille's and Racine's speeches memorized and had the sort of culture and knowledge of literature that was never inflicted on me in high school, which he had acquired from the brothers of the Christian schools (the celebrated "Frères quatre-bras") and from the Jesuits. He had this kind of direct relationship with French literature far earlier than me, and it was doubtlessly better. Still I had the good luck of falling ill one year, at the transition between fifth and fourth grade,[4] including a later relapse. I was prescribed fresh air (at Menton, a winter of dreams) and was to remain lying down or even immobile. This was a marvelous thing! I was able to read like crazy, everything or, rather, anything (Zola, Camus, Teilhard de Chardin, Stendhal, Pascal, Kierkegaard, *Miroir-Sprint*, detective thrillers . . . and the Bible), often without understanding anything at all. That did me a world of good and allowed me a little later to become "literary," thus pretty early on.

I have one very specific memory from my schooldays at the Sèvres high school: One day, probably in second grade, having to do a ten-minute presentation about *Micromégas*, I spoke for an hour, ending with a commentary on the Cold War and the failed Paris Conference! For the first time I discovered that I could *hold* an audience. Everyone was surprised, my classmates, the teacher, myself, and from that moment I was "literary" without reservation, playing this little social role consciously (I must have been pretty unbearable). But Sèvres was a high school where the supposedly innovative pedagogy of the time encouraged tacit competition between all

3. [Internment camps during World War II for people in France not willing to collaborate with the Nazi regime.]

4. [The French school system counts classes down instead of up, so the fifth grade comes before the fourth. First grade is hence the final one.]

the students and all the classes. In short, I read in a helter-skelter fashion, mixed everything up, and didn't understand a whole lot. I argued about everything and anything with total recklessness, but at least I was in deeply. That said, retrospectively I can see that from the beginning I did not write literature; everything went through the concept. Even so, the year of philosophy did not go well at all.[5] I was in conflict with the teacher, a young student [lit. a "normalienne," i.e., someone from the École normale] from Jordan, who was intelligent and ideological, proud to be working on a dissertation with Deleuze (obviously we hadn't the slightest idea who he was, but she often appealed to his authority). We were immediately involved in a kind of rivalry to see who would be the teacher. I never managed to make it through a class but would always be kicked out by the end of a half hour. Because I had other interests, I did not really start working until I was in the *hypokhâgne*, in the Condorcet high school. There also I still hesitated between literature and philosophy. Besides, even when studying with Beaufret I was never the first in philosophy but almost always the second.

Can you tell us anything about the first?

I seem to remember that it was often Alain Renaut who won. He was excellent and an orthodox Heideggerian at the time. I was still second in the *agrégation*. Never first. There was always a good reason for that, a sort of little gap, because I did assignments that didn't quite follow the norm, weren't entirely on the subject, went in a slightly different direction than the one expected. Indeed, literature was my passion, which I owe without doubt to another admirable *khâgne* teacher who taught at Condorcet, Daniel Gallois. He was a person of the novel in the strictest sense: He appeared in *Le foulard rouge*, where Gilles Perrault retraces some of the history of OCM [Organisation civile et militaire], a civil and military organization of the Resistance from the fashionable districts, of which Gallois was a perfect representative. He was arrested and tortured, but he did not speak, a true hero of the Resistance. Obviously he never talked about this.

5. [The preparation for the *baccalauréat*, the final exams in the French high school system, included a mandatory year of philosophy. Recently, this has been changed to apply only to those students pursuing a humanities track. Passing the highly competitive *agrégation* examination (see below) guaranteed a post teaching philosophy to students in their final year. The higher one passes, the more prestigious the school to which one is assigned.]

A legendary personality. No one who went through the *khâgne* under him will ever forget him. He taught me to be very rigorous in demonstration, plan, or conclusion, to make sure an argument is rhetorically sound. But he also had a feeling for poetry. He knew by heart—I think this is a true claim—everything worth anything in French poetry. During that entire period—and this feeling has never wholly left me even today—I told myself that I should devote my time to study either the poetry of the sixteenth century or the symbolism and poetry of the twentieth century. Thus, at the time of the entrance exams for the École, I was most at home in literature, and my first degree was a literature degree. I thus learned the French language and poetry with this formidable and exceptional lover of bow ties, the great Daniel Gallois (Daniel, like the prophet, we kidded), who terrorized us but truly loved us, as we found out at the end of the *khâgne*. I decided between literature and philosophy only very late, at the time of my entry into the École, because one day in the aquarium[6] my friends (at least Rémi Brague and Jean-Robert Armogathe) asked me very insistently to move to philosophy. Because I am obedient and easily swayed, I accordingly opted for philosophy.

Let's stay with poetry for a moment. What kind of authors do you like?

Ronsard, Maurice Scève, Du Bellay, Jean-Baptiste Chassignet, Jean de Sponde, and Baudelaire, Verlaine, Mallarmé, Rimbaud. Next to poetry, the novel in fact seemed to me a bit like liquor that has grown somewhat stale. Yes: Maurice Scève, Ronsard, Mallarmé, Claudel's poetry (obviously also his theater, but it is more like a staged or dramatized version of his poetry; one forgets this a bit). I also went through a period dominated by René Char, then more generally by contemporary poetry. Besides, among all the things I appreciate about the Académie française, there is power in always going back to the French language, in experiencing its absolutely inextinguishable and superior resources. For a long time, the challenge for me was to succeed in mastering several foreign languages for teaching, for lecturing, and for work, but, when all is said and done, I believe that one day I will try to learn French! I probably won't succeed, but that just makes it all the more urgent.

6. The attendees' nickname for the entry hall to the École normale supérieure, on the rue d'Ulm.

But it is clear that, in contrast to Levinas, for example, who began with novelistic projects, you were never tempted by the novel.

Providence has spared me that temptation, which would have led to disaster, hopefully to an obscure one. I have certainly, here and there, tried my hand at poetry, but without any success: One does not easily write a Mallarméan sonnet, and Mallarmé himself did not often succeed at it. Moreover, reading Heidegger's poetry (not to mention Sartre's novels) has definitely confirmed me in the conviction that one should not mix up the genres. In turn, for philosophy, I believe that I am now beginning to have an entry-level knowledge of more or less how one must undertake it.

To what would you attribute this incompatibility between poetry and philosophy? Descartes said that one does much better in metaphysics when one is less gifted in mathematics, and vice versa. It seems that this is somewhat the same thing.

Actually, I think that one cannot practice both of them or that one does so only with great difficulty. Even Valéry does not really manage it (even so, I know at least two or three indisputable exceptions). In the one case [philosophy], it is the concept that is determinative; in the other, it is neither allegory nor metaphor but the word. One must choose between the word and the concept. Their logic is not the same. In both realms one demonstrates, but one does not show with the same means or following the same kind of rigor. It is hazardous to claim to move from one logic to the other. Even when a poet moves over to prose, often he makes more (and better) prose poems than conceptual demonstrations. In short, in my view a conceptual literature means a bad literature. Inversely, a nonconceptual philosophy indicates a bad philosophy. The poem and the concept do indeed offer two registers of manifestation, but they remain irreducible to each other.

We will come back to this, because even so there is in your work a certain use of language and of words that requires further commentary. You say that you owe your philosophical vocation to Rémi Brague's appeal. Yet you already had Jean Beaufret as a philosophy teacher in the khâgne. *Do you remember his courses?*

Beaufret? He taught so well because he *thought* in front of you, directly, if I can put it like that. He said what he thought, or, more exactly, when he said something, he thought it. That was quite different from the teachers who told stories. Beaufret took at face value the Heideggerian principle of "not telling stories" and to speak only in thinking. For example, this translated into the habit of always citing authors in the original language. Beaufret would begin by writing Greek, German, and Latin on the board; then he would ask us to translate it. We would give a flat translation, and then he would help us see that each term had a history, a genealogy, and that one must reconstitute this history in order to understand its meaning. And then he would jumble the chronologies; accordingly, when he demonstrated something, relating a sentence in Kant to a sentence in Descartes and another one in Aristotle, he would conclude in an inimitable breathless voice: "You see, what they say is not alike, but they are saying the same; not the same thing, but *the same*." The students took notes (because he dictated) without really understanding, and Beaufret, inhaling from his yellow Gitane, then concluded with: "But what, did Aristotle read Kant?" The students thought the old man a bit tired after two hours of instruction, but he drew another puff and confirmed: "But yes, obviously, obviously!" And this "obviously, obviously," that is, that Aristotle had *naturally* read Kant, was decisive for me. It implied that the philosophers, especially within metaphysics, precisely respond to each other, that they remain in permanent correspondence. This is the correspondence that allows us to do what we call "the history of philosophy," that is to say, to show how metaphysics is unfolded. This was one of the main things with Beaufret. Yet what strikes me in hindsight is that in a sense he never spoke of Heidegger in class.

Even so, he is known for being the one who introduced this thinker into France.

Of course! But he introduced us much more to Heidegger by not speaking of him directly in class. As the good *khâgne* teacher that he was, he apparently limited himself to teaching us the history of philosophy to prepare us for the École entrance exams. But I discovered very quickly later to what extent this history of philosophy came from the Heideggerian history of metaphysics: He put Heidegger into our heads, but without citing him. It was more like a direct performance of Heideggerian thought than a course *on* Heidegger. That is probably why he had such an impact on us. It wasn't a commentary on or an explication of Heidegger, as if it were a matter of sustaining certain theses against others, but one found oneself *inside* of a thought in the process of thinking without always being fully aware of it. When I passed the entrance exams, I only knew some of Heidegger's texts, the *Introduction to Metaphysics*, the "Letter on Humanism." What one reads in the preparatory class. I did not know more, in fact rather less, of Heidegger than of Kant. I knew a little bit of Lacan, from which to draw pretty conclusions; I obviously believed myself to be Spinozist, like all the beginners who let themselves be taken in by appearances, and I droned on rationally at least once in each paper, but I had not read *Sein und Zeit* before arriving at the École. Nevertheless, I had actually already become more Heideggerian than I imagined. That is why it was necessary for me later, but then very quickly, to shake off this armor I wore without knowing it. I was only able to do this by writing *God Without Being*.

What memories do you have from your years at the École?

Very mixed memories. I entered in the theatrical group, the *Café de la gare* of May 1968, just in time to take part in the great half-improvised performance of the spring. I participated in this performance as a committed observer, or at least not as an uncommitted militant. Oddly enough, the May movement has taken on a magnitude that no one expected; at the beginning one thought of it as a bit of a schoolboy jest. It was not until the day that my roommate [*coturne*][7] (a specialist in Latin and in Gallic history, rather frail, about as far away from being an athlete or great warrior as possible) turned up wearing an enormous motorcycle helmet and announced to us, "I'm going there, and it will heat up," that I said to myself that things were beginning to gather force. Everyone was surprised, I as much as the others. After each demonstration, the École became the fallback for all the wounded, who had breathed in too much tear gas or had been clubbed too many times. We conveyed the wounded to the infirmary and sheltered the others in the dorms [*turnes*]. It was an unbelievable circus, halfway between the end of the Battle of the Alamo and *The Musketeers in the Monastery*. At the same time, I was not able to take all this seriously, not even politically, because I actually agreed with the Maoists, who stayed seated on the entry stairs to the aquarium while the whole world called them to action and who responded to all those who were outraged: "We have performed a political analysis: the situation is not even prerevolutionary!" They were right; the situation was not even prerevolutionary.

7. The colleague with whom a *normalien*, i.e., a student at the École, shares his room (*la turne*, in the *normalien* parlance). Play of words on the cot*h*urne with which the actors clothed themselves in antiquity.

Yet, the sociological and cultural consequences of this event were felt only later and were more important than what happened at the time. For two or three months, a kind of *commedia dell'arte* was played out as street theater. Even so, this theater brought my political education up to snuff; it taught me lots about the genealogy of the Marxist movement, about the different layers of all the Trotskyists of the world, about Joseph Stalin's doctrine of categories, about the Maoist distinction between poor peasants and average-poor peasants, and so forth. I learned how one manipulates a GM [General Assembly] and how one disinforms a public; I admired the virtuosos of beautiful lies and envied the fire breathers of effective slogans, who managed to get a whole crowd to chant the longest refrain ever attempted, convincingly and in rhyme: "Down with the Gaullist government, which is against the working class and cause of unemployment and misery. Down with . . . (back to the chorus)." Regardless, I learned a lot, but I never thought that we had experienced a political event in itself—except for the fact, which was certainly political and which constituted the paradox of the event: the ideological (or cultural, if one prefers that) undoing of Soviet Marxism and of the Communist Party. At that moment, the Gaullists, as they falsely called themselves—actually, they were partisans of Pompidou and others—swept the legislative elections of June 1968 by attributing the disorder to a Communist Party offensive. Instead, the events witnessed its defeat. I saw Aragon treated as a "Stalinist crook" by Cohn-Bendit on the steps of the Sorbonne chapel, if I recall correctly. And that day Cohn-Bendit said what we all thought, but he said it in a solemn manner, and the reason was definitely understood.

More than a political event, May '68 was fundamentally a cultural event that turned out also to have had certain political consequences. Ten years later, the whole issue of dissidents from central Europe arriving in Paris and being supported by a large part of the institutional left was to my eyes the most noteworthy effect of May '68, but that occurred only at that moment and could in no way have been foreseen (except by Clavel). In this context, one can count also as a positive, however minor, aspect of these days the period that I experienced with the "New Philosophers," around the years 1970 to 1980: when I encountered Maurice Clavel, Guy Lardreau, Christian Jambet, Philippe Nemo, André Glucksmann, and all those who came out of May '68. I found myself agreeing with them about many things, including the essential bit—the nature of the "revolution" that had taken place or, rather, that had *not* taken place.

Then you don't think that what Luc Ferry and Alain Renaut call and criticize as the "thought of '68" was a bad thing?

The denunciation of the "thought of '68" will remain superficial because, when it comes down to it, there was no single or coherent "thought of '68." The denunciation of humanism (Deleuze, Foucault, etc.) formed neither its stakes nor its property (this criticism goes back at least to [Heidegger's] "Letter on Humanism" or even to [Husserl's] *Crisis of the European Sciences*). The serious political stakes result from the end of the domination of the Communist Party over the left, from the breakup of this left into much more interesting tendencies, and, in the end, from the implosion of the Soviet bloc. Long before the politicians, the obscure actors of May '68 were the first to see this, and I was very lucky to be associated with them.

So you aren't affected by what the detractors of May '68 have called the "end of values," or "the end of the school," or the "end of authority," the "everything went to hell" view?

First, as you rightly say, it was a matter of values. And values, whether one is for or against them, never hold in and of themselves, because they depend on whoever gives them worth. What is particular to values lies in the fact that they have nothing of their own but depend entirely on evaluation, hence on the evaluator. On the other hand, in many respects, May '68 only confirmed what was actually already in place. The school "with neither God nor master," if I can put it like this, was already realized in the Sèvres high school in the 1960s when I was a student there. "Free creativity" and similar things already constituted the implicit (or explicit) ideology of my high school professors. Where it manifested itself most decisively, May '68 was sociologically not a cause but an effect, even a ratification of a state of fact. French society imagined itself to be still the same as in 1918 or in 1945, although that had not been the case for a long time: For the first time in a century and a half, a generation had grown up without war and in a period of unprecedented economic growth, peace had been established in Europe, the colonies were gaining their independence (and reciprocally France proclaimed its independence from the colonial empire), and so forth. French society simply admitted, officially, that it no longer was what it had been. May '68 did not accomplish a revolution but confirmed a state of affairs. It was an upheaval only for those who did not know this or who wanted to ignore the real situation in France. One can obviously debate the assessment of this evolution, but one should not turn it into a revolution.

You mentioned the "New Philosophers": What relationship did you maintain with this movement?

I was part of them, at the margins. The history of the "New Philosophers" is simple enough. Bernard-Henri Lévy was at the École at the same time as I was; we passed the *agrégation* together. He was then already what he still is today: an intelligent, lucid guy, courageous in his own way. In a sense, he had turned into a man of society and advertising by a mixture of ambition and intellectual modesty. For multiple reasons, he received a welcome at the Grasset publishing company. Responsible at the time for launching the collection "Figures" and having no authors available, he recruited among his schoolmates from the *khâgne* and the École. With Philip Nemo as middleman, he offered me a contract, which allowed me to do *Idol and Distance*. That book appeared between *La barbarie à visage humain* [*The Human Face of Barbarism*] and *Le testament de Dieu* [*God's Testament*], at the same time and in the same collection as that of the "New Philosophers." Thus at certain times I was one of them; at others I wasn't. What was interesting in this not always very philosophical nonmovement was to encounter Françoise Verny and Maurice Clavel, who stayed at the operation. Clavel saw this movement as a great war machine against everything that needed to be destroyed: "Destroy!" he said, and we were all charged with "destroying" something: Jean-Marie Benoist had to destroy structuralism, Philippe Nemo psychoanalysis, Lardreau and Jambet Maoist Marxism, Glucksman reserved Leninism for himself; as for me, I had to destroy Heidegger. A simplistic and completely delirious idea, but in that context amusing and maybe useful. After several months, we stepped into the breach. I, a bit protected and in retreat, because *Idol and Distance* seemed relatively less accessible than the other works in the same series, but acting also as a serious caution to the undertaking. I experienced this circus a little like I had participated in the theater of May '68: I was thirty years old, I approached the media and their in the end fairly superficial traps, their power and their relative powerlessness in the long run. This was an excellent initiation, which vaccinated me with a homeopathic dose of celebrity against the abuse of stronger and certainly deadly drugs.

How would you situate yourself politically at that time?

I was a Gaullist from my first moment of political consciousness in May 1958, and definitively. To the point that, after DeGaulle's death in 1970, I no longer had any enthusiasm or even decided political opinion. I am a nostalgic, like Chateaubriand, who knew that the monarchy would not return and that the royalist pretensions would themselves render it impossible. I admit that this position can today seem a bit too easy. But it comes from afar. My family was Gaullist. My mother and her brothers were part of the Resistance. My father was interned in a military camp established for those refusing to work for the Germans and for escapees, from where he came back in striped pants, weighing only forty kilos [about seventy-five pounds] and bearing permanent aftereffects. Under normal circumstances, he should not have come home, and my birth was a miracle. These kinds of things mark you. I have a very precise memory of a moment when my Gaullism was illustrated. In the morning of the very first night of the barricades, in May 1968, the students were assembled around the Ernest pool,[8] when the École was closed from the end of the night's fighting and encircled by the CRS, who threw tear-gas grenades over the railings. The question was whether the police would mount an attack against the École and, in that case, whether to protect the several hundred demonstrators still hidden in the dorms. What to do? as one said in 1905. The usual loudmouths proposed a plan, which actually worked: taking the refugees out as carefully as possible via the underground passages leading from the École to the science laboratories. But they thought it a good idea also to attempt a political analysis of each group before letting them go. I recall immediately having protested: "We are all in agreement to pull them out of this trap, but you can't require us to act as political commissioners." A great silence ensued, which put an end to the discussion. But upon leaving the general assembly, I was discreetly congratulated by some.

Were you able to work in the midst of such turbulence?

I spent 1968 reading *Being and Time* and working on Aristotle in the morning. The evening was more political.

8. The "bassin aux Ernest" is the fountain and pool occupying the court of the École normale superieure; the "Ernest" are, in *normalien* parlance, the red fish populating it, from the name of a director, Ernest Bersot, who directed the École from 1871 to 1880.

Did you read Sartre?

Not at all! From the time of high school onward, Sartre no longer existed. He never played the least intellectual role for me.

You soon devoted yourself to the study of Descartes, owing to your encounter with Ferdinand Alquié, a professor at the Sorbonne. How did you discover this philosopher? How did you decide to dedicate your life to him?

I did not decide this. One had to pass a masters, as one said. I had asked to do it in two years—at the time that was possible—a masters specializing in the history of philosophy, in order to have more time to devote to true research. But I had to obtain first, in double-quick time, a certificate in philosophy, which I would be able just to throw together, in that period of considerable laxity. Beaufret had convinced me during the *khâgne* that all the professors at the Sorbonne were stupid and ignorant. Nevertheless, having to find a director, and my friend Armogathe having led me to go hear Alquié, I discovered with surprise that there were exceptions to that rule. Not only was Alquié not useless at all, but there were several others of the same caliber (Aubenque, Gouhier, etc.). Like many others, I owe it to Alquié to have learned how to read a philosophical text, how to take it apart and put it back together, how to translate it, how to verify or to refute it, by example. At the time he was holding seminars on Spinoza and Malebranche. He showed us their evolution, even their contradictions, their ambivalent relationships with their predecessors or successors. I attended his courses and his seminar from 1968 onward until the end in 1975. In this very good schooling I learned the art and manner of working in the history of philosophy. It was there that I discovered the question that would interest me the most in Descartes, the doctrine of the creation of the eternal truths, which Alquié placed at the center of his interpretation. I suspected that even he did not assess its scope fully.

I discovered quite quickly in Descartes's 1630 letters to the Father Mersenne, in which he sets out the thesis of the creation of the truths, that in these letters, written in French, the few lines of Latin, except for two negations, are quotations from Suárez. Alquié (like other Descartes specialists) did not know this author and hence had not highlighted these quotations. This evidence was enough to show that Descartes had maintained a polemical position vis-à-vis his contemporary Suárez, probably the last of the great Scholastics. It was therefore necessary to look at Suárez. I knew one person at least who knew Suárez, Stanislas Breton, a Passionist priest, a professor at the Institut catholique de Paris, and a great friend of Althusser, who taught courses on Neo-Platonism at the École. Thanks to him (rather than going through Gilson or Vignaux) I was able to discover the second Scholastic period. Nevertheless, I quickly understood that one must begin at the real beginning, the Cartesian doctrine of science: I first devoted my master's thesis to the *Rules for the Direction of the Mind*, a text that has been remarkably little studied. And that was how everything started.

Ferdinand Alquié was a very colorful personality. Could you draw us a portrait of him?

He had kept a magnificent and inimitable Carcassonne accent that caused him to double his vowels; he only drank champagne, and on that topic his erudition seemed as inexhaustible as his reservoir of anecdotes. Under this surface, something totally different: an extremely serious philosophical sincerity and engagement, which he would summarize approximately like this: "One often asks me what my philosophy is. But I do not have my own philosophy. I only have the one and true philosophy, that of Plato, of Descartes, and of Kant, who in the final analysis say the same thing: being is not object and the object is not being." Basic, one might say. That may be so, but it was an efficient way of continually bringing together the history of philosophy with philosophy. It was also illuminating for the time of technology and for its exact thematic of the *same*. He spoke of himself as a "thwarted idler," a formulation with which many of us working were able to identify and that he illustrated to the very end: On his deathbed in the hospital until his final day, he corrected the proofs to the third and final volume of his edition of Kant's works in the Pléiade series. He was very friendly with the students he deemed worthy of his attention, he knew how to support them, to guide them, and above all to listen to them, to allow them to become themselves, even making them his peers and his friends. The list of research students, assistants, and the cohort of those whose career he helped attests to this; it includes Deleuze, Derrida, Birault, Philonenko, Brunschwig, Beyssade, Rivelaygue, Renaut, not to mention all the names that I forget or don't know. Following on many others (I was the last whose thesis he directed), he really made me work and progress. He was an extraordinary reader of texts. Besides, his books on Descartes (then his edition of Descartes), Malebranche, and Spinoza are flawless. They show how in order to reach his goal an author cannot, and even must not, always remain entirely coherent, how he hesitates, corrects and modifies himself, and begins again. When it comes down to it, Alquié really offered the opposite of Gueroult, who thought that understanding an author consists in making him systematic. In contrast, Alquié thought that understanding an author amounts to showing how he manages not to be systematic, to abandon expected, foreseeable, and a priori constructions, in order to recognize the things themselves as well as the demands and the flaws behind which they disguise themselves; the apparent contradictions often provide the symptoms of the essential paradoxes. This was a great lesson, for it is sometimes when an author wants to smooth out contradictions with all his might that he stops genuinely thinking. Alquié thus taught us to read the texts with a scrupulous honesty.

One must here call to mind his first thesis, *La découverte métaphysique de l'homme chez Descartes* [*The Metaphysical Discovery of the Human in Descartes*], a title in which except for the name "Descartes" all the words—"metaphysical," "human," and "discovery"—have a fluid meaning. This extraordinary book takes its point of departure from psychiatry to an unusual degree. In fact, in order to pass the *agrégation* in philosophy at Alquié's time, one had to have a certificate in the sciences, and the philosophers, not being great mathematicians, would undertake a sort of "peripheral" certificate. Alquié had obtained a certificate in psychiatry at Sainte-Anne, pursuing the lessons, the rounds, and the case studies with passion, while simultaneously being closest to the surrealists and a friend of Breton. He therefore thought that he had identified the mental illness from which Descartes suffered, a mental illness that turned him into a spontaneous surrealist by birth and physiologically. Alquié's entire thesis, which was truly surrealist, started with the hypothesis that Descartes was incapable of distinguishing dreaming from waking. Descartes was, so to speak, deprived of the obviousness of reality, hence surreal, and was making a heroic effort to get back to reality, recovering it via a constructed certainty. This is why Descartes begins with the practice of mathematics in order to reestablish contact with reality, but then he discovers that mathematics itself does not assure reality. From this comes the doubt, metaphysics, the creation (by hypothetical suspension) of the eternal truths, the *cogito*, the idea of the infinite, and so forth. This reading of Descartes, a bit surprising to common sense (and, as it happens, surprising for Gueroult), today actually appears profoundly right, even if maybe not necessarily for the same reasons Alquié put forward.

He was also really a master because even in his speculative boldness he maintained an extreme strictness in his reading of the details of the texts.

He shared this with Henri Gouhier, but with a much more conceptual weight than the latter, who was first a historian of ideas. Alquié avoids—to the point of excess or even caricature—pursuing an interpretation of Descartes read according to an artificial system. To the contrary, he put Descartes to work as a real thinker who, caught between the contradictory forces of things, tries to pursue them rigorously without a safety net. When I later spoke of the incoherence of the proofs for God's existence in Descartes, I was directly following Alquié, and this should have occasioned no surprise! For he taught us at the same time to read the texts with great precision and to admit that an author can be surprised without seeing this as an error of the interpreter or an offense to the thinker. His book on Spinoza remains in my eyes the best book that has ever been written on this man raging with systematicity, and, in the same way, his book on Malebranche offers a hermeneutic masterwork on a thought obsessed by metaphysical obsession itself. I am sorry that not everyone is convinced of this, but one will notice that Alquié's students (and there are many of them) have largely proven the fecundity of this method. Alquié, with his own means and within the limits of the very classical formation he had received, was capable of pursuing the rigor of things, of articulating the history of philosophy and philosophy, one on top of the other. I owe him, we all owe him, a lot.

Allow me to go back to this final phrase: "I owe him a lot." Would you say that you were lucky to encounter masters such as Jean Beaufret, Ferdinand Alquié, and others?

My colleague and friend David Tracy, the first Catholic theologian to be named professor at the University of Chicago, insisted on the fact that I had extraordinary luck in having had Ferdinand Alquié and Jean Beaufret as philosophy professors, as instructors (*caïmans*)[9] at the École Louis Althusser and Jacques Derrida, and then as lecturers Michel Serres, Gilles Deleuze, and Jacques Lacan. And, in theology, through the intermediary of Monsignor Charles, having also had as tutors, in the Oxonian sense of the word, Louis Bouyer, Jean Daniélou, Henri de Lubac, and Marie-Joseph Le Guillou. To have experienced such a tradition seems completely out of the ordinary to me. And we had this opportunity. One can be lucky to

9. In *normalien* parlance, a *caïman* is a teacher who helps with the preparation for the *agrégation* exam.

have great personalities available, but one must also have a certain capacity to recognize and see them. To achieve this, one needs another capacity, the most important and difficult one to handle, namely the capacity for admiration. Those who do not have the capacity to admire cannot receive what is there: They want to imitate or to confiscate the inheritance instead of receiving it as one should, namely as a task that is too great yet cannot be avoided.

Let me take a counterexample. At the École, there was a temporary teacher (*répétiteur*) for the students who were bad in German, which was the case for me, and he gave lessons teaching "der, die, das" to the absolute beginners. His courses were heckled in the worst way, and I also made a racket. Well, this man was Paul Celan! But nobody knew that Celan was Celan. I was overcome with shame when I found out too late that it was him. I therefore missed Celan as master. And by my own fault! Thus, if one does not have the capacity to admire, one remains closed and does not receive anything. In other cases, one places this capacity for admiration in false prophets: While one must have a capacity for admiration, one shouldn't be deceived about when to invest it. Providence must take you under her wing, and you must allow her to take you. The luck I had, together with some others, was to allow ourselves to be shaped at the right moment and with good minds. After a certain time, one is less deceived because once one has encountered true masters, one notices the small or false masters immediately; one is no longer easily trapped. Obviously one can speak of graduate studies—or even high school, for this can begin very early—as the moment when we are given the chance to encounter a master.

But what is a master?

A master? Maybe and above all someone who does not need disciples. This is in contrast to the "small master," who wants disciples in order to be reassured. A master teaches less his conclusions or his theses than his way of getting there. He teaches the right *manner*—the manner of working on the matters of thought, as one teaches how to plane down a board, how to ski, to sculpt, to paint, to run a business, and so forth. He teaches how to do it, but how to do *your* things, not his. The master lets you do your own thing and does not try to do it in your place; he also does not ask you to do his work in his place. He teaches you how to work and leaves you free. The master takes students, but that's not the same thing as having disciples. Disciples run your little shop in your place, selling and buying for you, playing the role of trade merchants and extolling the merits of the product; students learn the job in order to strike out on their own.

Now that you are in turn a master for a new generation of philosophers, do you still need your masters?

I always have them in mind. I do not write a single line without asking myself what Hans Urs von Balthasar, Jean Daniélou, Jean Beaufret, Emmanuel Levinas, or Michel Henry would think of it. When I do phenomenology, I ponder the opinion of two or three close friends in order to confirm what they would say in my place. If I imagine that they would disagree, I try to figure out why. To my eyes, Henry and Levinas, and in some way Derrida, remain living people with whom I am always in conversation. Heidegger obviously as well. One could say that what is distinctive about the masters is that they are never dead and that they teach even in their absence—according to St. Paul's magnificent formulation: "not only in my presence, but much more now in my absence" (Philippians 2:12).

Theological Training

This gives us a good transition to move on to your theological training and therefore in some way to the second part of your years of apprenticeship, which were spent near Mgr. Charles, who had you encounter Jean Daniélou, Hans Urs von Balthasar, Louis Bouyer, Henri de Lubac, and others. This Mgr. Charles was a charismatic personality?

Indisputably.

A man capable of leading the Catholic youth of his time. Could you talk about these years of your Catholic youth?

I come from a family belonging to a Catholic tradition of which I am very proud, that of Catholic Republicans. In modern Catholicism, after the Revolution, there were those who joined forces with the Republic and those who refused to do this. I belong to the first group, which rallied without reservation to the Republic, Dreyfusards, opposed to French Action, to Pétain and the French State, the tradition of Péguy, Bernanos, de Gaulle, Mauriac, and so on. In a sense, this was not the right, if one defines the right by French Action, the anti-Dreyfusism, anti-Republicanism,

Pétainism, and so forth. I was raised in the midst of these ideas with a strong leaning toward the "service of the State." I was a choir child at a very young age. I learned a lot and had decisive liturgical experiences that really marked me. I took the gravity of liturgical action seriously very early on. Then, in high school, I was very naturally taken along to participate in Catholic Action, the Christian student youth group [Jeunesse étudiante chrétienne = JEC]. I even founded the JEC chapter in my high school; that lasted about three or four years. In the end, as head of a fairly sizeable group, I noticed that I spent far too much time negotiating with others engaged in popular activism, that is to say, the UEC, the communist high schoolers. Moreover, their leader in the Sèvres high school was a very good runner, and we would race each other at the stadium. Thus we had lots of things in common, to the point where one day I had to admit that he and I did *exactly* the same thing: militancy for a supposedly just cause. In principle, the contents were different, even opposed, but the activism was actually the same. Thus, from that day on—I was in the first [i.e., final] grade—I stopped. I understood the mistake of "engagement." That was a very good lesson: the same method for two different actions can end up jumbling the contents. From that moment on, I became neutral and entirely opposed to any form of action, even, and above all, "Catholic" action. And as a result, when I arrived in the *hypokhâgne* and in the *khâgne*, psychologically quite fragile (as is normal), my friend Jean Duchesne said to me: "In the state you are in, you have to get out of the *khâgne*! I'm going to Montmartre for silent prayer before the blessed sacrament, come along!" And he dragged me there.

You encountered Jean Duchesne in the khâgne.

Yes, at Condorcet. I thus went with him to Montmartre. It was a bit harsh, a bit Spartan, because an hour of silent prayer in a place like Montmartre is not exactly what one naturally enjoys doing. But it was a very good discipline that I followed until I went to the École. Little by little I got to know the guy in charge of the place, Mgr. Charles, the former founder of the Richelieu Center, which he had established in 1945, just after the war. Then, appointed to Sacré-Coeur at the beginning of the 1960s, he revitalized the tradition of the place, the perpetual adoration of the Eucharist. Being an extraordinary leader of people—a great organizer and having the gift of gab—he attracted lots of people from all backgrounds. He had been trained at Carmes, the same class as Daniélou, and had acquired tremendous theological learning there. Nevertheless, he did not become a great theologian (although he would have been able to), because he was pulled too much by pastoral concerns and by evangelization. He was a man of action, not enough of an office person. His strength came from the tradition of the French school of spirituality—Bérulle, l'Oratoire, the Sulpicians. He had, if I may put it like this, the "technique" of the spiritual life and became a great spiritual director. When he took you in hand, he took you by the hand, and very effectively. This bracing little Périgourdin, who was both dominating and humble, did not bear the first name Maxime for nothing.

Mgr. Charles had left the Richelieu Center to his successor and spiritual son, Jean-Marie Lustiger, whom he had led to ordination. But, business being business, he had held onto *Résurrection*, a theology journal for students that he had founded, then reestablished at Montmartre, and that he wanted to strengthen. Having few people to put to the task, he asked Jean Duchesne to find some writers. At the start of the 1967 school year, Jean Duchesne, being at the École normale supérieure de Saint-Cloud and studying English, had to spend a year at Stanford as a foreign language assistant. As a result, Mgr. Charles entrusted the editorship of the journal to me in his stead, despite my panicked protests of incompetence, assuring me that I would learn the ropes. From one day to the next I found myself together with my little friends from the École entrusted with putting out an issue of several hundred pages three times a year. Dreadful and crushing work, because we had to deal with the Trinity and other very difficult subjects about which I at least knew nothing at all. We worked like madmen, guided by the strange and brilliant Georges Kowalski, the chaplain at the basilica and a professor at the Institut catholique de Paris, a Polish scientist and theologian. That's how we started; my first articles were published in *Résurrection*. When we did not understand each other or did not know what to say, we asked Charles for help. Very quickly, he would appeal to others more knowledgeable than himself, such as Louis Bouyer (who had left the "Catho" [common abbreviation for the Institut catholique de Paris] and had a brilliant career in the United States), Jean Daniélou, and others. Thus, from 1968 to 1973, I was in charge of that journal, and we "stuffed" ourselves with theology. There were four weekly working groups: one on exegesis, one on political theology, one devoted to the Fathers, and one on spirituality. This is how I added to the philosophical training I received at the École an equally intense theological training at Montmartre.

Was it new at that time to be interested in the Fathers?

No, because the collection "Sources chrétiennes" had existed since 1943.[10] But actually rather than doing classical Thomism (which seemed to us anyway too wrapped up in metaphysics, in Heidegger's sense), we were spontaneously inclined to a study of the Fathers and the history of spirituality. I recall having done workshops on the Epistle to the Hebrews, Dionysius, Saint Augustine, Maximus the Confessor. We really had no lack of daring. And each time when I didn't know anything about something, which was pretty much all the time, we went to see those who did know. That is how, for Maximus the Confessor, I participated in a working group led by Marie-Joseph Le Guillou at the Saint-Jacques Convent, where the journal *Istina* was set up: Alain Riou, Jean-Miguel Garrigues, and Christoph von Schönborn, who was named cardinal and archbishop of Vienna in 1995, were there. We also worked with Daniélou on Gregory of Nyssa and Saint Irenaeus. We saw Bouyer very frequently, either at the Villa Montmorency at the Oratorian residence or at the Lucerne Abbey in Normandy, where we did theological sessions every September. Then, in 1973, when, all fire and flame, I announced to Mgr. Charles that, since we were now graduates [*agrégré*—i.e., we had passed the *agrégation*], we could do a real theology journal, he dismissed me *illico*: "I don't want a professional theology journal, I want a journal for the people who pray at Montmartre to train themselves." He thus kicked me out. That was a little harsh, but it was the best lesson he could have given me. *Exit* Montmartre. Soon my thesis, *On Descartes' Grey Ontology* [*Sur l'ontologie grise de Descartes*], and the edition of the *Regulae* was brought to completion, and I became Ferdinand Alquié's assistant at the Sorbonne. Two years later, we began the equally foolhardy undertaking of *Communio*. But this time we had some skills.

Can you go back to Communio *and dwell a bit on Le Guillou, Bouyer, Lubac, and obviously Balthasar?*

Let's summarize. In the 1930s what is called "New Theology" emerged among the Dominicans, that is, a historical reading of St. Thomas, represented by the fathers Marie-Joseph Congar, Marie-Dominique Chenu, and some others, who were countered by the neo-Thomists in Rome. But at Fourvière, the Jesuits Claude Montdésert, Jean Daniélou, Henri de Lubac,

10. [A prominent series of Patristic texts with the Greek original on one side and French translation on facing pages.]

and some others also launched the series "Sources chrétiennes," whose first volume, Gregory of Nyssa's *The Life of Moses*, was published during the Occupation. This situation shows that the end of neo-Thomism as "Catholic system" (the formulation comes from Heidegger) happens on the one hand because of the rereading of Saint Thomas by the Dominicans and on the other hand owing to the rediscovery of the Fathers by the Jesuits of the "Sources chrétiennes." This long development was reinforced by the 1943 *Divino afflante spiritu*, Pius XII's remarkable encyclical, which freed Catholic exegesis in a decisive way by demythologizing in advance the historical sense of the Scriptures. All of this put in motion a movement that would end up leading to the Second Vatican Council. Congar, Chenu, Daniélou, Lubac, Bouyer (to speak just of the French) were all connected with its preparation. During the council, the theologians, who assumed the task of acting as theological consultants for the bishops, founded a first journal, *Concilium*, in which all the factions participated. After several years, tensions appeared among them concerning the "spirit of the Council." Some, among them Balthasar, Daniélou, Lubac, Bouyer, and the (then) young professor of systematic theology Ratzinger, decided to create a different journal, which was called *Communio*. Or rather it was a federation of independent journals, coming out in different countries. For unlike *Concilium*, which had a single edition translated into different languages, *Communio* was a federation of journals divided up along linguistic areas (German speaking, Italian, Dutch, American, Spanish, then also South American, Polish, Croatian, Hungarian, etc., today about fifteen). In contrast, *Concilium* was centralized, starting from the Low Countries, and was primarily edited by very established university professors in theology. *Communio* most often depended on lay people, some university trained but not only those, including women and some really young people.

Are you saying that Communio *was an anti-*Concilium*?*

Well, yes, in a sense, but less in terms of content than in terms of its structure and its organization. Curiously, *Concilium*, supposedly more "progressive," as one said at the time, and *Communio*, supposedly more "conservative," were opposed to each other above all by their staff, by their economic situation (one backed by institutions and a big international publishing company, the other without institution or subsidies), by the connection to cultural and ecclesial diversity (one being a journal of theologians, the other a journal of culture, very multidisciplinary, more open to the economic, political, and cultural realities). Instead of a pyramid-shaped system starting from above, *Communio* brought together from below independent journals, in different languages, which exchanged articles. As facts have actually shown thirty years later, this difference changed many things, and to *Communio*'s profit. This was clearer in the case of the French edition, which was born belatedly, after several aborted attempts, by great and dedicated figures and thanks to small hands like Jean Duchesne and myself, originally recruited as errand boys for Daniélou.

Daniélou's unexpected death at that time left us prostrate with grief but also relieved to escape the immense work we foresaw. Hans Urs von Balthasar, whom we knew a little bit due to *Résurrection*, for which he had encouraged us, was deaf in that ear: He summoned us (that's the right word) to discuss it with him in Basel. I still remember it: He invited us to eat lunch in the restaurant of the Basel zoo (an allusion to what awaited us?) in order to tell us that, without a penny, without any acknowledged skill, without any institutional support, we should nonetheless launch the Francophone edition of *Communio*. Our protest changed nothing in his decision. We were caught in the trap. That was the summer of 1974. We thus spent a year trying to gather together a competent editorial committee, a reassuring honorary committee, and we finally launched a minimal subscription. We set the bar very low: We would need five hundred preliminary subscriptions and five million of the old francs by July 14, 1975. On that very day, unbelievably, we had exactly five hundred subscribers and five million old francs. That was the hand of God—in other words, for us a catastrophe. We hence began in September 1975, and I hoped with all my strength for an honorable and especially for a quick failure, but by Christmas we had three thousand subscribers and were quite famous. From that day onward, the journal appeared six times per year without a single issue coming out late, without any other publisher but itself, without subsidies, without an institution. Nobody, neither among its friends nor its enemies, really understands how it carries on, but that's how it is, and it is going into its fortieth year.

What role did Balthasar play in Communio *and in the theological supervision of the little group you formed?*

Hans Urs von Balthasar was the inspirer, initiator, and unifier of all the editions of *Communio*. We came together once a year with him in Basel in the winter, for a work session of the editors-in-chief (about a dozen); there was also a larger meeting of several days on Ascension, each time in a different country. From this resulted intense work of international dialogue about the choice of themes, of authors, and of articles, about the orientation of what we wanted to say. It was also a very formative and interesting experience, which we lived through in all the languages (everyone was expected to understand what everyone was saying in his or her language) and which uncovered for us a complex theological (and cultural) landscape. That was a very rapid education, and one had to rise to the expected standard very quickly. There were several theologians in the French edition, but Lubac could not travel, and Bouyer did not want to appear directly. We, the kids, thus found ourselves in the front lines. But everything was animated by Balthasar.

Could you say a bit about Balthasar?

He was an extraordinary character. A man who at age thirty defended his thesis with Romano Guardini on *The Revelation of the German Soul*: two volumes, a thousand pages; everything, from Luther to Rilke! Then he went to Lyon to be trained by the Jesuits of Fourvière and showed, as if in passing, that the commentaries on Dionysius were not by Maximus the Confessor but by John of Scythopolis, which gave him a worldwide reputation as a great Patristics scholar before the end of the war. He was also a well-informed connoisseur and a great friend of Barth, who lived very close to him in Basel. Balthasar remains without doubt the best Barthian. One could call this ecumenism at the highest level. After having left the Society of Jesus, which ostracized him a bit, he only remained as student chaplain in Basel, which wasn't a huge job. He never became a university professor and was not even invited to the council! But, good came from ill. This allowed him to work much more, and he became the only partner or rival of Karl Rahner. An encyclopedic mind, truly and deeply spiritual, a highly gifted writer, he produced an oeuvre that dominates not only his own era but the one to come. In my opinion he has the stature of the greatest Catholic theologian of modern times. His humble and almost timid authority earned him any number of students but no disciples. For he was anything but dogmatic and had an erudition or, actually, a learning (which does not amount to the same thing) so sweeping that it gave you goosebumps. I have since discovered what it means to be learned with theologians. When one compares the majority of university lay people with theologians, there is no possible comparison: The theologians of this great era practiced multidisciplinarity seriously. They knew languages, philosophy, theology, literature, and obviously the Bible. Balthasar also knew music wonderfully well: I remember one time when during breakfast at his place, discussing some Mozart quartets with a Dutch visitor and disagreeing about a flat, Balthasar immediately suggested checking it (for he had Mozart's scores in the kitchen); he got up, looked for the score, checked it, made sure he was right, and picked up his coffee again. Such a scene dampens any conceit.

In what does the move from Rahner to Balthasar consist, which goes back to the alternative between the journals Concilium *and* Communio? *What was the basis of the conflict or of the debate between these two theologians who otherwise got along very well personally?*

The answer, such as I understand it, is as follows: Should Christian theology rely on a metaphysical fore-understanding, on logical conditions of possibility or impossibility? The transcendental Thomist, whose supreme heir Rahner remains, presupposes that there is in some way continuity between metaphysics, the question of being, even the transcendental subject, that is to say, the conditions of possibility for religious experience, on the one hand, and, on the other hand, Christ or God. In other words, the conditions of experience finally define Revelation itself. Balthasar's argument, to the contrary, states that Revelation has no conditions of possibility except itself. That is why he begins with the doctrine of the figure (*Gestalt*) of Revelation, which, according to him, provides its own norms. This intuition obviously agrees with Barth's starting point. God reveals himself—that means the self-manifestation of God from himself and according to his own rules. Balthasar is obviously right.

Reading The Glory and the Cross, *then, was decisive for you?*

Decisive. It was Jean-Marie Lustiger who, right in the middle of May '68, said to me: "You must *straightaway* read Balthasar." Which is what I did. Besides, in 1968, there were a bunch of us at the École reading Balthasar, not only the "Catholics" but also Emmanuel Martineau and Jean-François Courtine. We read him as the theologian who defined the concrete conditions of God's self-revelation. He described them much more concretely than Barth, who could get a little wordy. This definition was decisive because the figure of Revelation is then defined starting from its trinitarian dimension and leaves its mark in our experience, not always by becoming fulfilled in it (the infamous "Christian humanism") but often in contradicting it. This contradiction between Revelation and experience forms the core of the paradox of any revelation. Obviously, that permits a rereading of the Old and New Testament in *The Glory and the Cross*, which is all the same very strong.

From a more personal standpoint, beyond the Catholic education you received, did you in those years experience a "spiritual turning point"?

Of course. First, the discovery of the prayer of eucharistic adoration was a fundamental thing. Maxim Charles insisted on this point: It is a form of objective prayer, of objective mysticism. Its goal is to achieve or *develop* (in the photographic, psychological, and almost phenomenological sense) the link between, on the one side, biblical texts that convey God's words or, often, Christ's words and, on the other side, a totally real but perfectly silent presence. The whole work of contemplation consists in making these two coincide or at least to bring them closer together. It consists in putting into focus what will make presence speak, what will give to the words their referent. It is a labor of attention, of concentration, but one that is essentially desubjectivizing, where the *I* is erased before the one whom it observes speaking. That was a real and great discovery for me. The spiritual life, especially in the Catholic religion, seems to privilege interiority in opposition to the exteriority of action (apostolic or secular), but one must make it more than a subjective counterpart of what is real and is found in the world, with all attendant ambiguities. Yet, with eucharistic adoration, a fundamental psychological change takes place because it is a matter of putting words into the mouth of a reality, if I can put it like this, or of causing the words spoken to be really those said by Someone who is here now, before me, infinitely more than me. This makes the spiritual life first of all essentially dialogical—and not monological—and then gives it norms; it is neither arbitrary nor a daydream. That was the first discovery.

The consequence is self-evident: It gives you the conviction that God is not found elsewhere, in some other world. And even, in a sense, that you are the one who remains elsewhere, far from the stage where all takes place, but that God himself is already there where you cannot manage to go. This inversion of the relation of inclusion has a major significance, for the spiritual life becomes the objective space where everything else takes place and not a part, a margin, or a limit of the experience of the world. The consequence of this for intellectual life is not minor. One can no longer place speculative theology or neutral rationality to one side and the spiritual life to the other; now the same place encompasses both. It does so in such a way that any number of difficulties disappear entirely: The concern to figure out whether one is in a good spiritual disposition or is experiencing dryness, whether one "has faith," whether one is in a state of enthusiasm or depression—they all become secondary phenomena that change nothing about the substance of the matter.

Then came the day when I finally discovered that the crucial problem lies not in knowing or not knowing the existence of God but in figuring out whether I myself am sure of my own existence. For let's be serious: existence is the least thing we could dispute of God. The question would rather be whether anything that is not God could ever hope to be. There is a serious question for you. But the "question of the existence of God" is so badly posed that it cannot expect any serious answer. Rather, does *being* have enough meaning and dignity that it can be applied to God? Or at the very least, in what sense [could it be applied to him]? To take up the title of a formulation that has been used for translating one of Balthasar's books: "All is incorporated." There is nothing exterior, absolutely nothing that is not found already and above all given a norm by God, including the questions of his being and his potential existence. That is why it remains so difficult to call oneself Hegelian from a Christian point of view: When Hegel claims that God must externalize himself in order to become real, he makes the most anti-Christian statement possible because nothing remains exterior to God, not even the nothing. For the world is not created *outside* of God but inevitably *within* the Word—for where would you want it to be? The world is found *within* the Trinity, more exactly *within* the Principle, the Word, the Son. Whether one finds oneself there willingly or despite oneself—that, conversely, is a serious question. But be that as it may, everything takes place within the interior of God, and the world remains a subsidiary of the Word. The idea that there is anything outside of God has no meaning at all. That was for me truly a Copernican reversal, one about which I have never had the slightest doubt. When I wrote *The Erotic Phenomenon* it was with that conviction.

You realized this fully from the experience of eucharistic adoration to which Mgr. Charles introduced you?

For me, just speaking anecdotally, it happened at Montmartre with Charles. But this conviction isn't my own. Lustiger had it; every at least somewhat serious Christian has it. One does not "search" for God. This rhetoric disgusts me, just simply because it makes no sense. The people "who search for God" delude themselves: We do not search for God, because we are already within God, at the heart of God. We are within God—either we know it or we don't, either unwillingly or willingly; in short, our consciousness of it is more or less open. But one shouldn't reverse the roles: It is God who searches for us and not we who search for God. Consequently, the world has only a single logic, that of God. But this logic appears to us or does not appear to us; that's a different issue, which one can really debate. It is normal that it does not appear to us very clearly, but nevertheless there are no other kinds of logic. In short, this turnaround was and remains decisive for me.

Your lasting friendships with Jean Duchesne, Rémi Brague, and Jean-Robert Armogathe date from this time. In other words, could you tell us something of the famous Jean-Robert Bradurion to whom you dedicated your Prolegomena to Charity*?*[11]

Jean-Robert Brague-Duchesne-Marion—that was our little personal legend! We got to know each other in 1967; Jean Duchesne and I a little earlier, but I encountered Rémi Brague when he was still in the *khâgne*, then Jean-Robert Armogathe at the École. Since that time we have each done very different things. We have run two journals together, completed lots of publications; we have met up again on a thousand occasions. This relationship had something of the Three Musketeers. Rémi Brague, who did weightlifting at the École normale supérieure, obviously found himself in the role of Porthos. Jean Duchesne was always the noble father; I always had the impression that it was he who laid down the law for us, the serious older brother, a little bit of a lawyer: hence Athos. Aramis necessarily went to Armogathe: diplomat, priest, a man who knew everyone and whom everyone knew, the man who knows everything, who is always elsewhere, always where one does not expect him. For me was left just the role of Artagnan, with a comic and distraught side, and it doesn't really fit me that badly. And then Artagnan died at the siege of Maastricht.

The Career of Honors

You had a career. In a sense, the most brilliant career one can have in the French university system: assistant at the Sorbonne, professor at Poitiers, Nanterre, and finally at the Sorbonne, where you inherited the chair in metaphysics. With your

11. ["Jean-Robert Bradurion" adds the four names together: "Jean-Robert" for Armogathe, "Bra" for Brague, "du" for Duchesne, "rion" for Marion.]

work you also received a lectureship on the other side of the Atlantic, which earned you a chair at the University of Chicago. All that culminated with the Académie française in 2008.

In fact, this journey surprised me as well. I know that I won't manage to convince many people of this, but it is the truth: I never had any plans for a career, never! Nothing was programmed; I had no time or taste for anything like that at all. My university ambitions remained very modest at the beginning. When I was at the École, I understood that the best position possible was to be a head-assistant (one now calls them *maître de conférences* [head of lectures]) for life: never to write a thesis, hidden in a corner, able to write one's books quietly. That was my highest ambition and really without the slightest compunction. Yet I spent my time by being grabbed by the scruff of the neck, with orders that seemingly dropped from the sky, putting me in places I would not have dreamed of. So Alquié said to me one day, when I hadn't even yet passed the *agrégation*: "Do you want to be my assistant next year?" That was in 1969, and everyone was being recruited. I equivocated: "Sorry, but I have to pass the *agrégation* first." The *agrégation* in my pocket, thus assigned to teaching, I dropped off my application dossier at the Sorbonne, but I didn't hear anything. After some time, at the beginning of July, I finally went to see Pierre Aubenque, who was the philosophy dean, to ask him about the outcome of the candidacy. He answered me: "But, listen, obviously the election has taken place. Of course you were chosen. Don't you know anything about it? Have you handed in your course titles?" That's how things worked in those days, in the old university. Thus I began directly at the Sorbonne, completely surprised to be there.

That was in 1972; I was twenty-six. After some time the rules changed. One had to do a [doctoral] thesis [*thèse de troisième cycle*], without which one would have been kicked out. So I wrote *On Descartes' Grey Ontology* in 1974. I became head lecturer [*maître de conférences*]. Then Alquié retired and went to the Institut. Geneviève Rodis-Lewis replaced him. A bit later, wanting to be a bit freer in my schedule of courses, I did my *thèse d'État*.[12] Those were the first seven years.

12. [Second doctoral thesis, which qualifies one not just for teaching but also for the supervision of research. The French educational system had until fairly recently two separate, successive doctoral degrees, both requiring theses: the "thèse de troisième cycle" and the "thèse de doctorat d'État," the latter being far more highly regarded than the former and requiring more groundbreaking research but

Then someone sent me, as professor, to Poitiers. "Someone": that means Claude Bruaire, Ferdinand Alquié, and some others. And I discovered myself chosen for Poitiers without even having to campaign for it. I discovered a different world, for it was the first time that I had moved south of the Loire. I was surrounded by institutionally powerful characters: Jacques D'Hondt ruled the French Society of Philosophy, Guy Planty-Bonjour at the CNRS [Centre national de la recherche scientifique; a very prestigious French research organization], Pierre Magnard at the CNU [Conseil national des universités; the national council of universities]. On that stage, I played the role of the little guy.

I therefore learned the job, figured out what went on behind the scenes, which wasn't always pretty, for at stake were the battles between the show's producers, who chose the actors, the pieces to be performed, the prices, and the locations. (The actors or the authors think themselves important, but in truth it is the producers who are the important people.) Thus I discovered the world of the producers, in the exact sense of *showbiz*. Then followed all sorts of conflicts. That was inevitable, and I had to learn on the job. Poitiers was both a psychologically painful and an amusing experience. I became the assistant director of the Center for Research and Literature on Hegel and Marx, where I helped pass theses on Marx that were often quite eccentric. More seriously, realizing that knowing the history of philosophy is not enough to make one into a philosopher, I began to teach Husserl there because I did not know him. This allowed me to write *Reduction and Givenness*. Those were the second seven years.

Then Jean-Marie Beyssade's position (I had followed him as Alquié's assistant) at Nanterre opened up following his move to the Sorbonne. Thanks to his friendly support, I was chosen for it without problems. Nanterre had a completely different style. I assumed all the responsibilities there: I presided over the pedagogical committee, the recruitment commission, and the department. Obviously, the atmosphere there leaned left, full of culturally and traditionally "progressive" people, which caused repeated conflicts between the traditional (ex)communists and the offspring of all the leftists. But this produced an exemplary and sometimes touching concern

both being necessary for a senior teaching post in the university system; these have now been replaced with a doctorate and a "habilitation" (similar to the German system), the former allowing teaching and the second also the supervision of research, i.e., the guiding of doctoral theses. For more detail on this system, see Alan D. Schrift, *Twentieth-Century French Philosophy: Key Themes and Thinkers* (Oxford: Blackwell, 2006), 207–208.]

for the formation of students, an impressive dedication to the principle of the mission of teaching. Department meetings always lasted at least three hours, the same ritualized arguments came up again, regardless of what the agenda for the day was, but I learned lots about the university and the real ideological situation. In short, those were the third set of seven instructive and very cordial years.

When I left Nanterre, I recall well Georges Labica's very kind speech: "You leave us at the very moment when you have understood everything about the spirit of Nanterre"—the flatterer. I did both history of philosophy and phenomenology there; I reintroduced courses in the amphitheater. There were battles, but when I left Nanterre had a philosophy department that was really very good. We made Jean-François Courtine, Michel Fichant, and then Didier Franck come there. Finally, after two defeats, at the point when I no longer really hoped for it, and by a mysterious reversal of the situation, I returned to the Sorbonne, not to Alquié's position in the history of classical philosophy but to the position in metaphysics that had been held by Claude Bruaire, by Nicolas Grimaldi, and above all by Emmanuel Levinas. I had changed specializations without having intended to do so.

The international dimension of the work began very early. I was still assistant when Tullio Gregory with the Instituto per il Lessico intellettuale Europeo invited us to Rome, Jean-Robert Armogathe, Pierre Cahné, and myself, in order to demonstrate our use of computer lexicology for the history of concepts and of philosophy. Beginning in the anniversary year of the *Discourse on Method* (1987), the links with the university of Lecce and Giulia Belgioioso became regular and especially important. Then, beginning in 1986, I participated in the meetings of the Instituto di studi filosofici Eugenio Castelli at the university of La Sapienza in Rome: Levinas, Ricoeur, Michel Henry, Tilliette, Fessard, Bruaire were there; Lacan, Derrida, Appel, Habermas had been there. The great era! And it seems ironic to me that today I am the one to preside over the fate of this institution. Besides, being bored in Poitiers and scared to be buried alive there, I accepted invitations to go abroad with joy. That was first of all to Germany and Italy, then to Spain and the United States. First, they were general invitations linked to Cartesian studies, but, additionally, my book *God Without Being* had aroused interest as well as hostility both from the side of the neo-Thomists and from the Heideggerians, and it began to be translated into various languages. In the United States it was quickly and well translated by Thomas Carlson, published by Chicago with a preface by David Tracy (himself a student of Bernard Lonergan and one of the major figures of *Concilium*). Thus I was invited to visit as professor there, without having asked for it or even contemplated it, thanks to Daniel Garber (and Thomas de Koninck), to teach Descartes, phenomenology, and *God Without Being* all at the same time. These invitations were renewed with three-year contracts. Finally I obtained a regular position that was at the same time in the department of philosophy, in the Committee on Social Thought, and in the Divinity School. When Paul Ricoeur's chair opened up (in 2003), which had previously been Paul Tillich's, it was offered to me, although I had requested nothing there either, and I accepted. Since 2012 I hold a different chair at the Divinity School, which was that of David Tracy [the Andrew Thomas Greeley and Grace McNichols Greeley Chair of Catholic Studies].

So it seems to you that your career sort of happened by itself, not despite you, but . . . without you?

Experience has taught me that a career opens up or is cleared of obstructions when an institution ends up needing you more than you need it. The problem is that one cannot foresee when this reversal will happen. I was chosen for the Sorbonne for a different position than the one I long thought about and thanks to the decision of logicians and sociologists who had in no way supported me in the past, as is normal. For once, one must reverse the paradox in the Gospel: Do not ask and you shall receive—but that's the way it is. Yet what always matters, what helps steer clear of erecting a career plan on wishful thinking, are publications, if possible international ones, deepening one's knowledge of a field, recognition by other experts. Then, at some point, the institutions discover that they need you, precisely when you are no longer thinking about them.

This great lesson was continually confirmed for me, all the way to the Académie française, which I beg you to believe I never thought of until the very last moment. But a point arrives where everything teaches you that *hic est saltus, hic est Rhodus*.[13] Now in that case one must take a chance. In short, if I had to give any advice to the young people embarking on their career while their elders are still in it, it would be this: Focus on what you have to do, certainly not on your career. And, if what you do you do well, sooner

13. [A proverb conveying that one has to prove oneself at home, not just abroad.]

or later positive results will follow. Be careful in the meantime neither to become bitter nor to make yourself unbearable, but, if you work hard enough (that is, without stopping), you won't give in to that temptation and won't have the time to succumb to it. Above all, never ask yourself if you are a genius or even whether you are right; nobody knows, and nobody would be able to tell you. A final judgment would be necessary for that. That will happen, no doubt of it, but too late to give you any reassurance in this world.

Advice for a young generation that is too tempted by ambition and career plans?

I actually know many who have sacrificed their intellectual ambitions to an institutional project; often they had the satisfaction of a replacement. But that is a bad choice, the opposite is good. In Plato's *Apology of Socrates*, Socrates says something that one could translate as: "A career never produces virtue, but virtue produces the career." I do not know if I have virtue, but I know that I never put things together starting from career ambitions.

That is a new paradox!

Yes, but it bears saying and repeating: Many intellectual lives allow themselves to be ruled by identifying a theoretical problem with an institutional one, which ruins the intellectual project itself. For my part, I never had any conflict with institutions, and I never considered institutional questions as decisive. All the same, as regards institutions, which are indispensable and unjustly disparaged even by those who use them too much, I have observed that the more one finds oneself at their center, the freer one remains because in this way one precisely frees oneself from institutional problems. Just as in the case of whirlwinds, only the centers of institutions remain calm. I have never attacked the institution because it seems to me that it is inevitable anyway. The problem is not figuring out whether one belongs to an institution but to know the place one occupies in it, which institution is concerned, whether it fulfills a positive role, and whether it can be improved. Everything depends on the balance of power one maintains with it. That is why institutional reforms seem secondary to me compared to the relationships with the people who really make the reforms happen. It is never by changing the institution that one changes its content, but the opposite can be true if one changes the content by improving the people.

I have sometimes been told that I'm not a good politician. On the contrary, I think that I have proved to be an excellent one. I am a good politician because in a sense I don't get involved in politics and do not think that political decisions are determinative, at least in the intellectual life. There are neither good nor bad universities: There are good academics that make good universities and bad academics who ruin the most beautiful universities. Obviously, one can modify institutions, one can create new ones, but the institutional form as such matters less than the intellectual content. One can make an institution from nothing, and one can have very strong institutions for doing nothing at all. From this comes my skepticism about university reforms. I have seen a dozen during my career, and I am at present completely persuaded that the administrative management of a university is a sacrifice of understanding for those who agree to take it on. I am no longer certain that the battles of university power, which are nevertheless important because appointments have consequences, are absolutely decisive; I believe foolishly in the authority of the intellectual matter in institutions in general and in universities in particular.

In regard to what you have just said, what portrait or what image can you draw of the French university?

If one considers the best French students, I rather think that they are the best in the world! Maybe that's a surprising response, but experience makes it a necessary one. In fact, if what is at stake is forming individuals to have at the same time a good philological training, a real capacity of conceptual innovation, and an openness to the external world, the French system presents if not the best, then at least an excellent compromise. The American students develop a great capacity for discussion and a certain vision of their world, but their philological capacity remains insufficient; thus their broadness of mind and ideology always threatens them. At the opposite end, the Italians make marvelous philologists, but they lack conceptual power and positivism or historicism can limit them. The Germans have kept the tradition of conceptual debate alive but, like the Anglo-Saxons, they are less and less philologists. For (perfectly respectable and understandable) historical reasons, they tend to abandon their own traditions, and their conceptual debates become increasingly unreal, running the risk of turning empty. In the end, the French system with its preparatory classes, the École normale supérieure, and the truly international character of the scene, remains entirely admirable.

But what becomes of this famous French system, if one eliminates the preparatory classes, as is increasingly contemplated, and maybe even the great schools [i.e., the system of Écoles]?

To my knowledge, they aren't necessarily planning to eliminate the preparatory classes and the great schools. Rather, people are trying to incorporate the great schools and their preparatory classes into the universities, as is the case in Germany and the United States. That way, at the point of academic counseling for higher education we would not split, on one side, an elite that goes to the great schools from, on the other side, a crowd that enters a university, which actually exercises a disgraceful, slow, and frustrating selection by failure. It would be better for the university to put a selection clearly in place at the point of entry, maybe with paths of excellence that would not be separated in some watertight way from the other channels. In the American universities, the professional schools are, in some ways, great schools that are incorporated into the university, and that's not a bad system. In any case, in France, the great schools are actually invisible on the university map because they do not confer doctoral degrees, which they really should do and which would only be possible with the intervention of the universities. The universities themselves must introduce a system of selection by success and not by failure. How much time will all of that take? Maybe—this is the hypothesis of my pathological optimism—if one really were to take the autonomy of the universities seriously one might get there within ten or twenty years. But, contrary to the prevailing pessimism, I continue to think that the French system performs at the highest level. A good French student, I wouldn't even say a *very* good French student, when he arrives in the United States, appears to me indisputably far better trained than an American student of the same age. He just does not get as much support in France as he does in the United States.

Yet, don't you think all the same that the role of the humanities in the French university system is decreasing? We are being told that we no longer have the means to maintain humanities departments as rich and as high-performing as in the United States. Just think of the fact that the number of students in the L section of the baccalauréat[14] *drops each year. Are we witnessing the death of the humanities disciplines at the very heart of the university?*

14. [Final exams in high school; the L section refers to the humanities track.]

First, one must keep things in perspective. I believe that only a minority of the some two thousand American universities are real universities endowed with great humanities departments. If in ten years there are ten or twenty very highly performing humanities departments in the French university system, that would already be very good. That we have tiny departments of psychology, of sociology, or of philosophy in small provincial universities is not in itself a success. What is essential is that we have enough great poles of excellence in France. Also, one must really understand that the strength of the great American universities, that is to say the strength of ten or twenty among them, has to do with their decision to invest money in the humanities, financed by prominent scientific, medical, law, and economic divisions. The difference between a good and a very good American university has to do with the capacity to finance, apparently without regard for cost, the teaching of theology, for example, or of Chinese, of Assyrian archeology, of Latin, of Greek, and of Hebrew, and so forth. Thus, a very great American university almost always has an important religious studies department, which draws professors and hence students who come from all over America and the entire world precisely for *this* department! In comparison, our universities are still too single disciplinary in focus, even if one has tried to remedy that problem. And certainly one does not run a humanities department by closing a Greek department because there are too few students; one runs it by deciding to have better professors. That would be a great project, one that will draw students. One must pass from a logic of demand to a logic of supply.

Yet, to the extent that our university is itself understood as a social service, it is still to a large degree ruled by the principle of demand, even including the administrative reforms. It's a question of culture and of mentality. That said, the few universities that are ruled by the logic of supply, for example Dauphine or the Institut catholique de Paris, draw students by offering things that cannot be done elsewhere. Besides, if a university manages to think solely according to the logic of supply, that is because it sorely lacks inventiveness, for everyone thinks of the same thing, from the business schools to the law applied to business enterprises or to communication. Obviously there the market is very quickly saturated. Are we capable of inventing other things and of providing the necessary money? That will depend on the intelligence of the presidents. But I think that, if the French landscape is called to undergo a profound modification (as is the case), there is no reason why that would have to be negative; I think rather that it will be positive.

You are optimistic about the future of the French university, but maybe because you are a pathological optimist, to use your own terms! I would nevertheless like to quote some lines from your book The Erotic Phenomenon*: "As a child, I believed for a long time that I was not happy, even though I was; then, as a semi-grown-up, that I would be, when I was doing everything not to be. I believed later that success would make me sure of myself, and then, as I collected successes, I saw their insignificance and returned to my initial uncertainty."[15] This is indisputably a form of pessimism. Certainly, one does not speak of love except in the first person; certainly, also, the pessimism of those lines is toned down by what follows. But what a contrast to the optimism you show today! Would you say that you are a defeated pessimist or a "thwarted depressive," a little like Ferdinand Alquié, who, as you reminded us, called himself a "thwarted idler"?*

Bernanos said memorably: "Being optimistic or pessimistic are two ways of being an idiot." I think that's true enough. Really, the only certainty is that nothing is important because as we say at the end "death always wins." De Gaulle said: "Everything is magnificent and everything is possible if it comes from elsewhere; everything is useless, null and void, if we possess it." That's the paradox. Consequently, the true question becomes one of election. In other words, everything takes on a different meaning if what happens to me is given to me from elsewhere. In contrast, if what happens to me is a duplication and a product of myself, then even the most marvelous things lose their meaning. That is how one should understand success: Either it comes only from myself (from my ambition, from my gifts, from my will, from my cunning, etc.) and thus holds no interest (certainly, it is better to be rich and in good health than to be poor and dying, but in some way that doesn't prove anything), or the least satisfaction becomes a joy if it comes from elsewhere. Thus, in the end, it is the question of election that truly decides. But election, the acknowledgment of election, which forms the basis of erotic phenomena, of the intellectual life, and of the spiritual life, leads back to a matter of . . . what shall I say? A matter, let's say, where one must *believe*; it is a question of faith. Yet we live at a time when one imagines that autonomy is the best thing in the world. But autonomy, I think, is another word for suicide. If one instead thinks the world as essentially an experience of heteronomy, in other words as election, then everything is worth being lived, being expected, being desired, everything merits making an effort on its behalf.

15. Jean-Luc Marion, *The Erotic Phenomenon*, trans. Stephen E. Lewis (Chicago: University of Chicago Press, 2007), 15.

You just tried to respond to the call of the election?

Before trying to respond to the call, there is a more difficult thing, which is . . .

. . . *to hear it?*

It is to discover that there is a call, that is to say, being able to interpret what is *as what comes to us*. Then, at that moment, if that which is happens, then maybe it is a call. This decision to take things as calls—or the decision of not hearing the voice when it suits us better to justify relying on ourselves—decides everything else. The highest lucidity consists in discovering the call.

2. Descartes

Descartes Against Aristotle

You have devoted three large books to Descartes: On Descartes' Grey Ontology *in 1975,* On Descartes' White Theology *in 1981, and* On Descartes' Metaphysical Prism *in 1986. To this we should add several dozen articles gathered together in* Cartesian Questions I *and* II *(a third volume is planned) and a final book,* On Descartes' Passive Thought.[1] *Until recently you directed the Centre*

1. [*Sur l'ontologie grise de Descartes. Science cartésienne et savoir aristotélicien dans les "Regulae"* (Paris: Vrin, 1975, 1981, 1992, 2002). Translated as *On Descartes' Grey Ontology: Cartesian Science and Aristotelian Thought in the "Regulae,"* trans. S. Donohue (forthcoming, St. Augustine's Press). *Sur la théologie blanche de Descartes. Analogie, création des véritées éternelles, fondement* (Paris: Presses Universitaires de France, 1981, 1991, 2009). An English translation is forthcoming. The title translates as *On Descartes' White Theology*, although "blanche" also refers to "whitened out," "bleached," "clear/pure," "blank," or even "innocent." *Sur le prisme métaphysique de Descartes. Constitution et limites de l'onto-théo-logie dans la pensée cartésienne* (Paris: Presses Universitaires de France, 1986, 2004). Translated as *On Descartes' Metaphysical Prism: The Constitution and the Limits of Onto-theo-logy in Cartesian Thought,*

d'études cartésiennes [Center for Cartesian Studies], and you retired from the Sorbonne while you were holding the chair for the history of modern philosophy. Why Descartes? What brought you to this author?

First of all, a point deserves highlighting: I discovered only over time—it wasn't my initial motivation—that the way Descartes is interpreted during a particular period appears to correspond to the broader state of French philosophy at that time, in the same way, I suppose, as the interpretation of Kant in Germany or possibly that of Locke in England. To work on Descartes was hence a strategic choice, an unwitting one, but a strategic choice nonetheless. One could say that, beyond Descartes specialists, all the contemporary philosophers who really matter have an interpretation of Descartes. And, surprisingly, some who should play a central role, or claim to, have no such interpretation. In short, tell me who Descartes is, and I will tell you the state of philosophy in the era in which you work.

Could you give us some examples?

Every philosopher of the seventeenth century had an interpretation of Descartes (Jesuit, Malebranchian, Jansenist, empiricist, etc.). The eighteenth century is marked by divergent and often critical views, but Descartes remains central, even as he is challenged. Although Voltaire was Cartesian in the *Treatise on Metaphysics*, later he is so no longer. In a certain way, Rousseau is still profoundly Cartesian; without having read him very much, Kant remains marked by Descartes, just as German idealism obviously does—Hegel and, to a somewhat lesser extent, Schelling. It is less clear after that, but Schopenhauer read him, as did Kierkegaard. Nietzsche is again a great Cartesian, like Husserl and Heidegger. Moreover, in France the history of Descartes mirrors the constitution of modern consciousness

---

trans. Jeffrey L. Kosky (Chicago: Chicago University Press, 1999). *Questions cartésiennes. Méthode et métaphysique* (Paris: Presses Universitaires de France, 1991). Translated as *Cartesian Questions: Method and Metaphysics* (Chicago: University of Chicago Press, 1999). *Questions cartésiennes II. L'ego et Dieu* (Paris: Presses Universitaires de France, 1996, 2004), partially translated as *On the Ego and on God: Further Cartesian Questions*, trans. Christina M. Gschwandtner (New York: Fordham University Press, 2007). *Sur la pensée passive de Descartes* (Paris: Presses Universitaires de France, 2013). An English translation is forthcoming from the University of Chicago Press. The French text here says parenthetically "going to press." The book has since been published.]

(François Azouvi's research has demonstrated this). Descartes is chosen by the neo-Thomist revival as its primary opponent and by Victor Cousin as authoritative reference. In Husserl, phenomenology obviously tries to be more Cartesian than Descartes. Heidegger not only commented on Descartes, but he made him play several rather different roles depending on the period. In short, all later philosophers comment on Descartes, regardless of their nationality. The same cannot be said historically or even geographically for many authors: Maybe it can be said about Plato and Aristotle, or Thomas Aquinas (for other reasons), but not even always about Kant. By reading Descartes, then, one encounters all the great periods of philosophy and all the great philosophies. There was a different reason that pushed me to take an interest in Descartes: Right away, he seemed to me like an enigma, like an author behind in interpretation—that sounds a bit strange, but it is quite true.

In any case, it's paradoxical, because, before you, Descartes had been the subject of important research by Martial Gueroult, Ferdinand Alquié, Geneviève Rodis-Lewis, Henri Gouhier, and had given rise to memorable arguments among interpreters.

Absolutely. But Descartes interpretation had stagnated for at least two reasons. First—I already mentioned this in regard to the almost literal citations from Suárez in Descartes's 1630 letters to Father Mersenne—Descartes's link to medieval thought remained still largely unexamined when I began to work on him. It was thought that Étienne Gilson (and Alexandre Koyré, on Edmund Husserl's account) had taken care of things, which was not the case, because at the time of his 1913 theses Gilson was still writing under the influence of the Scholastic tradition and its polemical stance toward Descartes. Gilson remains a contemporary of Maritain, still dominated by the question of the critique of substantial forms, the question of the act of being, and some others. This means that in some manner his Descartes still really belonged to the nineteenth century—a Descartes that was in some way neo-Kantian, Voltairean, or Wolffian.

Moreover, what Gilson calls Scholasticism, that's first of all Saint Thomas Aquinas, while you shift the dialogue to Suárez.

When Gilson works on Descartes, his Scholasticism is still Thomist, and when he wants to oppose Descartes to the medieval thinkers, he puts Thomas Aquinas and his later commentators, Tolet, Suárez, Gabriel

Vásquez, and the Conimbres, on an equal footing, as if they all agreed with one another and with Aquinas (which is obviously not the case). I, for one, began by moving Descartes closer not to Aquinas (of whom I still had only mediocre knowledge at the time) but to Suárez. This allowed a much more complex landscape to emerge. On the status of mathematical and logical truths Descartes criticized Suárez but also John Duns Scotus and his own contemporaries, who held that the mathematical truths and the logical truths remain univocal, regardless of whether a finite or an infinite understanding thinks them. Consequently, Descartes entered into a much more precise relationship not only with medieval Scholasticism but also with the Scholasticism of his own time. One should never forget that Suárez's *Metaphysical Disputations*, which served as a reference work in the seventeenth century, dates to the year after Descartes's birth and that Suárez, a Jesuit, was still alive during the years when Descartes studied at La Flèche, also with the Jesuits. Philosophers like Suárez are therefore not distant authors but direct references. Furthermore, when I began to work, our understanding of Scholasticism (and of neo-Scholasticism) had been much modified by Gilson's final work in *Being and Essence*. Like de Lubac in *Augustinianism and Modern Theology*, Gilson very clearly opposed Aquinas to the authors of the fourteenth and sixteenth centuries.

So in your [doctoral] thesis you chose to treat the question of analogy. Could you take us back to the stakes of such a question?

The Cartesian doctrine of the creation of eternal truths raises the problem of knowing whether the same ideas that have the status of principles for a finite understanding keep this status of principles for an infinite understanding, assuming that one could speak with regard to God of an understanding or that one could distinguish faculties in God (something that is obviously denied by all the great theologians and by Descartes just as much). To understand it in the terms of medieval thought, one must retranslate it into a question about the ground of ideas, that is to say, about the analogy of knowledge.

So it is instead a question of the philosophy of knowledge?

At the beginning of my research for the dissertation it wasn't really metaphysics that interested me but a more ancient question, which had been unintentionally suggested to me by Beaufret. He insisted that Descartes's thought only becomes intelligible as a criticism of Aristotle; for him,

Descartes's theory of science can only be understood as a criticism of the doctrine of the *eidos* and of the identity of the known and the knower in Aristotelian noetics. For Aristotle there is only a single act for the knower and the known (as his *On the Soul* also stresses), while, with the doctrine of the object as constituted by the *ego* (I would not say *subject*, because Descartes does not use that term in the modern sense), Descartes establishes a noetics grounded on the distinction of what Husserl will much later call the two regions: the "region of consciousness" and the "region of the world." I immediately applied this line of questioning, which Beaufret had mentioned in class without developing it, to the Cartesian text that seemed most aporetic to me: the *Rules for the Direction of the Mind*.[2] It's an early unfinished text, probably from 1627–1628, in Latin, and characterized also by the strangeness of its vocabulary. Descartes uses terms in it that will later disappear, like the *intuitus*, which he would rarely employ later, and quasi-neologisms, like *mathesis universalis* and so forth. This text had hardly been studied and then only as a developed version of the doctrine of method in the *Discourse on Method*, published nearly ten years later—that is, as a commentary by its own author on a text that he hadn't actually written yet. And the translations testify to this underestimation: for example, Jacques Brunschwig's, which appeared in Descartes's *Œuvres philosophiques*, edited by Alquié and which is quite excellent, was marked by an interpretive tendency that does not hesitate to modernize Descartes's vocabulary.

Is that why you have retranslated the Rules*? To reach the text by dusting it off and freeing it from the underestimation it suffered?*

I wagered on an interpretive hypothesis—a restrictive one, but one that required rigor—by which one could translate this text only into the French that Descartes himself uses to the point of and including the *Discourse on Method*, and no further. This is why Pierre Cahné, Jean-Robert Armogathe, and I put together the first two computerized concordances to Descartes in Latin and in French, which allowed us to determine this vocabulary more exactly.

2. [*Regulae ad directionem ingenii*, translated as *Rules for the Direction of the Mind*, in *The Philosophical Writings of Descartes*, trans. John Cottingham, Robert Stoothoff, and Donald Murdoch, 3 vols. (Cambridge: Cambridge University Press, 1984–1991).]

And from there the fact emerged that the Rules *could or should be read as a criticism of Aristotle!*

Yes. I ventured the hypothesis that Descartes devotes himself to a term-by-term criticism of Aristotle's theses—first the theory of knowledge, then of logic, then of physics. That seemed necessary to me when I discovered that the first of the *Rules*, concerning the unity of the sciences, called into question a fundamental Aristotelian principle, namely that science is found only inside a definition of essence common to what he calls "a genre," that is to say, a region of things to know, and that no science ever passes from one genre to another. That means that there is no "transgeneric" science, hence no universal science. Now Descartes obviously claims entirely the opposite, so long as one reads the first Rule with Aristotle in mind.

In the same way, when Descartes says, in Rules II and III, that science concerns only objects that are certain, he directly contradicts Aristotle, who says there are sciences, such as physics, for example, that concern things that are essentially contingent because they consist of matter and hence entail change. By their very definition, these things cannot supply objects that are certain. In the same way, the *mathesis universalis* (which should be translated as "universal science," not as "universal mathematics") of Rule IV shows that what is at stake in the use of mathematics is not an "application" of mathematics to physics but the project of extending what is certain in mathematics to all the sciences (actually to *the* science) and thus setting it up as a universal science. This science would relativize the difference of genres, making the difference between the essences of things indifferent, provided they are known in *one* single science unified by homogeneous intellectual operations.

This is what is confirmed by Rules VI to VIII, which are entailed by the *mathesis universalis* and work out its implications. They do so by deconstructing the irreducibility of the essence of each thing by showing that *ousia*—which is often translated as "substance" but should be understood first as *beingness* [*étanité*], as essence—can certainly become relative because it is already a term relative to the accident and thus is exactly like it. This contradicts all of Aristotle's teachings. One can verify this by the fact that Descartes modifies the teaching of Aristotle's *On the Soul*, in which all the faculties of knowing depend on the thing, into a doctrine of modes of the ego (sensation, imagination, understanding, etc.). In short, I showed the profound coherence of the *Rules for the Direction of the Mind* as it appears as soon as one sees the rules as a series of refutations of basic Aristotelian theses, refutations that are concealed by the fact that Descartes never cited Aristotle's text nor even mentioned his name (with one exception).

Did Descartes have the same Aristotle available to him as we do?

Yes, for the most part, but also in a more Scholastic form. It's the Aristotle that we still teach (or *should be teaching*) to students starting at university: the *Categories*, the *Analytics*, the *Physics*, the fundamental arguments of the central books of the *Metaphysics*, and of course *On the Soul*. In any case, he had learned him very well.

But didn't you thereby leave yourself open to being reproached with interpretive boldness? After all, you confronted Aristotle and Descartes directly, as if nothing had taken place between the two. Unless maybe Beaufret's contribution was to authorize the assumption that the two could speak in direct dialogue?

Yes! I was fearless on this point, in accordance with Beaufret's thesis, which I acknowledged clearly in the preface. Oddly enough I was not subjected to discussions or criticisms in regard to this comparative lack of precaution, probably because in retrospect what I was doing appeared rather obvious. I dealt with the basic Aristotle, without subtlety in exposition and without a detailed account of reception history. But from Luther to Galileo, from Rabelais to Gassendi, the anti-Aristotelian polemic often proceeded like that.

You wrote that, while there are certainly underground channels that led from Aristotle to Descartes, you would not study them on their own terms. For a contemporary reader that seems strange.

I had understood very well that, before investigating the easily recognizable historical influences, one must know between which two poles these influences could play. Anyway, Pierre Aubenque, who was a member of my committee, agreed with this, as did Tullio Gregory. First one had to establish the two sets of theses; only after that could one uncover the channels in between. (Besides, that's what I outlined in the extensive notes to my translation of the *Rules*, published in 1977, two years after *On Descartes' Grey Ontology*.) Without establishing this relationship, one can see absolutely nothing. Since then I have become convinced that a philosopher should not only be read under a magnifying glass, in the manner of Gouhier or Gueroult, but also by telescope, in the manner of Beaufret. One must see him in comparison with distant peers and distant points of reference in order then to measure their differences. Later, that helped me a lot in reading the relationship between Descartes and Kant directly, without allowing myself to be distracted by the question of reconstituting what Kant could have read (or, rather, hadn't read) of Descartes. The same is true for the relationship between Nietzsche and Descartes. Regardless of who the intermediaries were, it's clear that Nietzsche was a very good reader of Descartes. So that was the verification of Beaufret's method, a method that was borrowed from Heidegger anyway (and equally from Husserl). In a sense, the great philosophers encounter one another in a direct relationship—not that there aren't a lot of foothills between the great summits, but one sees much more clearly and directly from one summit to another than from the top—far too low—of a foothill. Sometimes we have to leave even the most learned foothills of intellectual history in order to climb as high as possible on the conceptual slope of a summit.

This study of the Rules, *then, was the subject of your thesis [*thèse de troisième cycle*]?*

Yes, and this thesis became *On Descartes' Grey Ontology*, the annotated translation of the *Rules* and the concordance to the *Rules for the Direction of the Mind.*

So in the same gesture you set out both to establish a text that would be accessible to the Francophone reader and to interpret this text?

Absolutely. The two projects developed together—and quite quickly. I worked very hard, and I finished the actual writing in a year; the notes for the translation took longer because I was held back by many other things at the time. All the same, the whole thing was done rather quickly.

Descartes and His Metaphysics

Could you say a little more about the title of On Descartes' Grey Ontology*?*

As I worked, I discovered that the *Regulae* does not conduct an orderly criticism of Aristotle's doctrine of science. Rather, by opposing one theory of science to another, the Cartesian theory opposes nothing less than a doctrine of the thing in itself, an ontology of the *ousia*. It was necessary not only to reconstruct the epistemological requirements of what would become Descartes's theory of method, its practice, and its implicit metaphysics but also to elucidate how this epistemology is only put in place through the establishment of an ontology that does not say its name, which I therefore described as "gray."

With *On Descartes' Grey Ontology* I thus anticipated a question that was not really studied until several years later, namely an inquiry regarding the birth of a science that was actually called *ontologia* for the first time at the beginning of the seventeenth century, by Calvinist Scholastic philosophers under the influence of Suárez and Jesuit neo-Scholasticism. That said, I already guessed that Descartes's gray ontology represented first and foremost a theory of the known object. (This is a pleonasm, for the object designates the thing reduced to what can be known of it.) This is not a science of the being [*l'étant*] in itself but of being inasmuch as it is thinkable, of what from 1613 on (and even before) was called the *cogitabile*, of whatever is thought and thinkable—a science of precisely what Descartes calls the object! I consequently encountered a paradox that was confirmed by what followed: the ontology of the history of metaphysics, *ontologia* as *metaphysica generalis*, was actually always and from the outset gray because it was always a science that put being that can be thought [*l'étant pensable*] into the place of being that is defined by its essence [*l'étant pris dans son essence*], that is, being as being [*l'étant en tant qu'étant*].

You mean to say: a science that substitutes thinkable being (the cogitabile*) for the thing itself?*

Yes. The thing itself (which has traditionally been called the *ousia*, the *to on ē on*, the *ens in quantum ens*, i.e., being as being) in the gray ontology becomes being as known (*ens ut cogitabile* [being as knowable], *ens ut cogitatum* [being as known]). Berkeley's justifiably celebrated formulation systematized this: *esse est percipi aut percipere*, "to be is to be perceived or to perceive"—an eminently Cartesian formulation. Being is either the one who cogitates (*ego sum* or, also, God) or the cogitated object. The truly initiating gesture of ontology is thus found in the *Rules*, and that's what immediately interested me. It allowed me to raise the question: Does Descartes belong to metaphysics? This question had become central in the 1970s because the French revival of Aristotle interpretation after [the publication of] Pierre Aubenque's doctoral thesis (*Le problème de l'être chez Aristote* [*The Problem of Being in Aristotle*]), in other words, with the added influence of Heidegger, brought up the question what in it was attributable to the history of metaphysics and what to the history of being. Many others raised similar questions: Jean-François Courtine, Rémi Brague, Alain de Libéra, and then, in their own way, Bruno Pinchard, Vincent Carraud, Olivier Boulnois, and Jean-Christophe Bardout.

Now from that point of view Descartes posed an odd problem. In the dominant interpretations of Descartes—from Victor Cousin, then Brunschvicg, and even Hamelin, to Gueroult, Gilson, and Maritain—the whole world agreed that Descartes was not interested in the question of Being [*l'être*]; whether one blamed him for it, as the neo-Thomists did, or whether one congratulated him, as Gueroult or the French Kantians in the lineage of Léon Brunschvicg did, either way, all these readings agreed in their conviction that Descartes had put in brackets the traditional (and scholastic) questions of Being [*l'être*] and of being [*l'étant*] and was interested only in certainty and hence in the constitution of the object, in its knowledge, in mathematics and physics, and so forth. One thus discovers a Descartes not really doing any general metaphysics, a Descartes for whom God merely hits a button on the machine of the world (as Pascal is supposed to have put it) and for whom special metaphysics remains a mere pretext. And in a sense one could and *should* have affirmed, as late as the 1960s (in Gueroult's case, at least), that Descartes was not a metaphysician and hence was not inscribed in the history of Being [*l'être*].

Had Alquié not already detected the gap in Descartes between the object and being?

Yes, but in remaining, if I may say so, quite superficial. As we saw, Alquié asserted that his personal philosophy resumes the one true philosophy, that of Plato, of Descartes, and of Kant, and that this philosophy is summarized in two theses: Being is not the object; the object is not being. But, apart from the fact that this thesis is found with difficulty among those authors, assuming it were correct, the *ontological* difference between the object and being would still have to be explained; obviously, Alquié did not do that. But everything changes if, as *On Descartes' Grey Ontology* demonstrated, the theory of the object calls for an ontology, even a subtle one, of being as object. From that moment on the question is raised insistently whether there would be a special metaphysics in Descartes, that is, whether a metaphysics of the highest being, what is called a special metaphysics, can be added to the general metaphysics (the equivalent of a science of being as being, that is to say, the doctrine of science interpreting being as object in general). Thus, several years later, I finally again took up the enigma of the 1630 letters, which raised the question of the grounding of finite knowledge, whether absolute or not. I again applied the method of thematically comparing not Descartes with Aristotle now but Descartes with the medieval authors who wonder about analogy. And that became *On Descartes' White Theology*, which begins by showing that the 1630 letters raise the question—in the same terms as Suárez and Duns Scotus—whether the mathematical truths and the logical truths would remain immovable in the absence of God (*etsi Deus non daretur*) but then respond to it in the opposite direction.

Could you briefly take up again the content of the 1630 letters?

At the end of a letter from April 15, 1630 [to the priest, theologian, and friend Marin de Mersenne], in which Descartes refuses to speak of theology (he claims to confine himself strictly to philosophy), he suddenly announces, employing this term for the first time, that he will speak of metaphysics and asserts that the mathematical and logical truths that Mersenne calls eternal have been established by God (and hence are not eternal) and that they are only true because God has established them. By doing this Descartes turns upside down one of Suárez's propositions. Suárez said that the truths are created by God because they are true, and not the reverse; Descartes says that they are true because they are created by God, and not the reverse. Descartes adds that we should never say, because it is blasphemous, that "two and three equals five" *in itself*; "two and three equals five" *appears* necessary (and is necessary) only to our understanding because it is finite, but our understanding remains created by God in the same way that God creates the mathematical truths (and the things of the world), which correspond to it and which seem fixed to it. Mathematical truths are actually objects that are suitable, i.e., finite, to an understanding that itself is also finite. And all of this relies on what Descartes draws by contrast from a formulation that one will find again in 1640 and all the way to the end: "the infinite and incomprehensible power of God." Thus rationality, *our* rationality, remains created, finite: It cannot have access to its principle, which takes the face of power and not that of reasoned and reasoning reason [*raison raisonnée et raisonnante*] (and also, contra an enduring misinterpretation, does not take the face of divine will, the supposedly Cartesian voluntarism wrongly denounced by Spinoza, Malebranche, and Leibniz). Power becomes the place and the meaning of the infinite. Now the infinite remains, by definition, incomprehensible to the finite. The divine power, being infinite, imposes itself incomprehensibly on any finite understanding.

This doctrine certainly seems very strange. Descartes does not prove it; he presupposes it. He takes it up again in the majority of his works but without mentioning it as such in the *Meditations*. He will never cite the 1630 letters; he will never argue about this point, which he cites from time to time without demonstrating it. And what is most surprising is that this thesis will be rejected by all the philosophers who identify themselves with Descartes in whatever way after him. Leibniz repeatedly criticizes it. It is done away with by Malebranche, for whom the truths are identical with the divine understanding without being incomprehensible because they are necessary even for God; God as Word is the universal law of God as Power—that is, the Father (Power) obeys the Son (Word). As for Spinoza, he considers resorting to the incomprehensibility of the divine will to be the refuge of ignorance, which contradicts his entire philosophical undertaking.

Descartes's thesis hence appears as very provocative, and in my opinion one will not find its equivalent before Kant: Kant will take up the absolutely determining status of the difference between the finite and the infinite, between the "archetypal understanding" and the "ectypical understanding," and the a priori conditions of knowledge remain unextendable for us because they mark finitude. Anyway, Kant often holds positions completely identical to those of Descartes, without saying or seeing it. I thus began to study the medieval background of this question, showing that the thesis according to which the mathematical truths would be true even if God had not been known was, since at least Duns Scotus, classical, certain, and maintained by Suárez, Vásquez, and the majority of the medievals because Duns Scotus was the first to reason *etsi Deus non daretur*, i.e., as if God had not been given. This thesis would actually offer one of the possible replies to the question of the analogy of knowledge: Are the ideas of things in God the same as ours? If not, how do we ground the truth of our knowledge? The late Scholastics stated, against Thomas Aquinas and Bonaventure (and hence against the previous tradition), the univocity of being (i.e., being is spoken of in the same sense whether one speaks of God or of creation) and the univocity of knowledge (i.e., true ideas are the same for the divine understanding as for human understanding).

This position constitutes one of the responses to the question of analogy and of the divine ideas developed entirely differently, for example, in Thomas Aquinas or in Augustine. Descartes then appeared to criticize radically and turn upside down the late Scholastics' dominant position on the problem of the relationship between the truths and God; as a result, strangely enough, he is in a sense closer to Thomas Aquinas than to Suárez. Even more surprisingly: I have tried to show that Descartes's contemporaries, whether scientists (Kepler, Galileo, and Mersenne) or even theologians (Bérulle and others from the mystical movement), also maintained, albeit for different reasons, a kind of univocity of knowledge between mathematical truths (and logical truths) and the ideas in God, which would be the same as those that we know ourselves.

Consequently, by maintaining the irreducibility of the infinite to the finite, Descartes appeared to be an author against the trend of all his contemporaries. It is on this basis that, in the second part of *On Descartes' White Theology*, I attempted to reread the entire metaphysical foundation of 1641, of the *Meditations*, and of the "Replies to the Objections." From this emerges a Descartes who raises the question of special metaphysics as such, that is, the question of the grounding of finite knowledge, which has, for example, considerable consequences for the proofs of God's existence. Accordingly, I tried to show that the three proofs of God's existence correspond to the three definitions of God, each of which are not really compatible with the others: The first proof ("Third Meditation") presupposes the infinity and the incomprehensibility of God, hence that God is certain inasmuch as infinite, that is, inasmuch as incomprehensible. On the contrary, the second proof ("Fifth Meditation") joins with the "ontological argument" (as Kant will later call it) in upholding that the existence of God is deduced from his essence like a mathematical property from a definition, which presupposes that the same type of mathematical intelligibility is found again, with its certainty and its evidence, even in the case of the proposition of the existence of God—but then the existence of God is discovered as situated at the same epistemological level as a mathematical truth, which contradicts the creation of the eternal truths! As for the final proof ("Replies to the First Objections" and "Replies to the Fourth Objections"), it is concerned with God as *causa sui*, thus presupposing the inclusion of God in the principle of causality (and thus anticipating Leibniz's principle of sufficient reason, as Vincent Carraud has demonstrated). This determination of God by causality maintains quite nicely the interpretation of his essence as an infinite power, and in that respect incomprehensible, but it also postulates that God is no exception to a universal rule, which states that everything that is must have a cause (or a reason exempting it from cause). Therefore, here also, God, although infinite and incomprehensible, is submitted to the common regime of all being. One finds God's transcendence also put in question there.

The awkward compatibility of the three proofs and of the three definitions of God only appears if one thinks that Descartes has seen from the outset the supreme importance of the distinction between the finite and the infinite. If this question does not appear crucial, one will not discover the tension between the proofs of God's existence. This is why I said that theology remains undecided in Descartes. It is simply a "white [*blanche*] theology," like a blank [*blanc*] check that can be endorsed by different signatories. But who is the signatory here? Who is the God who endorses Descartes's rational theology? Is it the God subject to the principle of sufficient reason or, at least, already subject to the principle of causality? Is it a God who is a mathematician and mathematizable or, rather, the incomprehensible and infinite God? And anyway, what is the first principle of Descartes's special metaphysics? The ego or God? Both interpretations of Descartes remain possible and have been defended. The principal concern of all his successors was to reconcile these two hypotheses by identifying one with the other. Rational theology, special metaphysics, seemed indeterminate—thus a white or blank theology. In any case, I reached the two moments of a Cartesian metaphysics and, as an essential result, Descartes is then found rightfully reintegrated into the history of metaphysics.

You arrived thus at your third investigation into Descartes, your "autonomous work," as you write (the first two having been [doctoral] theses): On Descartes' Metaphysical Prism. *You subject Descartes to the question of figuring out whether he belongs to the history of metaphysics, and you bring up to date the way the two onto-theo-logies interlock in his work: the onto-theo-logy of the* cogitatio *and the onto-theo-logy of the* causa. *The point obviously was to synthesize the results of the previous investigations and to give them a more systematic formulation. Why subject Descartes to the question of whether he belongs to metaphysics, and what do you mean by defining metaphysics as onto-theo-logy?*

On Descartes' Grey Ontology and *On Descartes' White Theology* provoked different reactions: the first, shorter, study, although it was not ignored, still did not provoke specific reactions. It was generally acknowledged to be a useful demonstration.

All the same, even among those who find things to object to in your work on Descartes, On Descartes' Grey Ontology *is the work most readily accepted!*

No doubt because it concerned a supposedly minor text, it remained precise and technical, without particular development, and because the consequences did not seem to put in question the standard interpretation of Descartes but even seemed to reinforce and emphasize his opposition to

Aristotle. It was a bit different for *On Descartes' White Theology*: the work appeared to place Descartes into a theological perspective. One might wonder whether it did not suggest an interpretation that was too theological (which remains a bad word). And, in my mind, what is at stake is not at all a theological interpretation but a *metaphysical* interpretation, renewed by a perspective that takes into account the theological debates of Descartes and his time period, debates that until then had been ignored or weren't well known. It was nevertheless clear that a certain number of questions are raised. Above all, the readers at the time did not see what seemed obvious to me: The conditions were assembled for finally responding to the question whether Descartes belonged to metaphysics. Theoretically, I had tried to establish, on the one hand, that there was a general metaphysics, that is to say an ontology of the object ("gray ontology"), and, on the other hand, a theory of grounding, a special metaphysics in the shape of a rational theology in competition with a doctrine of the ego or "rational psychology," to use Kant's language ("white theology").

Why do you mention a theory of grounding?

I want to speak of a theory of the grounding of knowledge and of universal ontology in regard to a privileged being. Now among the three privileged beings of special metaphysics (the soul, the world, and God), Descartes had pointed out two that could be ultimate: either the soul (the ego of the *cogito*) or God. It therefore became almost inevitable to ask the following question: What sort of relation is there between the "gray ontology" and the "white theology"? My thesis was that it was a matter of two of the traditional elements of a special metaphysics, such that Descartes indisputably belonged to metaphysics. Yet, what shape does his metaphysics take under these conditions? At first I studied the different uses Descartes makes of the terms *metaphysics* and *first philosophy*, in order to situate them within a history of these concepts. I insisted on the fact that Descartes had a very particular vision of *first philosophy* (which historically is one of the rival names for *metaphysics* as also for *ontology*), that he considered it a philosophy of first *knowledge*: what was first, what caused a being to be privileged so as to ground all the other beings—this was its primacy in the order of knowledge. Once one had done this, once one had tackled the general problem of the cohesion of Cartesian metaphysics, it became impossible not to confront Heidegger. In a celebrated text Heidegger had defined metaphysics as an onto-theo-logy. He thus went back to a term utilized by Kant and some subsequent authors like Schopenhauer: In Kant, onto-theo-logy referred to one of the arguments intended to prove God's existence. Heidegger will impart a wider and more precise meaning to it: "Onto-theo-logy" names the logic that articulates ontology, that is to say, the doctrine of being in general (being as being) and the doctrine of the highest being, with the understanding that the highest being could be God but could also be any other first being if there is another—such as the ego.

I hence asked the question in these terms: There is a metaphysics in Descartes because he develops a general metaphysics (or its equivalent) *and* a special metaphysics; he therefore also unfolds an onto-theo-logy. Yet how to describe this onto-theo-logy? A difficulty arose here. For Heidegger, onto-theo-logy forms a kind of circle: If I define being in general as what has an essence, the highest being will be the being that is, that exists, by its essence. In Aristotle and in some way in Thomas Aquinas, this being cannot, by virtue of its essential definition, not be in act. This leads to a circle: Any being is according to its essence, and there is a being for whom essence implies that it exists—it will then ground the others. Can one reason like this in regard to Descartes? Can one transform a universal determination into a determination that would justify, in accordance with the necessity of essence, the primacy of one of the beings that grounds all the others and that is simultaneously the illustration of the way in which all the others are? The tension between two hypotheses in regard to the first being, the being par excellence, obviously becomes inevitable there: Is it the ego or God?

Quite a few interpreters, beginning with Gueroult, keep going back and forth between the two imperceptibly, as if that did not present any problem whatsoever. Descartes establishes for the first time the primacy of the ego over everything that is known to it, the ego as first principle (this is the title that is given to it in certain texts), and, despite everything, God remains for him the first principle as Creator and as the only eternal, necessary, and infinite being. The reconciliation of these two possible first principles nevertheless remains very difficult: Descartes's successors all worked at it, always, in fact, sacrificing one or the other of the first principles. I hence ventured the hypothesis that there was not only *one* single onto-theo-logy in Descartes but *two*. According to the first onto-theo-logy, the one where all the beings are defined inasmuch as they are known, that is, as objects, the first being is the being that exists inasmuch as it knows them—that is the onto-theo-logy of cogitation: every being is a *cogitatum* or a *cogitabile*, as the ontology after Descartes will say, and, in turn, the one who assures the nature of the cogitability of all beings itself comes to be endowed with primacy. One obtains a complete onto-theo-logical circle, which will be developed in a perfect fashion both by German idealism and by the neo-Kantianism of the Marburg School. The finite mind (tangentially infinite) takes the role of first foundation and thus maintains—in the name of what metaphysics called rational psychology—the function of first principle. This first onto-theo-logy operates in Descartes in the first two Meditations and in several other texts. Nevertheless, Descartes proves the existence of God by introducing the notion of causality, whether in the "Third Meditation" or the "Replies to the Fourth Objections": In this case, if God is the cause of any thing and, in this sense, is what grounds all the other beings, he himself is first inasmuch as he needs no other cause than his own essence. He is hence tangentially thinkable as *cause of himself*. Thus, from the point of view of causality, God becomes the foundation and introduces a second onto-theo-logy—the onto-theo-logy of the cause.

How to explain this doubled representation, these two onto-theo-logies? Of course, one can simply say that one of them is too much and that the reconstruction is not correct—Heidegger never envisioned the possibility of several concurrent and simultaneous onto-theo-logies. Yet, I have maintained this interpretation for many reasons. The first reason is that when classical and soon afterward Scholastic metaphysics became established, it was set up on the basis of the irreducibility of two principles, the principle of identity and the principle of sufficient reason. The principle of identity decrees that nothing can be thinkable if it contradicts itself. That is the case for cogitations: Everything that is, is identical to itself, and only what can be thought without contradiction is possible. Yet that is the principle of the first onto-theo-logy. Furthermore, the principle of sufficient reason posits that no proposition and no being are true and certain without a reason or a cause why they are such and not otherwise—that is the principle that supports the second onto-theo-logy. This distinction, made explicitly by Leibniz, then sanctioned by Wolff, still known to Kant, will give rise to a debate concerning whether one can reduce the principle of identity to the principle of sufficient reason, or the inverse—a completely classical debate as old as metaphysics itself—because it defines it. These two principles really show that an irresolvable tension could be found in metaphysics itself, from its Scholastic formulation onward. Thus it may not be entirely unbelievable that this tension would appear at the beginning of Scholastic metaphysics, that is to say, with Descartes.

The second reason why I maintained this interpretation of Descartes as following two onto-theo-logies is because it is perfectly possible to articulate them. In fact, the onto-theo-logy of cause does not simply repeat the onto-theo-logy of cogitation; it goes beyond it. Descartes shows very well that the finite mind, as the first and foremost principle of cogitation, itself also turns out to be open to an overdetermination as the effect of a cause; it is indeed first according to the onto-theo-logy of cogitation, but, as it remains finite, it can also be a being derived from an effect, at the interior of an ontology of the cause, where it will never play the role of first cause. Certainly the ego of the *cogito* can in some way aspire to the role of the *cogitatio sui* in accordance with the first onto-theo-logy, but in no way can it aspire to the role of *causa sui* in accordance with the second. Two primacies are therefore possible, which correspond to the two representations, to the two irreducible principles of the order of reasons, and also to the two principles of metaphysics. It is this hazardous link, although inscribed in the texts, which characterizes, it seems to me, Descartes's metaphysics and maybe his alone. (Aristotle remains the counterexample.)

I showed, then, not only that Descartes was part of the history of metaphysics as the history of Being [*l'être*] and of being [*l'étant*] but also that he accomplished an essential moment in the process of setting up and of constituting metaphysics such as Heidegger defines it, namely as onto-theo-logy. This reading validated and complicated the Heideggerian model of metaphysics and corrected it just as much. (That is why it is ridiculous to call this a *Heideggerian* interpretation of Descartes, as some did and still do.) This hypothesis appeared all the more appealing to me given that Descartes's followers became more intelligible if one took into account the link between these two onto-theo-logies. Without going into detail here, one can say that Spinoza, for example, can be summed up in an attempt to make the logical deduction—that is to say, the ontology of cogitation—coincide with the causal consecution of the effect and the cause. One meets up with the same effort in Leibniz, but in a more complex manner. Nothing is more striking in Malebranche than to see God himself doubled into two principles: first, the Word or Wisdom of God, who is the place of principles and develops an onto-theo-logy of the cause where the divine Word is understood as a *cogito*; second, the Power of God, the Father, who must be regulated according to necessary reason and abide by universal laws of order, that is to say, the first onto-theo-logy, that of cogitation.

In the case of Malebranche, it is then, in contrast to Descartes, the onto-theo-logy of the cause that submits to that of cogitation?

Absolutely.

Is such a submission possible in Descartes?

For him, the two onto-theo-logies are linked, but they do not cover each other. His successors try absolutely to identify them or to subject one to the other, as in Malebranche, where power (the Father) yields to cogitation (the Word) in a strange Trinity, one that is inverted and without the Spirit.

These post-Cartesian attempts to recover the doubling of onto-theo-logy in Descartes hence correspond to the disappearance of the thesis of the creation of the eternal truths after Descartes?

Exactly. And the function of the creation of the eternal truths in Descartes consequently becomes completely unintelligible. It means that the incomprehensible power (what will become the onto-theo-logy of the cause) grounds what appears as the first principle, though only at the interior of the onto-theo-logy of cogitation, namely the mathematical truths and the logical truths thinkable by the ego. Thus, in a sense, the hypothesis of the doubled onto-theo-logy reinforces the coherence of Cartesian thought.

Why do you speak of a metaphysical prism *of Descartes?*

Because the prism breaks white light up into specific lights. *On Descartes' Metaphysical Prism* broke up the apparent or unquestioned unity of Descartes's thought into its different dimensions. For example, as we have seen, I show that the Cartesian proofs for God's existence put into place three definitions for God that are not completely compatible with one another. The so-called ontological argument ("Fifth Meditation") falls under the onto-theo-logy of cogitation because it places God at the level of the mathematical truths, the proof by *causa sui* ("Replies to the Fourth Objections") depends directly on the onto-theo-logy of the cause, and the proof by the idea of the infinite ("Third Meditation") articulates the two according to the relation of the finite to the infinite. I have also tried to show that the definition of the ego and of the very complex relationship between its finitude and its will (at the same time one of the modes of the thinking and infinite thing) is explained by the fact that the ego itself is also situated at the border of the two onto-theo-logies.

In what sense can anything escape onto-theo-logy at that moment? Maybe God, understood as infinite?

I have not yet come to a conclusive response in regard to the position of the infinite. In fact, two of the proofs for God's existence will chiefly be developed further after Descartes: the one that inscribes God into the onto-theo-logy of cogitation, namely the celebrated "ontological argument," and the one where God, seen according to the second onto-theology, appears as cause (or even *causa sui*). The argument according to the idea of the infinite hence tends to disappear (Fénelon is the exception). Why? How? Is it because it was the weakest? I believe, on the contrary, that for Descartes it was the strongest. Maybe it has to do with the difficulty of forming a notion of infinity, which in fact requires an enumeration of the finite and of the infinite. For in some way the infinite can only be conceived as incomprehensible, forcing us to conceive incomprehensibility as such. Maybe that would explain why metaphysics, when it wants to be closed in on itself, must give up thinking the infinite, which is necessarily beyond its grasp. The question of the fate of the infinite is thus left over. In other words, one must still figure out whether there is a philosophy beyond metaphysics.

That is why *On Descartes' Metaphysical Prism* ends with a new look at the connection between Pascal and Descartes, where Descartes appears within the topic of the three Pascalian orders as the representative of the first and the second order. The first order, the order of bodies—in the sense at the same time of the body of politics, of affairs of the world, and of material extension—defines precisely what the ego can understand and construct of the extended thing. The second order, the order of thought—of mathematical truths, of logical truths, of philosophical truths, of metaphysical truths—defines the order of the thinking thing, philosophy in the sense of Descartes and what Pascal himself also admits as philosophy. The third order, the order of charity, to which only the saints have access, remains outside metaphysics, and Descartes has no access to it, according to Pascal. In his theory of the three orders Pascal accordingly allocates a place to Descartes's metaphysics, namely the second order. This means, however, that Descartes's metaphysics does not encompass everything and that one can describe something outside the metaphysics constituted by Descartes. This opens another direction, this time not toward the rational theology of metaphysics (special metaphysics) but toward the theology of Revelation.

But in that case for Descartes there was at the very heart of the double onto-theology a kind of sally out of metaphysics, namely the infinite?

That is the hypothesis I suggest.

Do you then meet up again via a historical investigation with the results that Levinas's phenomenology had established in showing that the infinite is exempted from totality and from metaphysics?

Oddly enough, at the moment when I worked on *On Descartes' Metaphysical Prism*, I had not yet really seen the connection with Levinas—maybe because Levinas's use of the idea of the infinite in order to show the way to exteriority was not yet entirely established. Let us not forget that Levinas's text on the idea of the infinite was published in the tribute to Alquié, *La passion de la raison* [*The Passion of Reason*], which dates to 1983.

Yes, but Levinas's analyses on the infinite in Descartes date already to 1961 in Totality and Infinity *. . .*

When I studied the idea of the infinite, I certainly knew that Levinas had spoken of it, but I had not personally seen to what extent he remains Cartesian on this point. Later that obviously became evident to me. Does the infinite open a path to get outside metaphysics? I raised the very same question, but instead through the intermediary of Pascal, an astute reader of Descartes, who immediately applies the most precise diagnosis to the ambivalent aspects of the Cartesian position. When that book was published it triggered a real debate: some criticized it for being a Heideggerian tale forced on Descartes.

Yet all the same, as we have already suggested, you complicated and qualified the Heideggerian interpretation of metaphysics!

Of course. Having said that, those who criticized my hypothesis were not always terribly familiar with Heidegger's thought or texts. Once again, one could and should have just as much interpreted it as an approach in opposition to Heidegger. First, because the onto-theo-logical constitution found itself transformed into a *model*, a model that one could complicate and adapt to different authors. Moreover, an implicit question resulted from my proposal: Are there authors for whom the onto-theo-logical constitution does not work? If yes, would these authors still be philosophers, even if they are not metaphysicians? Is philosophy identified entirely and exclusively with metaphysics (as Heidegger suggests) or not? Now, by other paths and in the same period, I came to see and tried to show that in a strict sense one cannot pinpoint any onto-theo-logy either in Anselm or in Thomas Aquinas. Finally, I argued that there is also no onto-theo-logy in Augustine. Once more, it is in clarifying the model of onto-theo-logy historically that one can verify, specify, or refuse it, surely not by ignoring it or by disqualifying it on principle.

The criticism that accuses you of being a Heideggerian philosopher thus falls on its face and doubly so: On the one hand, because you showed in God Without Being *(1982) that one must remove the question from the horizon of Being [*de l'être*] within which Heidegger had wanted to raise it, and, on the other hand, again, because in your work as a historian of philosophy you contested or clarified Heidegger.*

I am not at all and have never been a low-browed Heideggerian, supposing that there are any and that Heidegger's thought would allow one to become so. Heidegger throws such a light on the question of metaphysics that in this light itself one can thoroughly discuss his analyses or complicate the models. My admiration for him precisely allows me to take the freedom (which he won for us and taught us) to transform his hypothesis as far as the texts require doing so. Obviously under these conditions the reproach of Heideggerian overinterpretation seems a groundless accusation to me. Nonetheless, the research pursued by others or by myself since then on the medieval thinkers (Saint Thomas, Duns Scotus, Suárez . . .) and the Cartesians (Pascal, Spinoza, Malebranche . . .) have shown the validity of my hypothesis.

The Center for Cartesian Studies

In fact, your studies on Descartes came to throw a light on Pascal first, then on Malebranche, and the results you reached were afterward validated by other research on the Cartesians, with the exception of Spinozist studies, which have remained a bit at the fringe of the movement. The dynamic you launched was decisive during the 1980s and 1990s in the history of Descartes interpretation in France. The importance of your work also relied on the Center for Cartesian Studies, of which you were an active member from its creation before becoming its director. Can you go back to Father Costabel's putting in place the "Descartes Team" and the founding of the Center for Cartesian Studies?

Thank you for allowing me to say something about this. The first remark is that, paradoxically, the Center for Cartesian Studies has never constituted a very strong or heavily administratively structured entity. It always stayed a section within a research group connected to the department of philosophy, then to a doctoral school of the University of Paris-Sorbonne. There is hence a discrepancy between the intellectual results of the Center for Cartesian Studies and its administrative status. This disproportion, as I have already explained, corresponds completely to my vision of university affairs and to the very weak role that I concede to the administrative structure. Besides, this flexible and free functioning matches what I have found at the University of Chicago. The second remark is that the Center for Cartesian Studies was able to expand and to endure because it was not monolithic and did not defend an ideology or even a theory. For a long time, it was directed by my friend and predecessor Jean-Marie Beyssade, whose disagreements with my interpretation of Descartes were widely recognized. We have remained in more or less vigorous discussion for years.

Other examples still come to mind today. There was accordingly neither a dominant orthodoxy nor a closed position, which is what permits other researchers belonging to other institutions and with other preoccupations to become involved in our debates. Besides, it also helped spread my hypothesis that one could criticize it at the very heart of the team that I (together with others) animated: Taking a position for or against some hypothesis or other did not determine whether one was on the inside or the outside of the Center for Cartesian Studies. This has permitted many research studies to become involved with other ones, either for verifying or for falsifying certain results but also to draw closer to other authors: Montaigne, Hobbes, Spinoza, Malebranche, Pascal, Leibniz, and up to Kant. In the history of metaphysics, one must also think big and in the long term.

How did the internationalization of Cartesian studies take place?

The Center for Cartesian Studies was international from the beginning because even before its founding we worked with the Lessico intellettuele europeo at the University of La Sapienza in Rome, a celebrated research center directed by Tullio Gregory. Then there were relations with Giulia Belgioioso and the Center for Studies on Descartes and the Seventeenth Century at Lecce, with Daniel Garber and his important American network (at Chicago, then at Princeton), with the Dutch in Utrecht gathered around Theo Verbeek, then the Germans, the Spanish, the Japanese. This internationalization also allowed us to test out a great many hypotheses, including my own, on very exact philological grounds owing to the translations, editions, and concordances already published or in the process of being worked out, during the conferences that we organized once or twice a year always on very specific topics. In this way an uninterrupted process of validating and verifying one another's work occurred. Besides, my *Cartesian Questions I*, *Cartesian Questions II*, and soon (if the time is granted me) *Cartesian Questions III*—and a final book of which we will speak in a moment—resulted to a large extent from this increased activity. These collections of studies allowed me to verify, to complete, or to correct overall hypotheses, for example, on the theory of substance or on the status of the ontological argument. Accordingly, the interpretation of Descartes was constantly refined, put back into perspective, and completed. That is how I was able not only to contribute to reintegrating Descartes into the history of metaphysics in the strict sense but to show how there was a *Cartesian moment within metaphysics*, which lasts until Kant at least and which corresponds to establishing the notion of *ontologia* for the first time with the two principles of metaphysics: the principle of reason for the onto-theology of the cause and the principle of identity for the onto-theo-logy of cogitation.

What connection do you establish between Descartes and Kant?

Between Descartes and Kant passes exactly the time required for trying out and exhausting all possible solutions that could resolve the difficulties, the aporias, and the tensions of the metaphysics set up by Descartes. After the failure of all these paths, Kant took Descartes's position up again (I know that this theme of Alquié can seem paradoxical, but I accept it) and systematized it in the shape of the *Critique of Pure Reason* (and not only in the "Dialectic," even if it is there that the resumption of Descartes is best expressed). I remain convinced that Kant was the most authentic and the best Cartesian. What Descartes calls the "method" Kant calls the "critique." Kant's "categories" correspond to Descartes's "simple natures." The tension between the transcendental ego and its finitude (hence the postulation of an infinite knowing) is found in Kant and in Descartes. It also runs through their common definition of the "I" via its relation of finite understanding to infinite will. In both, imagination works first in the service of mathematics, not only reproductively but also productively, in the constitution of objects. One can read all of that as the permanent traits of critical reason, that is to say, as a radical thought of finitude. Anyway, it is no accident that after Kant all his self-proclaimed heirs will endeavor to subvert his fundamental theses as unanimously as Descartes's successors contradict all his fundamental theses. One knows the result: a radicalized return to Kant's positions with Husserl and Heidegger. It is a strange paradox to see how the great philosophers determine their reception for a long time, the time it takes all the attempts and all the hypotheses to get out of the aporias (or of the truths that coincide with the aporias) that they have raised: a great philosopher is recognized by the efforts his successors still undertake in order to escape the conclusions he has established. Yet, when all the evasions and all the compromises have run aground, one carries out a return to the theses of the great philosopher by deepening them or even by claiming to surpass them. Locating these constants and their sequences is the only thing that permits scanning the history of metaphysics in a coherent manner.

What state of Cartesian research did you find when you entered it? The history of the "Descartes Team" had not yet been written at all. It would be good to sketch its outlines a bit.

When Jean-Robert Armogathe and I began to work on Descartes, we obviously wanted to get a sense of the production of Cartesian research outside of France. That was done very little at the time, for our great masters, caught in a prestigious and competitive cohort, did not take much notice of foreign studies, which were then quite secondary and very dependent on the French ones anyway. Yet some of them appeared to us all the same to illuminate many things: the German (and Italian) studies on the history of metaphysics or on the reception of Aristotle, on the late Scholastics, on the *minores*, and so forth. Armogathe, who was already very open to the international scene (he studied very early on in Germany, in America, and in Italy), had the brilliant idea of putting into place an international bulletin for making an inventory of writings on Descartes (which with the support of Vincent Carraud led later to his indispensable *Bibliographie cartésienne [1960–1996]*).[3] But we needed to be guided, especially myself in the history of science, because I worked on the *Rules*. We therefore went to see Pierre Costable, a reserved, calm, and immensely learned scholar at the CNRS. We forced his hand, and although he was not in the habit of getting on soapboxes, he found himself involved in this business. Then Geneviève Rodis-Lewis, having been appointed to the Sorbonne, straight-

3. Jean-Robert Armogathe, Vincent Carraud, et al., *Bibliographie cartésienne (1960–1996)* (Lecce: Conte Editore, 2003), to be continued.

away agreed to support the undertaking. Everything hence worked from the ground up, if I can say it like that.

What is strange is that Geneviève Rodis-Lewis, an eminent historian of Cartesian philosophy, did not share any of your commitments or of your presuppositions about Descartes. She worked permanently at restoring Cartesian thought as faithfully and as precisely as possible, even at the risk of repeating it—which was the opposite of your willingness to favor interpretation.

Very learned about Descartes, Malebranche, Arnauld, and Leibniz, among others, she was in fact also interested in exploring and in restoring the small Cartesians, as in restoring the almost literary spreading of Cartesian themes in second- or third-tier authors, of whom she was a great specialist (together with Jean Deprun).

Thus, Geneviève Rodis-Lewis reconstructed, and Henri Gouhier worked on the history of ideas. And Gueroult? What opinion do you have about his work?

Gueroult was no longer very active in those years but was occupied with constructing (that's the word) a general theory of the history of philosophy. Gueroult's great period had been the 1950s to 1960s, but in the 1970s he ruled without governing. I have read him but without thinking of him as a decisive interlocutor. The problem with Gueroult was that he proposed (really imposed) a closed, because systematic, interpretation. One had to be in agreement or possibly not, but one could not really discuss his theses. Moreover, his disciples saw to it that any challenge would be extinguished: Those who risked it paid dearly. Gueroult was more at ease with Spinoza, for Spinozism as a hard doctrine obviously corresponded much better to his very static methodology, all the more as the professional Spinozists were ecstatic to discover a well-armed and finally closed interpretation of an author they considered as closed. And Gueroult's antihistoricism suited the antihistoricism of the French interpretation of Spinoza perfectly, while I took a different orientation. In regard to Descartes I asked: Are there new textual questions, constructions of the text to be made, editions to redo, ignored sources, and so forth? Are there interpretations from abroad to discuss and take into account? (For example, should one not criticize studies like that of Harry Wolfson on Spinoza?) Are there possible influences on the author, perhaps discussions of this author with other thinkers, whether known or unknown and in any case underestimated? All these questions remained completely foreign to Gueroult's approach. As for turning to Heidegger or to Kant, comparing Descartes to Aristotle, that would have appeared completely foolish to him. Gueroult was also not—in terms of *method*, I insist on that—a reference.

Moreover, in Alquié's school you learned to pay attention to the ways in which the system malfunctioned, while Gueroult did everything for the system to hold together perfectly.

When there was an internal discord in the author, he would construct a concept that would allow one to cover up the problem. For example, in regard to the question we already encountered: "Is the ego in Descartes the first principle?" he responded by distinguishing a subjective *cogito* from an objective *cogito*, a completely invented distinction that is without textual support. He clearly saw the problem, but he resolved it by the forced introduction of plugs into the framework, of Scholastic *distinguo*. Even so, in a different sense, Gueroult did prove one thing negatively: that when one turns to distinguish two senses of the same concept or of the same thesis in an author, it is because the interpretation does not fit.

Was it to distinguish yourself from this way of working that you went to look among foreign interpretations?

Yes. There were Italian studies (Giovanni Crapulli) on the *Rules* that based themselves on the reconstruction of a Dutch translation contemporary to Descartes's text. (This is also the methodology used today by two new editions of the *Recherche de la vérité* [Descartes's *Search for Truth*] one edited by Ettore Lojacono and the other by Vincent Carraud and Gilles Olivo.) When we began to work, it was those kinds of results that we wanted to study, in relation to the research on the systematicity of the notion of metaphysics, taking place especially in Germany in different areas at the same time (for example, those by Wilhelm Wundt, Peter Petersen, Ernst Vollrath, E. Zimmermann, Wolfgang Röd, etc., which were occasionally passed on to us by Jean-François Courtine's lucid scholarship). Thus, the international and scholarly dimension became central. All of that convinced us that interpretation can be simultaneously speculative and philological in a very exacting way, without there being be the slightest contradiction in that. We thus needed a new network and a new work tool: that became first the *Bulletin cartésien*, which appeared for the first time in 1971, then the Center for Cartesian Studies, which was created in 1974. That's how everything got started, without us having to spend our time filling out forms for forming an entity of the CNRS, initiating the usual administrative procedures, which are complicated, restrictive, and, especially when successful, often sterile, so much does the organization (and the sacrosanct assessment) of research today end up replacing research by masking its absence. We immediately organized conferences, almost entirely without financing. But everything went off smoothly. The international network put into place very quickly took up considerable room, for the French debates were thus able in some way to be confronted with the international public opinion or, better, with the Republic of Humanities [*République des lettres*], the name our Italian friends still rightly give to it.

What kind of confrontation do you have in mind?

The positions are relatively simple: Either Descartes belongs rightfully to metaphysics, raises and takes up again the question of being, remains via the neo-Scholasticism he criticizes in a strict relation with the great tradition that precedes him and can hence be read starting from the symptomatic judgments of his successors; or Descartes must be read as inside a self-referential system, as an orphaned beginning and an accomplishment without descendants, someone gloriously autistic, exposed to all the ideological repetitions, in short a "French philosopher." This final option gets its authority, I hope mistakenly, from Cousin, from Brunschvicg, and from Gueroult, with a "Spinozist" methodology, obsessed with the question of internal coherence, which *must* be systematic. On the flipside appears the ambition of an open and hence more instructive and more complete reading of Descartes, taking contemporary models of interpretation to cast a contrasting light on the arguments that the whole world thinks it knows by heart. The debate between Derrida and Foucault on the madness in the "First Meditation," explained by Jean-Marie Beyssade, was a good example. One could also cite passing remarks by Lacan on Kant and Descartes—maybe false or strained, but illuminating. More widely, Nietzsche often proves to be a very good reader of Descartes, even if he has read him very little: When he says, for example, that the concept of substance in Descartes is deduced from the ego and not the opposite (as almost all the modern commentators claim), he is perfectly right, and anyway Heidegger will agree with him. And a reading of Descartes from a Thomistic or medieval standpoint, even if it is critical, might be unjust or force the texts but can still show a decisive point. In this way all these theses, at times drawn from his contemporaries but often from outside viewpoints, can be extremely instructive on Descartes himself. In conclusion, it seems to me that Descartes is a central author in the history of metaphysics, in the history of being, on the same level with Aristotle or Kant: If the result is acknowledged, we will not have wasted our time.

But now really, what remains to be done? What would be the subject today of a final or penultimate investigation of Descartes?

I have just finished a final work that will doubtlessly be called *Sur la pensée passive de Descartes* [*On Descartes' Passive Thought*]. For an aporia remains in Descartes: The final part of his oeuvre, which includes the *Passions of the Soul*, morality, and the question of physiology, still seems underinterpreted, not at all because few people have tackled it (reference works are not lacking from Geneviève Rodis-Lewis to Denis Kambouchner, to mention only the French) but because the relation between this final trajectory and Descartes's previous paths do not always emerge very clearly. And that is easily explained. For, if Plato was right to say that a philosopher requires two sailings,[4] then one must count to three in the case of Descartes. As I have said, I hope to have succeeded in articulating the first two sailings: the neo-Kantian Descartes, so to speak, where the ego constitutes objects without wondering about itself, the sailing of the theory of science, of the *Rules*, up until 1637; and the Descartes where the ego does wonder about its metaphysical status, the sailing of the *Meditations* and the *Principles*. But a third one is left there: the Descartes of morality, a third ego that enters into morality. Yet this ego bears very strange characteristics because it does not practice abstraction from the senses, is not identified with the distinction between extension and thought, but, quite the opposite, finds itself or rather experiences itself via the union of soul and body. How does he get from the first two sailings to the third? Where does he call into port? Is it a matter of a discovery despite himself, of a turn late in life, of an unforeseen crisis? Does Descartes with a single blow change into a thesis what remained an aporia in his preceding system? How can one find coherence here between contradiction and development? Does the order of reasons govern Descartes's final cruise? Gueroult himself seems to doubt it, who, after devoting two equally huge volumes to his commentary on the *Meditations*, does not explain either why the "Sixth Meditation," the one that precisely treats the union (but also the distinction), merits a second volume

4. [In Plato's *Phaedo* Socrates refers to "two sailings," designating two successive attempts at developing a methodology for the search for truth.]

for itself, or how it can then be separated from the first five meditations, or above all whether such a union, operated as conclusion of metaphysics, does or does not continue in the *Passions of the Soul*. It all seems as if the end obstinately resists the system.

Descartes himself demanded that one read the first five meditations in one go.

Yes, but why the first *five* and not *also* the final one? I am currently working on the following hypothesis: From the beginning Descartes defines the thinking thing, the *res cogitans*, by five modalities without privileging any of them, placing them all on the same level: doubt, pure understanding, will, imagination, sensation. In fact, the first five meditations correspond to the first four modalities while the "Sixth Meditation" takes up the fifth modality, that of sensation, of feeling. But why would feeling be a modality particularly reserved to a meditation reticent to the order of reasons? A hypothesis emerges here: The first four modalities all correspond to an activity of the ego. For it is up to the ego to doubt, to understand (to think according to pure understanding, by abstraction from the senses), to will, and to imagine (for imagination produces). In contrast, the final modality, feeling, reveals a *passive* way of thinking. In fact, it does not depend on the ego to feel: that comes to it from elsewhere, *aliunde*, not from its own initiative, *invito*; sensing [*sentir*] and feeling [*ressentir*] do not attest to a power but to a passion, a passivity. Yet, strangely, passing from an active power of thinking to a thought via passivity requires more, or something else, from the ego. It needs ways of perceiving, of feeling, of receiving; the passivity of sensing requires equipping the ego with instruments of passivity, of receptivity, of adding to it what one could call today, in computer terms, a peripheral. And this peripheral is found in that part of extension that nonetheless belongs to the passively thinking ego, in its living body. The final Cartesian paradox derives from this that there is a part of extension related to thought where the ego experiences itself passively and which functions *on behalf* of thought. This part of extension, which is *among* bodies but which is not *a* body, cannot be interpreted correctly except by recognizing in it by anticipation what phenomenology since Husserl calls the *flesh*. That is what I would like to reconstitute. If I am right, Descartes would remain coherent all the way to the end but would have reserved for the end the description of the modality of thinking that is the most distant and most difficult to conceive in relation to its point of departure: sensing as passive modality of thought. I feel myself, therefore I am. Nietzsche's word—that it is the body that thinks—Descartes almost said it beforehand.

Thus you question Descartes from the side of phenomenological results that you have already elucidated elsewhere and in other respects: the ego's passivity and destitution of power?

Yes. That gives us a lesson on what a decisive philosopher can accomplish. A decisive philosopher is someone who says not only more than one would have understood before him but more than one believes to have understood with him. On the one hand, inasmuch as he determines the tradition of metaphysics, he continues to determine us. On the other hand, simultaneous with what he says, he carries all the problems that he leaves unresolved or open and that, in their very aporias, precede us. From that point of view, Descartes is one of the *very* great ones. A great philosopher is always right and gives us to think even in what he does not manage to think, while a philosopher is limited to responding, hence to dissolving questions. There are three kinds of philosophers: those who do not respond to questions and hide them through ideology; those who respond to questions that they did not themselves raise and hope thus to clear up; and those who raise questions that no one ever thought of raising, insoluble questions that open the future. Descartes is one of these latter ones. That is why philosophy remains a continually open game.

3. Phenomenology

Reduction and Givenness

You completed your great cycle on Descartes with On Descartes' Metaphysical Prism *in 1986 [published in English in 1999]. In 1989 you published* Reduction and Givenness *[published in English in 1998], which is a collection of essays on Husserl's and Heidegger's phenomenology.*[1] *In a sense, this book has produced paradoxical results. Although it claimed to be an erudite study in the history of Husserl's and Heidegger's phenomenology, it gave rise to important reactions, as if you had hit upon something absolutely central that could not but elicit reservations from several phenomenologists. What led you to phenomenology after your work on Descartes? Does not your interest in phenomenology and in Heidegger date all the way back to* Idol and Distance?

1. [*Réduction et donation. Recherches sur Husserl, Heidegger et la phénoménologie* (Paris: Presses Universitaires de France, 1989). Translated as *Reduction and Givenness: Investigations of Husserl, Heidegger, and Phenomenology*, trans. Thomas A. Carlson (Evanston, Ill.: Northwestern University Press, 1998).]

For several years I had done phenomenology like Monsieur Jourdain did prose: without really realizing it, essentially using Heidegger's practice. But, oddly enough, as I progressed in the study of Descartes, it became increasingly clearer to me that I had to tackle philosophical positions as such, if only in order to continue to work in the history of philosophy. Although the history of philosophy proves indispensable for philosophical education, just as the knowledge of chess games played by the great masters in the past is necessary for the training of a chess player, the goal still is to play chess, not simply to repeat previous games, even if they are famous. It had always been my intention at some point or other to attempt to practice philosophy directly, if I was capable of it. Thus, as soon as my second thesis [*thèse d'État*] was finished, upon my transfer to Poitiers, I made it a rule each year to teach an introductory course in phenomenology, obviously in very traditional fashion by beginning with Husserl. Although it was pedagogically unremarkable, for me this course counted as a new personal beginning.

Why Husserl? First, because the study of Descartes leads (or should have led) almost inevitably to an encounter with Husserl, who had read and considered Descartes and thought of himself as Descartes's most authentic heir. Second, because, among the possibilities of theoretical practices—to use the language of the time—we had only two styles of philosophy available, as is still the case today. To simplify, let's say the analytical style and the phenomenological style. It was entirely natural for me to choose the phenomenological style because it wasn't unknown to me and also seemed to me the most coherent and the most consistent. It had the great advantage over the analytic tradition to grow by a cumulative effect. That is to say, each phenomenologist in some way managed to add new results to the preceding descriptions and, whatever the occasional disagreements, each continued on a path opened by his predecessors, without having to shut it down or even to leave it. Even in his worst polemics against Husserl, Heidegger follows in his steps. Sartre and Merleau-Ponty each seem to me to be first of all commentators on *Being and Time* and *Ideas II*. Henry and Levinas answer each other because each in his way responds to Husserl. In fact, they all focus on specific and common phenomena, which remain "things themselves" for them and for their readers. One cannot say the same thing about the analytical tradition, which has been so multiplied, criticized, and divided that it becomes really almost impossible to assign a body of teachings to it or even just a predominant direction. Besides, maybe its principal philosophical value lies in this education and this asceticism of argued indecisiveness, of refined skepticism. But, not being able to do without things, I went to phenomenology.

Therefore I started to teach Husserl. I began by reading the *Logical Investigations* in the most traditional way. Then I went on to explain the Heidegger of *Being and Time* in the most complete way I could. In preparing these lectures or these rereadings for the first time in an organized fashion, I was not only interested in the details of the authors' development of thought but rather in what could be called questions of method: How exactly does one do phenomenology? In what does this *doing* consist? What are its workings, considering we are dealing with a style in which philosophy in good Cartesian fashion proceeds on a path it builds gradually (that's the meaning of meth-*od*)? By what operations and actions does one end up seeing what one thinks and think what one sees? Of course, philosophy aims at knowing things such as they are, but this definition itself, "the things such as they are," already constitutes an operation. One cannot speak of things "such as they are" or of "being as such" without performing an operation, because one *reduces* what appears to what it is or, rather, to what is in it. The supposed immediacy of appearing itself results from an operation, even if just an interpretation.

The immediacy only appears—if I can put it like that—if one suspends its already implicit mediations or those used in a given moment for producing it. Also, the return to the things themselves indicates that the things themselves are not given immediately. Their immediacy hence must be gained via mediation, to the extent to which one must precisely go back to it via a leading back, a reduction. It is an illusion to think one can do without philosophy because immediacy is never given and the given is never immediately available. One must search for it. Otherwise, why should it be necessary to go back to "the things themselves"? Where would they have gone? Where would we be? What distance would separate us from them? It is in order to resolve these questions that I was interested in phenomenology and its operations, especially that of the reduction. But in saying this I realize that today there is a certain tendency in phenomenology that wants to do without the reduction. Yet, without it, everything collapses—and not only by regressing into naturalism.

What exactly is the reduction?

In the technical sense, the reduction consists in not taking everything I perceive for granted and in not receiving everything that happens to me with the same degree of evidence and thus of certainty but in each case to question what is actually given in order to distinguish it from what is only pieced together, inferred, or, so to say, acquired in a roundabout way, indirectly. And in saying this I'm trying really hard to avoid a different word, the second word that one must introduce together with "reduction," namely that of "givenness" [*donation*].

What is it that I perceive when I perceive this window, then see this lawn behind and through the window? Actually, if I think like an empirical metaphysician (that is, precisely as an empiricist), I would have to say that I only perceive blotches of color and some basic forms. In reality, I perceive much more. I perceive not only these sensible givens but also, and for a start, that there is a lawn in front of a house, thus of a house inside of which I am and from where I perceive. If I hear noise, I perceive not only or first of all a pure (or composite) sound, but I immediately identify this noise as construction going on around this house (the roof is being repaired) or of a job being done on the inside (someone is cleaning). Consequently, I never perceive "sense data" but always already a unity of meanings (that of the house and of the people in it and the work they do). I perceive green only as that (or as those, for there are a thousand nuances) of the lawn or of the falling leaves, the red as that of the leaves that have already fallen to the ground, and the gray as that of the bars of a window. One must distinguish between what is given as such and what is given only indirectly. The reduction will, first of all, allow me to separate them in order, then to reconstruct the degrees of givenness of the whole and of each of the components that appear or do not appear. That is to say, those that appear in person or appear in outline, whether by signification or by fulfillment, whether by a signification that is either empty or partially filled or saturated, whether by an inferred signification rather than one immediately observed, and so on. This work of classifying the appearing in a hierarchy releases what is really at stake for phenomenality. Ultimately, it seems to me, the degree of givenness of each of the components is what is really at stake in the reduction.

I discovered very quickly that one must remain very precise on this point especially because it is strictly a matter of determining the degrees and the figures of givenness, of not confusing degrees with figures or with a different authority than the given itself. Yet, in reading Husserl, the reduction enables us to authenticate that which, while really given first, ends up allowing the constitution of the phenomenon or its reconstituting of the object as *object*. But what link does the given maintain with the object? Must every given become an object? Does objectness exhaust the face of any given? When Heidegger takes up the operation of the reduction in his own way (he does so more rarely and more implicitly, but still, I think, indisputably), he ends up interpreting the phenomenal given in its different degrees and its different types of status as always a *being* [*étant*], that is, from the point of view of Being [*être*]. The being, inasmuch as being, thus results from an operation of reduction of the given, but it is a reduction that is no more self-evident than that of the given to the object. When Aristotle raises the question of a science that would consider being *as* being, one must understand that this being inasmuch as being results from a reduction, from an interpretation of the given by an *inasmuch* that recognizes a being there. But no one has ever seen a being straightaway or immediately; we see trees, a lawn, the bars of a window, a house. We always see essences that are already determined, existences that are already identified by essences. To consider the unity of these essences or of these individuals as beings, one must reduce them to what they are not, that is, to a pure and strict being, to the detriment of what they are, namely essences identifying existences. As strange as this may seem, the [particular] being [*l'étant*] is not a being [*un étant*], because what is, is a thing always identified by an essence. No tree is ever a being; it is first of all a tree. To consider it as a being presupposes that one would place in parentheses or that one would reduce what one would have to call its *treeness*. And in the same way, the *houseness* of the house must allow itself to be put into parentheses for the house to be reduced to a being. Similarly, I would have to "de-window" the window in order to see it as a being. A reduction of the phenomenon is therefore necessary in order for the house, the window, or the tree to appear to me *as beings* rather than *as themselves*. One sees clearly that, in order to interpret the given not only as an *object* (in Kant or Husserl) but as *being* (Aristotle and Heidegger), one must undertake a reduction, a *certain* reduction. Reducing, yes, but toward where and to what?

Inevitably, I posed the question, or, rather, it imposed itself on me—and Husserl's very vocabulary justified the terms of its formulation right away—why the given, such as it appears, would find itself reduced to a different authority than to the given itself. Why does the phenomenon, a phenomenon given and reduced as given, find itself finally at the last minute interpreted either according to objectness or according to beingness? (I prefer the term objectness to objectivity here because objectivity comes from the theory of knowledge, while objectness refers to a determination of the thing itself.) Why is beingness or objectness arbitrarily and without specific justification privileged for characterizing the given [*le donné*], givability [*la donnéité*], or givenness [*la donation*]? For Husserl very frequently and even systematically employs the term *Gegebenheit*, which one can translate literally as "*donnéité*" (the character of being given) or simply as "*donation*" [givenness]. He speaks also of "givenness in person" (*Selbstgegebenheit*) or "self-givenness in the flesh" (*leibhaftige Selbstgegebenheit*), a term used to mark the irreducibility of the most indisputable presence. Thus, in Husserl's approach the reduction has the goal of reaching and of isolating the irreducible core of the most intense givability possible in what appears, the goal of referring the visible given to the indivisible kernel of phenomenality within it. In *The Idea of Phenomenology*, a short and crucial text written at the height of his career, which he presented as his "critique of reason," Husserl clearly suggests in certain formulations that the reduction aims to reach the most pure givenness.

I proposed a principle from this, which can be formulated as follows even if not exactly in Husserl's words: "as more reduction, so more givenness." This principle echoes a different formulation, albeit by radicalizing it, which Husserl had picked up from one of his predecessors (from Johann Friedrich Herbart in this case): "as much appearing, so much being." Consequently, appearing itself implies in some way to be to a certain degree. This is not a philosophical version of "no smoke without fire" but of an acknowledgment of the dignity of the given—no showing up without appearing, no appearing without being given. But on one condition: namely, that one must know the degree of givability of this appearing, the point to which it gives and is given. Only a reduction that is accomplished all the way to the end manages this (and not one that too quickly makes do with an object or a being).

Husserl would thus almost have betrayed his own project by arriving at a reduction to the object rather than arriving at a reduction to givenness . . . But how do you explain that Husserl's initial project was to turn toward the constitution of an object*?*

That is a question that must obviously be raised, for it really seems that by spontaneously thinking or formulating any phenomenon in the horizon of objectness, Husserl reproduced Kant's gesture, for whom it is self-evident that phenomena remain a specific case of the object because the object is the highest concept. As the conclusion of the "Analytic" in the first *Critique* declares and postulates, it is the encompassing concept for any possible phenomenon, even for ourselves. Kant's decision was in some way taken up by Husserl, who accordingly speaks the language of all of his contemporaries (Natorp, Cohen, but also Lask, Rickert, Twardowski, and obviously Meinong, with his famous theory of the object). They all thought phenomenality in terms of objectness. Husserl hence only upholds what I would call the language of metaphysics. This is metaphysics in its final stage, in all the senses of "final stage," because metaphysics here means a philosophy that dies of a cancer of the object, of a multiplication of objectness under all of its forms and in all of its uses. Everyone thinks only about extending the field of objectness. (This still remains, and increasingly more so, the horizon of contemporary restorations of metaphysics in analytic philosophy, which recklessly manages the inflation of objects without realizing that it is only dealing in counterfeit currency that will lead to a stock-market crash of the concept.)

But then the phenomenology of the object is still metaphysics! Thus there would be no opposition between metaphysics and phenomenology? The distinction between metaphysics and nonmetaphysics would cross phenomenology itself?

I have always upheld that phenomenology cannot get out of metaphysics the way one crosses a border or escapes from prison. Husserlian phenomenology was born in a totally metaphysical climate and at the heart of the debate about the theory of the object and its extension, about the broadening of the realm of formal logic, about the accomplishment of the ideal of a rigorous science in philosophy, about the recovery of the young Descartes's dream of a *mathesis universalis*. All of those are properly metaphysical questions, for the metaphysical project is accomplished in modernity alone: the ancients and the medievals, who knew nothing about objectness, barely caught a glimpse of it. (That's what makes them so interesting.) From this results a difficult, heroic, and fascinating effort, one that really has to be studied: How Husserl, pushed by the truth itself—to go back to one of Aristotle's formulations—little by little and thanks to phenomenology, had to leave himself and his point of departure, that of rigorous science in philosophy. And how this effort was continued by Heidegger and his followers, really one step at a time, having to figure out just how far to go. At least a part of philosophy, its best part, for a century has tried heroically to exit metaphysics. It has been a slow and at times brutal, unremitting development in a continual and maybe always unfinished self-critique, which surely always has to be pursued further. Husserl sees givenness. He sees that one can only reach givenness via reduction, but to a large extent he stays within the presupposition that the given is a matter of objectness, of a theory of the object. From Mount Nebo, he sees the promised land that he will not enter from his still transcendental standpoint. Only Heidegger, not without violence, began to make the walls come tumbling down.

I have therefore asked myself whether instead of linking reduction directly to objectness—that is to say to the pair noesis-noema, thus tied to all the traditional problems of the constitution of the object—it would not make more sense to connect it directly to givenness itself. How great was my surprise when I found the question of givenness clearly raised as a central enigma by the early Heidegger from 1919 onward! This is actually obvious if one reflects on it carefully, but I was unfamiliar with this text when I was writing *Reduction and Givenness*, which was thus confirmed retrospectively. In fact, he raises the topic of givenness *as such* from his very first courses in Freiburg onward with this famous question: "What is the given, and what is givenness? Givenness, this magic word of phenomenology and the stumbling block for everything else." In this way, Heidegger encounters givenness very early on, at a point when everything begins for him and when Husserl is still at the height of his powers. Heidegger immediately responds to the question by brilliantly intensifying it with the device of the *es gibt*, "it gives." We translate this *es gibt* poorly and lazily with the "*il y a*."[2] Thus, he leaves normal space in order to enter into the field of givenness.

Examining these two major phenomenological figures, *Reduction and Givenness* produced studies that all turned on one another rather than offering systematic expositions of Husserl's and Heidegger's thought. These studies were able to tie all the inquiries into one result: Can phenomenology continue beyond Husserl and Heidegger not simply by going back to its initial operation (because up to this point it had not yet been accomplished as such) but by attempting to perform the reduction inasmuch as it aims at determining the degrees of givenness and nothing else? Objectness (Husserl) and beingness (Heidegger) only offer specific and possible cases, but surely not the most legitimate ones, of the naming of givenness.

Thus you tried to go back to the most authentic project of phenomenology, bypassing the recoveries it has undergone?

Husserl's initial impulse already led him further than objectness, that is to say, further than his own project and maybe occasionally further than Heidegger, who was held in beingness by the *Seinsfrage* [the question of Being], long (but maybe not always) assumed to be a fixed horizon. From this I derive what I realize is a somewhat provocative but to my mind unavoidable thesis: that Husserl's reduction to objectness (first reduction) and Heidegger's reduction to beingness (second reduction) can and must

2. [Literally, "it has there"; usually translated into English—just as poorly and lazily—as "there is." Idiomatically the three expressions function identically but use different auxiliary verbs in the three languages.]

make way for a third, more original reduction, which thus appears only in a third position, namely the reduction to givenness. From that moment, my sole goal became to describe this third reduction.

*The Gift and the Given Self [*Le don et l'adonné*]*

At the end of Reduction and Givenness *you state these three reductions very quickly, without explicating them, without clearly articulating them, but opening the door to the future. This articulation will be made in* Being Given *in 1997,*[3] *where you conceptualize givenness starting from its own difficulties. The difficulty had to do with the fact of describing givenness, and for this you proceeded via the description of the phenomenon of the gift. To think givenness one must first think the gift, but without falling back on a metaphysical logic, because it is the calling of givenness to escape this logic. Thus, in a sort of circularity, one must think givenness starting from the gift but also think the gift starting from the logic of givenness and not starting from a metaphysics of exchange or of economy, for which Derrida had distinguished the aporia or even Mauss himself in* The Gift. *Could you first go back to these links between gift and givenness and then describe the phenomenon of the gift?*

All this gave rise to an animated discussion. Paul Ricoeur once said to me, almost threateningly, that phenomenological givenness could have no link with the question of the gift and that I should not bring the two together. Dominique Janicaud and some others found the third reduction phenomenologically suspect, or at least questionable, because if there were a givenness, then there would inevitably have to be a giver, in such a way that the reduction to givenness seemed to them to establish a first metaphysical principle. And Jacques Derrida insisted on the idea that the *given* itself always had to be deconstructed until it is shown to be impossible. The standard objection issued by analytic philosophy is added to this, buttressed essentially by the critique of the "myth of the given": You reintroduce a given, they say, but in fact this given has no validity for knowledge as soon as it is constituted as an object, except if it belongs to the indescribable subjective. That was the cluster of objections I received and that obviously still persists among uninformed readers. For in philosophy one can always wear oneself out by responding to objections, but many people still continue to

3. [*Étant donné. Essai d'une phénoménologie de la donation* (Paris: Presses Universitaires de France, 1997). Translated as *Being Given: Toward a Phenomenology of Givenness*, trans. Jeffrey L. Kosky (Stanford, Calif.: Stanford University Press, 2002).]

be more attached to their objections than open for a serious discussion. Thus one must wait for the objections to develop or for them to dissolve on their own. That's what I did.

But how does the phenomenology of the gift respond to these objections?

The phenomenology of the gift does not respond to these objections but complicates matters further! I began by thematizing the three reductions in the first part of *Being Given*, trying to show textually how the horizon of givenness had already determined Husserl and Heidegger, despite the fact that they had covered it up again in the end via objectness or via beingness. But I showed how givenness frees itself from itself in certain cases (those of the painting and of the work of art) that can only be described in terms of givenness. Then, I tackled the question of the gift.

The theme of the gift became famous after Mauss's *The Gift* (which, moreover, had been republished with a quite critical preface by Claude Lévi-Strauss). Furthermore, between *Reduction and Givenness* and *Being Given*, Jacques Derrida had expressed reservations in regard to my concept of givenness in several texts (among which was *Given Time*). In his view, givenness would have to be deconstructed because the gift itself would have to disappear in order to remain really a gift. The conditions of possibility for the gift were also the conditions of impossibility for the gift. The argument can be summed up as follows: In the case of the gift, the giver always discovers himself in a real or symbolic way paid in return for his gift. Either he is really repaid (as in Mauss's *potlatch*, where the gift actually triggers a delayed exchange), or he is repaid by gratitude (a gratitude that lasts as long as the debt itself) or by self-respect (in the case of the debt denied by the recipient). It thus becomes unavoidable for the gift to turn into an exchange; it is impossible that the giver is not repaid in some way or other. Thus Derrida concludes that the gift must be unfolded in a horizon of gratuity for it to remain a gift. Thus it would be neither visible nor even conscious. Henceforth, the impossibility of the gift coincides with its condition of possibility. There is only a gift if there is no phenomenon of the gift. A magnificent exercise of deconstruction.

How should one respond to this? One would have to show that in order to be understood the gift itself requires first to allow itself to be reduced to givenness: one must submit the gift to the test of a reduction. I conducted this reduction by showing that each of the three elements of the gift can be eliminated by turns (the thing given, the giver, and the recipient) without preventing a gift from continuing to work, even though there no longer is any exchange. The proof that the gift does not come down to a figure of exchange oblivious to it arises when one eliminates one of the dimensions of the exchange, so that the exchange disappears but the gift remains. Thus one reduces the gift to givenness and tears it loose from exchange. There are a thousand examples of a gift without giver: inheritance, the right hand not knowing what the left gives, and so forth. The giver without recipient is attested if I give via the intermediary of a third (an NGO, an association, etc.) or if I give to my enemy, who I am sure will not give anything back to me. (It is curious that in this case my enemy gives me the gift and its verification.) As for the case when the given gift itself becomes eliminated, far from invalidating the gift, it defines it in general: What one gives actually coincides only rarely with the thing itself whose ownership one transfers to someone else. Quite the opposite: The majority of the time the given thing remains the possibly expensive but often negligible token and sign of what one is really giving and what is not a thing. When I give my time, my life, my affection, my word, my loyalty, in short, my love, that is, the only things that we really would like to receive from the other, they precisely do not concern mundane things one could possess, stockpile, or keep in a box. Thus to mark these "nonthings" in phenomenality (such as time, love, one's word, loyalty, etc.), I really do give them, [but] I give a *different* thing, actually a first *thing*, which serves as the pure and simple symbol for the nonthing that is actually given (a ring, a jewel, a certificate, a signature, etc.). That was the response to Derrida.

The gift, then, isn't of the same order as economic phenomenality?

The gift does not belong to the order of exchange, even as an exchange unaware of itself or an impossible exchange. It falls under a different phenomenality. And this other phenomenality is characterized by the fact that the gift does not demand reciprocity. Instead it demands nonreciprocity; the gift does not enter into economy but remains destabilized and uneven for good. Yet, and that is the path of access to givenness in the larger sense, this character of asymmetry of nonreturn on the investment of the gift (irreversible in time and irretrievable in space) unveils an essential characteristic of the given in general. That was the response to Ricoeur.

Having liberated the gift from the danger of being just a figurehead and appearance of exchange, having restored the phenomenality of the gift according to givenness, in the third part of *Being Given* I was able to start showing the characteristics of the given as such, of the thing as given in such a way that it is distinguished from the object, in such a way that it is distinguished also and especially from being. One can pinpoint several characteristics of this: facticity, unpredictability, irreducibility to its constitution as an object and compared to it. For in all these cases it is the given itself that imposes on me the place and the moment from which it can be seen. This is what I call the anamorphosis: There is only one place and one moment where I can see the given as such, and I cannot fix or change this place, repeat it or reproduce it by projections like the subject in the transcendental position. Only the event of the phenomenon that gives itself is able to do this. From this results the fundamental character of the given, namely that it is given starting from itself.

By saying this I recover in some way the definition of the phenomenon introduced by Heidegger in §7 of *Being and Time* against its thematization as object in Husserl (and actually also in Kant). Heidegger defines the phenomenon as what shows itself from itself and as itself. But this inevitably raises a question, albeit one Heidegger does not raise explicitly: Under what phenomenological conditions can a phenomenon show itself *by itself*? If the phenomenon shows itself *in itself* and *by itself*, one does not need to be a great Kant specialist to understand that a phenomenon in and from itself constitutes a radical contradiction in critical philosophy. What is in itself and by itself is the thing-in-itself, and the phenomenon is precisely not by itself because it is *by* the *I* who constitutes it as object. How, then, can Heidegger attribute a *self* to the phenomenon and consequently eliminate the difference between the phenomenon and the thing-in-itself? The fact that he is perfectly right to attempt this does not absolve him from describing this *self* more fully. (For does he really completely accomplish it when he holds on to Dasein's ontic and ontological primacy?) Yet in some way Heidegger never defines the self of the phenomenon because he remains too preoccupied with thinking the self of the phenomenon (actually of *one* phenomenon, *Dasein*) as a being [*un étant*], as the beingness [*l'étanite*] according to Being [*l'être*]. As a result the implicit and silent question raised by this definition remains. This is why a further step has to be taken: If the phenomenon is shown in itself, one must admit a self for it, but this self is only attested in what *gives itself*. In other words, to give *itself* only becomes effective in what *gives* itself. Consequently, nothing shows itself that does not give itself in itself, but nothing can give *itself in itself* that does not *give* itself.[4] That is the given that I tried to examine in *Being Given*.

4. [The last couple of sentences could also be translated as passive rather than reflexive: "In other words, to be given only becomes effective in what is given. Consequently, nothing is shown that is not given in itself, but nothing can be given

Does this imply withdrawing any initiative from the ego, *that is to say, denying that the* ego *would constitute the phenomenon inasmuch as it is given? Would it be possible to explore a little more the odd position, in which I am when the given gives itself? We have said that the given is given* by itself, *but it is no longer given* by me. *As in the anamorphosis, I orient myself to it; it does not orient itself to me, and I do not command it. Am I in a kind of passivity that contradicts the position of the famous Kantian or Husserlian (or even still Heideggerian) transcendental subject?*

We can have two attitudes in regard to things. On the one hand, the most widespread attitude, the one for which we are trained, which consists in reducing the chances that those around us will surprise us; consequently, we continually learn how better to control them. Whatever happens, we really count on being able to anticipate situations and accidents, to be able to react, to control, to correct, to secure, as one says, the chaotic dance of things around us. Besides, the majority of the time we discover ourselves surrounded only by objects, which, being essentially functional, function because they are intended and conceived to function to our advantage, whether it is a matter of technical objects or even of the improvement of natural things around us. All is done so that we are at the center. In a car that works well, the security systems operate in such a way that whatever happens the car responds via technological means (ABS, EPS, alarm systems, etc.), ultimately to allow me to be in charge of driving. That is also why nothing happens in a house that functions well, that is to say, only what I can decide and constitute happens. Knowledge, education, mastery of a science consist in ensuring that nothing happens that could not be immediately intelligible or that could not quickly become so. Thus, we live in a world that we organize such that we retain from it only those things that can be constituted as objects, only what we can grasp with our intelligibility, under the control of a quasi-master and possessor of nature. This is a Cartesian project because by doing this we acquire certainty and thus security. We obtain certainty or security by ruling out danger. Yet what does ruling out danger mean if not keeping away from the unexpected? But what is this unexpected, if not that which cannot be constituted as object, that against which one cannot protect oneself? The transcendental subject

---

in itself that is not given." The two constructions (passive and reflexive) are identical in French. In what follows, either construction will be used, depending on the context, but the reader should keep in mind that in French *se donner* always has both connotations: being given and giving itself.]

is actually and correctly defined as that figure of the *ego* which passes its time at protecting itself, thus thinking ahead. Knowing is thinking ahead; security is thinking ahead; if I want peace I prepare for war. The transcendental attitude aims to anticipate perceptions. Metaphysical rationality is used for thinking ahead.

That's all well and good, but this rationality, which only holds on to what concerns it [*qui garde seulement ce qu'elle regarde*], only what it can anticipate, does not want any of the rest, which it voluntarily ignores, which it actually even tries to annihilate after having rightfully discredited it. It only retains this layer of reality that one can call the object. But the object offers a very thin and superficial layer of things. It leaves to the side, at the bottom and on the margins, everything that it cannot foresee, everything it cannot anticipate, what is said to be unknowable. Abandoned by reason, it becomes analogous to lawless zones beyond vague and menacing borders that one dare not cross. What interests me personally and what philosophy should mobilize are these lawless zones, there where one could no longer enforce the process of pacification by objectification, there where unforeseeable things—events—survive. That is where the given is displayed because it characterizes what among things resists objectification and is given by its own initiative.

I would like to go back for a moment to what you have thought under the term anamorphosis, *that is to say, perceiving a feature in a painting that is only possible if the subject, the spectator, is oriented by the feature. The painting does not show itself to the spectator, but the spectator obeys the instructions that the painting draws up for him or her: I am commanded by the features; I do not command them. This analysis permits us to clarify the position of the subject, of the* I.

Yes, anamorphosis defines the distinctiveness of a painting that, if one puts oneself in the head-on position of the normal observer (that is, of the transcendental subject), does not yet offer anything to see except complete confusion. Instead, one must walk along this very painting, look at it from very complicated angles, until, by feeling about, one finds certain places where the effect of deformation and of inverse perspective offsets the apparent disorder of the spectacle seen head-on and, all of a sudden, allows the painting to become visible and, finally, normal. There are paintings where one must place oneself entirely to the left, or completely below, or entirely to the right in order for the thing suddenly to appear. There is an example in Rome in the cloister of the convent of Trinity-on-the-Mount. The painting has a secret point where one must be situated, one that is determined by the painting and not by the spectator. The spectator must obey the painting in order to see it.

In the given, in the phenomenon inasmuch as it gives itself according to its character as nonobject, in the unpredictability, irreversibility, inequality of its appearing *by* and *in* itself, a place and a moment are described where the ego must know how to allow itself to be found and which it does not decide. In this way the ego leaves its transcendental position, obeys the event, and sees without foreseeing. That reverses our objective relation with the world, where we always command (or believe and hope to command) the world. In the case of the given, we find ourselves commanded by the thing, summoned to come experience it. I must be there "at the false moment" or "at the right moment." There are people to whom something always happens, those who have the gift of always putting themselves into impossible situations; they always find themselves in the right place (I was going to say the wrong place) and at the right moment (that is, the wrong one). The philosophers of the future will have to find themselves there.

A whole range of situations is possible. When the phenomenon is given [or gives itself], I can say that it is an accident. It can even be a matter of an illusion where I believe that the phenomenon gives itself while in reality nothing is given. It can remain intentional from my side, if I am exposed in such a way that what I really very much want will happen to me. And then, maybe someone had the intention that such or such a thing would happen. One can imagine anything, and there are all the gradations, from complete illusion to perfect election. Between the two: an accident, an encounter, a stroke of luck, misfortune, good reflexes, the pure unforeseeable, the unheard of, the call. In short, the event. Watch out, I am not trying to reenchant on the sly a disenchanted world—for the world only seems disenchanted to those who expect magic from it. I am evoking a relation to the world that is neither one of commandment nor one of transcendental possession toward objects, a relation that insists on the idea that at the core all the shadings are revealed to be possible and must be described.

Does that mean that the I *is passive?*

On the one hand, there is certainly a situation of historicity, of unpredictability, of fait accompli, hence of passivity. But, on the other hand, the term *passivity* is not good enough because I precisely cannot remain passive in front of the event: I make myself available or I avoid it, I take a risk or I run away, in short, I still decide, and I respond even by refusing to respond. In order to become passive in such an encounter, a certain kind of activity is required; one must leave oneself exposed to things with a certain amount of courage. It is hence not just a matter of passivity. To speak of "passive synthesis" or of "passive consciousness" is no longer enough because such an understanding is limited finally to reversing the transcendental activity and to imagining its total absence, even though it is not a matter of a simple undoing. One must go against, leave oneself exposed, turn toward, and so forth. Certainly, first of all, one can restrict oneself polemically to the praise of pure passivity—many philosophers have done it—but the stakes are much more important and open a different regime of phenomenality imposed on a different regime of subjectivity, without the transcendental posture that foresees or controls what it has reduced to the rank of an object. When the reduction goes beyond objectivity and beingness, all the way to the given, it is necessary that subjectivity itself changes stature, that it would receive itself from what it receives. This is what I propose calling the *adonné*.

Saturated Phenomena

But someone finding himself facing an event discovers that in some way concepts won't work because, if he has prior concepts available from his experience, he would command it, he would understand it perfectly. The event that happens to him surprises him in some way, and he has no preliminary concepts at his disposal for arranging it. It is this lack of the concept linked to the self-giving phenomenon that you think under the category of the "saturated phenomenon." Could you go back to this category and tie it to reduction and to givenness?

The first metaphysical definition of the phenomenon, that of Kant or Husserl, conceives of it, like Plato's chariot, as the encounter with a messy, haphazard intuition that is received passively with one or several concepts, defining an intelligible and still abstract signification. Why do these colors appear spread out here? How do the lawn and then the red leaves that fall on the green of the lawn appear? I have already given one response by using concepts that identify the intuitions sensed as *the* green, *the* red, *the* wind that stirs the leaves. It is thanks to these concepts that I organize the manifold of intuition, which would otherwise remain disorganized in itself and absurd. But I bring my perception under control as a perception of this or that thing because I immediately have concepts at my disposal that allow me to arrange the intuition. Let us suppose that the given that is given as an intuition appears in such a way that I no longer have any appropriate concepts available. What happens? For Kant, concepts will be used anyway because they remain a priori and precede the experience. Metaphysics in fact always seeks to settle the conditions of possibility for experience in a priori fashion by such a priori concepts. Descartes maintains the same thing with the "simple natures."

But the question remains: Do we always have a priori concepts available to us, and can we always get to the bottom of every intuitive given with these a priori concepts and manage to organize them in order to constitute them into objects? How can we simply set aside the cases where we do not have any a priori concepts or any number of other cases where all the concepts that we could summon up would fall short of the givenness that is imperturbably given? But these cases are not all that rare or exceptional. There are circumstances where one cannot settle the signification of a phenomenon, where even the question of an adequate or univocal signification, a sufficient and comprehensive question, makes no sense at all. That is true for aesthetic experience: No one can claim to explain *why* a painting is beautiful and another isn't. Neither *why* some music is beautiful or more beautiful than some other piece of music. One can suggest reasons, but one cannot prove them conclusively. The beautiful pleases without concept, as Kant says.

This situation is valid a fortiori for one's personal life. Why do we love someone or why do we not love? Why did we make one decision in a given situation rather than another? Very often, the more the decision matters, the less can one give reasons that justify it or provide a *why*, even retrospectively. That leads us, moreover, to regard the practice of moral philosophy with some skepticism, where one refines the search of reasons for decisions, causes, or beliefs, as if it were self-evident that we make up our mind to believe or to act based on reasons or following on particular causes, in short in accordance with a *why*. Instead, it might be best to find (and search) for reasons *after* having decided to believe or not to believe, to love or not to love without reasons or causes, namely in order to justify them a posteriori. This is not because we would have acted entirely without cause or reason but because the highest decisions by far *surpass* sufficient reasons and efficient causes, which can do nothing.

But does that not turn you into a philosopher of irrationality?

No, obviously not. Quite the opposite. I think that in a good many cases it is irrational to claim to search for reasons *before* the decision because it is actually the decision itself that allows us to find reasons for it. When one has to make decisions concerning objects (for example, do the needs of the market call for the production of this type of object?), the reasons precede the decision because one is speaking of objects. But, when it is not objects that are at stake, then there is no longer any great rationality in strictly beginning by searching for causes or even for reasons. When the point is to decide to respond to the question "Will I love someone or not, will I get married or divorced, will I have children or not?" it does not seem very responsible to speak of causes or reasons. Serious matters demand much *more* than that. At that moment, what's at stake does not hang on concepts that we could work out independently of the event, i.e., of the given phenomenon. We often lack concepts, and frequently the decision does not proceed from a concept but itself brings about rationality.

Let us take the phenomenon of an event, for example, the typical case of what I call a "saturated phenomenon": With the event something happens that we could not have foreseen. Thus, the attacks of September 11, 2001, were (apparently) not foreseeable. Yet, when this unpredictable something *actually* occurs, when it seems a priori that our concepts cannot conceive it, it is truly impossible, because the possible is equivalent to the conceivable, to the *cogitabile*. Consequently, this invalidates the metaphysical principle according to which only what is first possible becomes real. Here something becomes real about which, even once it has taken place, we say: "That isn't possible." The event remains outside the horizon of *our* possible, even if and precisely *because* it proves itself real [*effectif*].[5] When the towers collapsed on 9/11 (I found myself that morning in front of the television in the midst of my students at Boston College, in the city where the terrorists boarded their flights), everyone saw quite well that they were collapsing, nothing was more real, yet at the same time we said that this is impossible. Why? We wanted to say that it is inconceivable, without any concept adequate to the enormity (i.e., as absence of any norm) of intuition. A very strange thing therefore occurs in such an event: Once this impossible becomes real, it continues to be impossible to conceive its possibility, but it nevertheless becomes possible to redefine the field of the possible starting from it. Consequently, a new beginning opens up; one can and must say that a new era begins at that moment—and other grandiose formulations.

Here givenness produces rationality. It thus does not depend on it?

In fact, it does not depend on it; it is epoch making. The event is defined in this way: I have to make up my mind in regard to it because it is not

5. [Marion employs the terms *effectif* and *effectivité* in the sense of "actually taking place" or "really happening."]

determined by me. The rest of the time, I decide or can at least pretend to decide. But here the event is what decides, and at best I respond to it.

When something comes to meet us, does an event occur at that very moment?

At that moment, the event in fact imposes a new horizon of possibilities that one must attempt to rationalize. To the extent that concepts remain at the pitch of the intuitive given, to the extent that concepts find themselves given at the same time and at the level of intuition, to that extent nothing happens, everything can be constituted, and I am the one who thinks, who decides. Yet, when an imbalance arises and I find myself lacking concepts, something else happens, something that decides, that I cannot directly comprehend and in regard to which I must make up my mind in response. My decision will always be only a response to the incomprehensibility of the event itself. That is what I call the *saturated phenomenon*. And no one better tell me that they have no clue what I'm talking about.

Would phenomenology also allow us to describe the coming of the impossible?

Absolutely.

The impossible accordingly comes by producing a new category of thought, but the description is then not hemmed in a priori by concepts, because the event is imposed a posteriori, even as the supreme a posteriori.

Yet the event is not the only saturated phenomenon. There is also what I call the idol as the intensity of bedazzlement, the icon as the face of the other, and the flesh as the capacity of being affected.

Let's take one of those examples, the flesh.

The flesh is based on the fact, as Heidegger said, that I am always in a situation where I am affected, under attunement, attuned. I am never neutral, without state of mind. I am comfortable, uncomfortable, anxious, anguished, not anxious, open to some project, lifeless, attentive, distracted; in any case I am never in a neutral position. I am not only affected by the exterior world but also by an internal attunement. How can I always be affected? Actually, I am not first affected by the external world; rather, the external world can only affect me because I am intrinsically open to being affected. This intrinsic determination of affectability describes a superior, primordial, intimate passivity; this internal attunement attests to an intrinsic passivity. Yet this interior passivity (according to a rather Heideggerian analysis) can be attributed (according to a more Husserlian analysis) to the distinctive fact that my body is *mine*, that it is myself under the modality of passivity. Among all the extended bodies in the world (to speak like Descartes), there is one body that has a special property, that is mine, and that is affected.

Let's take an example: I touch the armchair on which I am seated, and my hand touches its armrest. One could always say that my hand and the chair fall under the same materiality, that they share the same space and thus that I am one thing in the world among others. Yes, but a huge difference remains: When I touch the armchair, the chair does not sense my hand that touches it; it senses nothing, but although my hand remains a part of the world like the chair it touches, it senses the chair, and it alone does so. Indeed, it only senses the chair because it senses itself. Or rather, I sense myself when I touch the chair and therefore in touching this chair I sense two things: the chair and especially myself as the one sensing. Not only can we not sense anything without sensing ourselves, but this sensing of the self alone makes possible the sensing of other things, and not the reverse. I can sense other things because I can sense myself. The proof? Anesthesia: when you do away with self-affection, you put an end to affectivity. I have the privilege of "sensing myself," and the distinctive feature of this part of the external world, of my body of flesh, consists in what is not external but internal *to itself* because it senses itself. This is myself, what one calls the flesh, and I only know one flesh personally, namely my own. The flesh consists of this part of materiality that is the jurisdiction of the mind or the soul. That's the paradox.

Yet, this materiality contradicts one of the basic principles of a priori concepts, of Kant's categories: According to Kant, we can never perceive an object in experience, a phenomenon of the type of the object, without setting it in relation to a different object. For example, this armchair can only be conceived because it stands on the floor of a room. There is no chair in-and-of-itself but always a chair at such and such a distance from another object in space. I could possibly in a dream perceive the chair floating around all by itself, but when awake I must always put it in relation. Very well, yet even so there are absolute, nonrelative phenomena. I experience within my flesh the privileged case of the nonrelative, nonrelational phenomenon that has no a priori concept. My flesh finds itself affected and self-affected in itself, by itself, and independently from everything else. Everything else just comes along with this capacity for auto-affection (to employ Michel Henry's language this time) but does not depend on it. The flesh remains nonrelative, and the concepts of relation do not apply to the flesh. In this sense, the flesh establishes the very type of the saturated phenomenon. Infinite modes of self-affection are possible, all relative to nothing. Being hungry or thirsty, running a temperature, or being anxious are all cases of self-affection that are not relative to anything external, that I cannot link to anything, even if they rub off on the things around us. And the greatest self-affection comes with the difference between life and death, between birth and absence, which I cannot refer back to anything in the world.

*My flesh is always my flesh, and this self-affection is always exercised. This means that the saturated phenomenon is something extremely commonplace [*banal*]. There is then an extension of phenomenology to everything that is given and not only to the object or to a being. Thus, one must not think that the phenomenology of givenness is only reserved for absolutely exceptional or even impossible cases.*

That is really something on which I should have insisted and that it took me a while to understand: Saturation is very mundane [*il y a une grande banalité de la saturation*]. Saturation is not limited to exceptional phenomena but consists above all in understanding phenomena otherwise than as common objects. The simplest phenomena can already appear as saturated! When you smoke a pipe, as I am doing at this moment, a saturated phenomenon can already be at stake—everything depends on how you are smoking. Ask Baudelaire or Molière. Or take as another example the two masters of saturated phenomena in contemporary literature: James and Proust. The most minor things described by them become saturated phenomena. Why? Because they show you that this mundane [*banale*] and common sensation can become an event and that this event, besides its limited objective sense, can have an increased meaning, which refers to past experiences, to very complex tonalities, to networks of unlimited referrals. Everything can then become a saturated phenomenon as long as the manner in which it is given is not closed down into univocal objectivity, as the everyday routine of the world of technology requires it.

When Proust writes, "And all of a sudden a memory came to me," is he describing a saturated phenomenon?

Of course! Again, the doctrine of the phenomenon as given, thus sometimes also as saturated (for not every given saturates its concept), does not unleash a category of exceptional phenomena but instead the exceptional character of any phenomenon, when it is seen as being given in itself beyond a concept, not as constituted and reduced to the status of an object. One can then come out of the pair external/internal, objective/subjective, in short, one can emerge from the appalling assertion according to which the real world would be objective because supposedly external and everything else would be subjective because internal. This distinction defines objectivity; all the same it is plainly false: The world is neither internal nor external when it is not objectified—and that's really never the case. The distinctions between internal and external, between subjective and objective, come from the fact that one imagines nothing other than constituting objects.

*And because the event happens by itself, I have to make up my mind in regard to it, as you said a moment ago. I am thus the one given [*l'adonné*], that is to say, the one who in some way receives himself from what he receives.*

To understand the *adonné*, one must think of the response that Leibniz gave Locke in regard to the principle of the empiricists, according to which there is nothing in the understanding that would not first be in the senses. Leibniz responded that, certainly, there is nothing in the understanding that has not first come in through the senses—Descartes also said this—but with one specific exception: the understanding itself. The understanding must be there in order for it to receive everything from the senses. The understanding remains the place of the a priori. But one must add that, in order for the understanding to be already there, it is necessary that it itself is also discovered as already given. The weakness of empiricism is equal to that of intellectualism, both presuppose that the understanding is already there, one unconsciously, the other consciously. As a result, one must bring this presupposition to light by saying that only the given is there, including the one who receives the given. In some way, the moment when I discover myself given remains strictly and always contemporary to the moment of the reception of my first given.

One can put this differently. Philosophy has with good reason paid great attention to the phenomenon of the possibility of death, that is, to death as a determination of life, of the present: I am the kind of being that is destined to die. All the same, this description should liberate its presupposition, namely that I exist in such a way that I will die *because* I exist in such a way that I have begun by being born. Therefore there is a phenomenology of being-born as being that has always had to be given because it had to appear. The *adonné* precisely designates being born of an event. Being born means being oneself as a necessarily original event. The *adonné* is defined as the one who begins, as the being [*l'étant*] in accordance with being-by-birth [*l'être-par-la-naissance*], just as much as in accordance with being-toward-death. To say that we are fated beings oriented toward death requires by right that we think ourselves *first* (from the beginning) as the being that happens as an event. And the being that has always already happened is in accordance with its being-born, being by birth, by the native event.

What birth illuminates in death has to do with what it shares with death and what it adds to it. We know nothing about death except that it remains incomprehensible. But because it has not yet arrived, we can say to ourselves (yet without believing it too much; still, it's a bit reassuring) that, when it arrives, either we will no longer be there to see it or at least we will maybe comprehend it. Yet birth is no less incomprehensible, although it has already happened. It was an event that in some sense the whole world witnessed except for me. In short, the event that saw me show up remains an event I never attended. Besides, nobody is born in my place, but everyone saw it, and I, who come from it, will never have any idea about it. The claim that it should always finally be possible to reduce the incomprehensible to the comprehensible admits of one huge exception: There is at least one incomprehensible that will never become comprehensible, namely my birth. What unbelievable facticity! Here is a structural phenomenon, one everyone has known, and of which there is intuition—I have access to a sufficient number of givens for the circumstances of my birth to be able to explain my character, my traumas, my dispositions, and so forth—enough to feed scores of psychoanalysts, of psychiatrists, of pediatricians, of genealogists. The whole world can say everything about my birth, about its circumstances and its outcomes. But that does not prevent the fact that there will always be a lack of concepts both for the observers and a fortiori for myself.

This incomprehensible event remains no less an absolute event. It has no adequate concept, but it sets down all of what is possible for me. Here there is, then, a saturated phenomenon that no one can deny because no one living can deny his or her own birth. Consequently, I am myself an event, am myself a saturated phenomenon, thus myself in the situation not of the transcendental ego but well and truly of the *adonné*. This new figure of subjectivity allows me to describe a number of situations that govern neither the theoretical attitude nor the constitution of the object. For example, let's take the figure of the witness: He knows absolutely what he says, to the point of risking his life for upholding it, but he hasn't necessarily understood what took place. Yet, the majority of the time, we are in the position of the witness, in the position of someone who is certain of what he or she has seen and who nevertheless cannot resolve the enigma of what he has seen and did not ask to see. There is also the attitude of someone who sees himself invested in an event, in the sense of the rhetoric of commitment: Should I participate? Should I not participate? Am I or am I not responsible? This somewhat nauseating rhetoric of Sartre's time acquires meaning here. Or also, the ethical question according to Levinas becomes entirely rational starting from the situation of the witness and can be formulated in terms of obligation: those I have chosen and those I haven't chosen, those who precede me and those I call forth. The linking of ethics to theory then becomes perfectly intelligible. One could say the same thing for political questions. Obviously, all these questions escape the transcendental domain.

A multiplication of modes of rationality then becomes possible. For it is certainly not a matter of leaping into irrationality. Quite to the contrary, irrationality arises from a very narrow definition of rationality, which limits it to objectness and to the transcendental constitution, expelling an immense crowd of phenomena into the shadows of supposed irrationality, phenomena that might very well have been able to enjoy full citizenship in a more generous kind of rationality. But the best objectness of the world can only give what it has, as the best daughter of the world. And it cannot give much; thus it bars many from its favors. Actually, to defend that objectness and objectivity constitute the limits of rationality amounts to placing the infinite in the field of the irrational and to considering it merely a threat. Our society, obsessed by technological security and by objectivity, causes insecurity and violence in exactly the same way.

An Open Rationality

Does that mean that irrationality correlates to a rationality that is too narrow? Is that our society's ill?

We are in fact paradoxically in a very irrational society. The most blatant case is the irrationality of the market economy: Supposedly offering the non plus ultra of self-regulation, it continually contradicts the technical criteria by the passions of consumerism for the natural system, by the passion of accumulating for the system of speculation. But let's not take a situation of financial crisis but instead the situation of a developed and stable capitalist economy: In order to expand consumption, and hence growth, the market must not only produce the most rational technological objects but above all transform them into objects of desire. In the final account, the irrational *uselessness* of desire becomes the true engine of growth (even if desire is said to operate by way of "consumption," in the end is there any other engine?). One must sell cars to people who do not need them, and with useless results, if only because the sacrosanct security precludes it. What is really being sold? The objectification of a fantasy, a brilliant object of desire. Thus, the irrationality of the consumer gives rise to and fosters the production and the sale of a rational product. This contradiction, intrinsic to modern economy, appears very clearly in the superimposing of two determinations that cross the technological *and* corrupt object itself: on the one hand, the technology of rationality in its concept and in its production; on the other hand, need, thus also the fantasy of the consumer who obeys the logic of desire. Between these two a contradiction internal to the rationality of the market arises, a contradiction that is much stronger than its purely economic contradictions. Here is a case where the narrow-mindedness of our definition of rationality calls forth irrationality and thus, in the long run, violence.

Is this weakness in terms of objective rationality what you call negative certainty*?*

Not exactly, for negative certainty first allows us to describe the facticity of the saturated phenomenon from the point of view of the recipient. We have seen that the saturated phenomenon is neither a being nor an object constituted by me but an event that happens to me and surprises me. But, one may ask, how can I then still achieve the least certainty, considering that, traditionally (metaphysically), objectness lays down the conditions of certainty? Actually, certainty exceeds the limits of objectness. *Sometimes* at least, it is still accessible, even with a saturated phenomenon. There *can* be cases where I achieve an absolute certainty without having an object available. For, *sometimes*, negative certainty gives the reverse of that of which the saturated phenomenon shows the obverse. This is what happens in the case of the event (or) of the gift. The gift always remains possible (in the realm of reduction to givenness), whatever happens. Why? Because it is not subject to conditions of possibility: It is fulfilled with certainty, but with a certainty that is precisely without object, a negative certainty. We obtain a wide range of phenomenalities there.

Are these broad phenomenalities tied to the opening of a field of rationality by the saturated phenomenon, and therefore they do not give less certainty than the metaphysical certainty of Cartesian objectness?

Actually, what is most strange and what basically interests me first in a philosophy has to do with what in it cannot be thought or described and what nevertheless often remains perfectly accessible. For example, philosophy cannot describe life. Besides, it is not at all certain that one could ever have a *concept* of life. Of course, many philosophers appeal to life and presuppose it, but rare are those who venture to define it (not even Michel Henry). Does life *exist*? Even biology, above all biology, gave up defining it long ago, and no one today imagines that it could, or even should, still speak of it. But philosophy also cannot say what joy is. But, what is more important in life than joy? As we have seen, philosophy cannot say for what *reason* I do or do not succeed in remaining faithful to a person, to a conviction, to an orientation. Yet this is a decisive point, a crucial point, which remains very mysterious. How and on what grounds can I remain the same over time while also changing entirely? That is a thing that I do not comprehend. Philosophy in the metaphysical scheme is limited to distinguishing between substance and accidents, transforming the question into the response, thus owning up to the fact that it does not have adequate concepts at its disposal. Yet how can I be deeply sad or serenely joyful and maybe sometimes the two at the same time? What happens when we submerge ourselves in these affective tonalities that, after all, constitute the depths of our life?

The basic problem of philosophy according to its metaphysical version is summed up in this, that the more it was developed and the more it produced and spread rationality, the narrower, thinner, and weaker this rationality became. It certainly has always produced more rationality and extended it everywhere, but it is still always and everywhere the same rationality, that of objectness. Nietzsche named this poor and impoverishing reason when he said that the "true world," the forged world of objectness, has become a "fable." It is a world of objects, that is, of alienated things; their very existence evaporates, just as the final breath of air is futile. Under its metaphysical form, philosophy was able to say a lot about things, provided that they only exist very little. In order to broaden its will to comprehend, it has reduced the greatest number of things possible to what exists the least, namely objects, by denying existence to those things that refuse objectness. We find ourselves surrounded by an infinity of things that exist very little but which, for that very reason, we comprehend very well. Thus grows the desert.

Why were you interested in phenomenology? Was it precisely to get out of the world of poor and perfectly controlled objects?

When I began to meddle in philosophy in high school, without really understanding anything, only one thing really interested me: finding texts, formulae, or questions that I did not understand. As soon as I understood a text, I no longer found it strong enough, hence, like a type of liquor, not really very interesting anymore. I fed on finding paradoxes defying common sense and told myself that, if someone very intelligent could have said such a strange and incomprehensible thing, there must be something serious, something precious, there. Actually, it is this quest for paradoxes that has always guided and motivated me in philosophy. Thus, as soon as a philosophy bores me, when I see it coming and can anticipate its conclusions, I almost persuade myself that it is not worth the trouble to study it. It bores me when it says what everyone knows very well or says things that are neither true nor false but plausible and that make sense, make "good sense." There are thus many contemporary philosophers who bore me to tears. They have nothing to say to me, even if they can sometimes say it with talent.

It always seemed to me that the role of philosophy consists in helping us see (and understand) things that one does not see at first glance—paradoxes. As Heidegger insists, phenomenology becomes indispensable when we face up to precisely the things that do not show themselves at first and the majority of time. One cannot say it better. Without doubt that is also the reason why theology has always interested me: It concerns—indeed it cannot but concern—paradoxes, and that is what makes it so fascinating, so logical, so serious. Theology always ends up ensuring and accepting that even that which is visible is not comprehensible. It does not yet show anything but ensures and accepts that who shows and what shows *itself* remain, first of all, invisible. This paradox is certainly disconcerting, but it fits the experience of everyday life. What really holds and merits our attention in daily life? Not what we see but instead what we do not understand in what we see and what we must understand in order to see what we see. Thus what we do not understand *orients* us (it points us to the Orient, where the sun rises).

The saturated phenomenon appears as a paradox because, first of all, we do not understand it; we remain low on concepts. Even so, it offers the reserve of possible rationality by requiring an invention of concepts because it lacks them, so that, if one concentrates on it, it will maybe remain incomprehensible, but it is also possible that it will give rise to a rationality around it. It becomes a center of potential rationality, while the technical phenomenon exhausts its rationality immediately in its function: As soon as one knows how to use it, there is no longer anything else to understand in it, to the point that the technical phenomenon only becomes noticeable (in the doubled sense that one must then pay attention to it and that it gives to think) when it breaks down, as Heidegger described very well, or when it allows us to react to an event. But then it only becomes interesting owing to this event and, by a stroke of good luck, it also acquires the status of paradox.

Your works, as much phenomenology as history of philosophy, are full of paradoxes or paradoxical formulations. Is that because, according to you, the paradox is the very character of the given?

Exactly. The given itself exercises a paradox; otherwise it would give little. A nonparadoxical given, maybe one could call it "doxal" or *doxic*, corresponds exactly to the opinion or the expectation that one already has of it before it, which amounts to saying that there isn't much to expect from it.[6] Actually we are really all only interested in paradoxes. When one goes to visit a museum, what does one look for? One looks for paintings that one does not understand because one has not seen them or because one has seen without understanding them, and thus one must go to look at them again. Maybe the event will happen from a painting not in my guidebook or from one I wasn't able to see up close. I walk right past *The Coronation of Napoleon*, which I have already seen a zillion times. But, quite the opposite, the last time that I *stopped* was at the exposition "Gertrude Stein" at the Grand Palais, in front of three apples painted by Cézanne in 1873. Suddenly I remembered that Courbet started painting apples in 1871 in his prison cell in Sainte-Pélagie, where he served a sentence for his activities in the Commune and where he wasn't able to paint very much. This is what struck me: Why did these two men paint apples at almost exactly the same moment? Is there something particular about their apples? And why didn't the others paint any apples?

This is how the phenomenon appears: It might be extremely mundane [*d'une banalité extrême*], yet it can still hold you by its unintelligible, unforeseeable, paradoxical aspect. When philosophy is not interested in paradoxes, then it also is not worth an hour of trouble. In what lies our fascination with Descartes or Kant, if not in their paradoxes? The *Critique*

6. [One of the meanings of the Greek term *doxa* is "opinion."]

of Pure Reason and the *Meditations* string together paradox upon paradox. How dare they uphold that space and time are forms of sensibility and not characters of the world? Or that I exist only inasmuch as I think, while the whole world knows very well that one must first exist in order to think? These are paradoxes! This is serious philosophy!

A Philosophy in Dialogue

At the same time as this permanent concern with the paradox, that is, with the given, your work seems to have been occupied with discussions with other phenomenologists. Could you tell us something of your connections with thinkers like Levinas, Henry, Derrida, or even Ricoeur and Heidegger?

As regards Derrida, Levinas, and Henry, I would say that I encountered them on the way. I knew them well enough before, I read them and even saw them frequently, but at some point in my work it happened that I came across some of their positions and discovered that I could not think through mine without theirs, either to catch hold of them or to push against them in opposition (like climbing between two rock faces in the mountains). For example, when I had the idea that the direction of the gaze is inverted (what I call counterintentionality or icon), I turned to Levinas. Oddly enough, when I put the saturated phenomenon in place, I reread Michel Henry a bit. For the question regarding the difference between distance and différ*a*nce, I had to work on Derrida, from the time of *Idol and Distance* onward. I thus had the good fortune not only of encountering these three philosophers but of meeting up with them again at crucial moments of my own journey. I was delighted and relieved not to find myself alone in the difficulty. For when one is on a path where there is nobody else but then one suddenly notices that someone else went through it, it is reassuring to know that one hasn't completely lost one's way. Not that one would necessarily have to go in the same direction or choose the same route, but at least one knows that it is sensible to find oneself in that place.

A certain number of encounters resulted from this—I was very lucky—and it all happened very simply. For example, I sent *Idol and Distance* to Levinas (I lived very close to him, on the rue d'Auteuil), we saw each other, then we met each other again at conferences. We spoke together—I scarcely dare say it like this—as people who deal with the same sorts of things, each asking the other how things were going: "How do you manage to put these things together?" I suppose just like two joiners or two masons swapping tips with each other. It was the same thing with Michel

Henry, with additionally the common interest we had in painting. He was a genuine collector; we didn't just talk about auto-affection! It was even simpler with Derrida because my relationship with him at the École had been the very unremarkable one of student to *caïman*: he corrected my papers (actually not very much because we weren't pestered too much). We saw each other a little bit (thus he entrusted me with the first editing of *Ousia et gramme*) and we spoke; in short, we had a good relationship, but (or because) I was not his disciple. He seemed to me indisputably very intelligent, very discerning, very learned, "bluffing," if I dare say so, even more than Lacan or Deleuze, who nevertheless were given triumphant welcomes at the École. But I was no disciple of his.

One day, in the 1990s, I received a handwritten letter from Derrida, four pages written in a hotel in Japan, where he told me that he had finally read *God Without Being* and had at the same time reread *Idol and Distance*. Contrary to what he had been told, he realized that these essays were not at all written against him, that instead I had understood what he wanted to do very well and that we had questions in common. Thus to his death we basically remained very much in contact. We certainly had many debates between us but no personal conflicts. The debate we had at Villanova in 1997, although rough and even exhausting for me, still proceeded from a genuine cordiality.[7]

Polemics always arise from those who understand badly or who do not want to understand, rarely from those who have an objection or a serious question. Polemics come from people who are unsettled by what one has told them without aiming at them or even thinking of them but who react because they discover their positions to be weak or even already crushed. It is therefore most often advisable to read them on an ideological, that is, ultimately psychological level. Real interlocutors rarely prove polemical or aggressive, because they have no need for it: They really see what you are doing, they see to what extent it goes their way or not, they ask you one or two questions, they think what they want to think, and that's it. Our paths meet, and then each goes his or her own way again; sometimes, one even goes part of the way together.

7. [This was the first Villanova Conference on Religion and Postmodernism on the theme "God, the Gift, and Postmodernism"; proceedings edited by John D. Caputo and Michael J. Scanlon under that title.]

In the front of your book The Visible and the Revealed, *published in 2005,*[8] *there is a dedication to Michel Henry and Emmanuel Levinas: "Reference points"—maybe with a play on words! In what way were they "reference points"?*

Starting from my own questions or from those that the authors of the tradition have left behind, many times I believed myself lost, and I was very happy to find myself back before them again and thus to note via traces or writings that they had already been through it. I realized that I was not lost, and I found my bearings through the connection with them. It was a little different with Derrida, if I may say so, who wasn't someone with whom one could find one's bearings; he himself passed his time trying to lose himself and to lose his reader, according to the logic of deconstruction. In contrast, one could and one still can, one even must, find one's bearings when approaching Husserl, thanks to the works of Levinas and of Henry, who are after Heidegger the two greatest possible interpretations of Husserl and even the two greatest accounts of the history of metaphysics. This is possible because, even if they happened to have doubts like any philosopher, they nevertheless remain perfectly confident in what they have conquered. I accordingly had the habit of regularly meeting Henry and Levinas, almost once a month. We also met at presentations at the conferences to which we were invited. With Levinas, I spoke essentially of philosophy and of theology. With Michel Henry, as I said, I also discussed painting, food, and wine.

Does the fact of being in charge of editing Levinas's collected works carry symbolic significance for you?

It's very unsettling because there were several reasons why I first thought of declining: I am not, properly speaking, a Levinas specialist, I am not his disciple, I am not Jewish. In the end, other factors intervened: Someone was needed who held a university position, someone in whom Levinas had confidence, with a general competence in phenomenology, familiar with publishing, sufficiently distanced for making people work together, and someone with nerves of steel so as not to go crazy when things get tense, which is inevitable in the course of such an enterprise. I thus accepted out of duty, and I will continue as long as it remains useful.

8. [*Le visible et le révélé* (Paris: Cerf, 2005), translated as *The Visible and the Revealed* (New York: Fordham University Press, 2008).]

Did you meet Lacan?

No. I did not want to have personal connections with either Lacan or Heidegger; that seemed much too dangerous to me. I saw up close certain disciples of Lacan and Heidegger, those who came too close to the master and were burned to a cinder by doing so. I did not want to burn myself, in any sense of that term. Consequently, I knew to keep my distance. I could easily have gone to see Heidegger. Besides, Beaufret had brought him a copy of *On Descartes' Grey Ontology* during the summer of 1975; obviously I could have accompanied him and delivered my book to Heidegger personally. According to Beaufret, upon seeing the book Heidegger said: "That's very good; I also have worked on the *Rules*." Which is perfectly true, but we didn't know those texts at the time, which have since appeared in the *Gesamtausgabe*. Without doubt, he would also have found it judicious to read Aristotle in the *Rules*, to treat them as a palimpsest of Aristotle. I thus received unction in absentia, but still I did not want to become a Heideggerian. And I never did become one.

Reading you, one has the feeling that your Heidegger is above all the Heidegger of Being and Time. *Why this discretion in your work in regard to the second Heidegger?*

On the contrary, I am very interested in that at the moment. I have just devoted several years of courses in Chicago to it and will continue. The second Heidegger, all the same, seems much more difficult and maybe even more rigorous than the first. Therefore, few people really venture to read him. The serious reading of this part of his work is quite recent in France and it is owing to the publication of the lecture courses and of the *Gesamtausgabe*. In the 1980s, Didier Franck and I were among the first to devote a seminar to the reading of the whole of *Being and Time* at the École normale supérieure, a seminar that I redid in Chicago. I also devoted myself to reconstructing the complex history of the ontological difference from *Being and Time* all the way to the end, through the "Letter on Humanism." The very final texts are left over, which are at times very problematic, even for readers such as Jean-François Courtine or Didier Franck. The central and radical nature of scholarly texts such as *The Anaximander Fragment* or the *Bremen Lectures* would demand even more patience and silence. The work still has to be done, but I am beginning to have some plans for fundamental discussion in this field. Moreover, when writing my recent book on Saint Augustine and by working again on Descartes, I discovered evidence to the effect that a good part of the *existential analytic* arose from a theological origin. To what extent can the *Seinsfrage* appropriate theologoumena to itself and neutralize them in accordance with its unavoidable "methodological atheism" without either rendering them ineffective (because outside their own proper field) or jeopardizing itself with theology? And in the end, must one grant Heidegger that philosophy is finally summed up by metaphysics or rather that the question of the *es gibt* (*il y a*/there is) falls back onto that of Being, or even of the *Ereignis*, without leading to the thought of givenness? Thus I'm not done with the question of Heidegger—and the polemics, which ritually return every ten years like the chestnuts every year, do not change anything about it.

The study of this work therefore, in your view, need not be closed down again by the polemics about his position in regard to Nazism?

Levinas, who was quite right, said this about it: "It's annoying, but the greatest philosopher of the twentieth century was a Nazi." I would add: This is facticity, this is nihilism—when the truth is darkened, good and evil are mixed up, and the universal assessment ends up by scrambling everything into the indistinct enormity. This calls forth several remarks. First and at the bottom of the list, let's acknowledge that in the general situation of Germany in the middle of a suicidal Europe between 1920 and 1940, the waste and the debris of the Great War had stockpiled so much flammable fuel that very many things, that almost anything, could have set things off like fire in the underbrush. And several fires were lit. Nazism was one of them (but not the only one; we French know something about it, too). According to this point of view, Heidegger caught fire from the side of Nazism, while other intellectuals caught fire from some other side. In this blaze, Nazism was just as much the effect as the cause of a fatal illness affecting all of Europe, an absolutely fundamental crisis that we have scarcely managed to pass through. Next, and within this context as an individual, Heidegger was a member of the Nazi Party. The texts have appeared in the *Gesamtausgabe*, and there is nothing else to debate. Heidegger was wrong to do so at that time and even more wrong never to have acknowledged it later. Finally the essential thing for a philosopher is left: his thought. Did it have a privileged connection with Nazi teaching, either in terms of influencing it or in terms of coming from it? While it would give far too much credit to Nazism to suppose that it could have produced concepts and gone beyond the ideological level, one must admit that at least at certain moments Heidegger could fall into ideology. To my knowledge he only did, if he did it at all, in some brief passages of some texts in the 1930s, for instance, in his *Introduction to Metaphysics*. But for the rest, responsible proof, although often attempted, has not yet led to any convincing results, for a doubtlessly quite simple reason: Heidegger's most determined opponents are not usually the ones who know his thought best, to put it mildly.

But how should one think of a "salvageable" thought, of a thought that could be salvaged, on account of its vagueness? Is the philosopher responsible for the possible misappropriation of his thought?

One is always, if not responsible, at least to some extent implicated in the misappropriations that are brought about by one's own thought, if just for having produced the thoughts themselves open to being misappropriated. But one only attributes great responsibility to Heidegger because he was Heidegger. Had he been a little philosopher, the whole world could care less; no one would attach the least importance to it. In the same way, one can wonder whether Shakespeare was anti-Semitic because of *The Merchant of Venice*. This question, however, is only raised because we are talking about Shakespeare; otherwise no one would care. The recurring polemics concerning Heidegger's *political* attitude presuppose what they would like to erase, namely the exceptional importance of Heidegger's *philosophical thought*. As far as I am concerned, one thing seems clear to me: Ideologies do not produce concepts but live parasitically on the backs of philosophers and philosophies; they consume them, they damage them, they reuse them, they vulgarize them in all the senses of the term, but they do not belong to the same world, to the same rule, and to the same order as the concept. There are certainly some common sources between Heidegger and Nazism, and Heidegger was partially bound to his time. But I do not understand what chronology one wants to establish. After all, *Being and Time* dates to 1927, not to 1933. It would thus have been necessary for Heidegger to have been under the influence of a possible Nazi doctrine set up in the years 1920 to 1925? That hypothesis remains at the very least dubious. Stop searching for thoughts that Nazism has led astray: Nietzsche and Wagner would provide a better study than Heidegger, and by far.

One thing at least is indisputable: Heidegger lacked political sense and political courage. One can doubt that he was a prince in the first Pascalian order, as one cannot doubt he was in the order of the mind. But there are other things that Heidegger did not see or did not want to see. His very ambiguous relation to Judaism and to Christianity offers a perfect example of this.

What did he not see, in your opinion?

Obviously the order of charity, Pascal's third order. It seems that he had no access to it. He was a prince of the second order, but he remained a prince of the second order. Numerous are the places and the moments when Heidegger did not see. In my opinion the clearest example of this is found in his reading of Hölderlin. Commenting on poems like "Patmos" and "The Only One" without referring to Christ or on "Bread and Wine" without allusion to the Eucharist would appear scandalous if it were not a symptom of a more essential refusal. One just needs to know exactly of what or of whom.

4. Theology

Idol and Icon

Idol and Distance *straightaway opens a theological path in your work.*[1] *Besides Bernard-Henri Lévy's request, how did this book come to be?*

Idol and Distance was written very quickly in 1976, although it relied on material already worked out over several years, especially arguments that had been put to the test in articles published in *Résurrection* during the years 1970 through 1973. In this sense, then, it was an occasional book, but it tackled a haunting or even stubborn problem, one that occupied me and many others for years—the question of the "death of God." I ended up approaching this paradox—How can God die, if he is really a god, that is to say, immortal?—by three convergent paths. First, predictably enough, Nietzsche, whom I had started to read very closely, first of all because of

1. [*L'idole et la distance. Cinq études* (Paris: Grasset, 1977). Translated as *The Idol and Distance*, trans. Thomas A. Carlson (New York: Fordham University Press, 2001).]

personal interest, more prosaically because he was included in my schedule for the *agrégation*. There was also Hölderlin, the poet of exile and withdrawal, whom I discovered through Heidegger and via the encouragement of Jean-Miguel Garrigues, OP. Finally and above all, I had been impressed for a long time by the aforementioned "negative theology," especially since leading a seminar on *The Divine Names* at Montmartre. The conceptual possibilities, which one right away sensed to be powerful in it, intrigued me especially. In that way the material and the arguments were already available. One only had to connect them into a coherent and, if possible, strong hypothesis.

Just a comment: Understood literally, the "death of God" conceptually speaking clearly is a contradiction in terms. For if God dies, that is only because he is not and never really was a god, even less the true God—and hence all this amounts to the destruction of an idol. Consequently, the "death of God," taken in the standard sense, does not have any validity against the true God. This "insane" [statement] really does not say anything sane, except for providing a negative evidence, which all the same exerts the indispensable purifying function of smashing idols, making the hills low and the rough places plain in order to prepare the way (*via negativa*) for the announcement of a true god, of the God who would be *true*. Yet can one grant a purer meaning to the predicative word, grant a more positive credit (*via affirmativa*) to Nietzsche's saying "God is *dead*"? For in the end this positive sense is necessary: the Christian Revelation really and truly relies on the "scandal of the cross," that is to say on the fact that Christ incarnates God. Thus, apart from docetism or illusion, if Jesus Christ dies, then God passes through death, enters into death, descends to the tomb in him and *as him*. It is thus necessary (and there is nothing optional here) for God's divinity to be *manifested* still and even precisely in Christ's death, as death of God. Yet, because God cannot die, Christ's death must accomplish what it signifies, namely the death of death. The Resurrection is itself inferred *analytically* from the "death of God," of course assuming that it is a matter of the death *of God*.

How should one think and express this paradox grafted on a contradiction? By undergoing the evident and inevitable conclusion: The "death of God"—obviously as understood by faith, that is to say, by the revelation of Christ as the man in whom God becomes human in order to deify humanity—is one of the figures of God's manifestation. For me it is the ultimate figure because it enters into our deepest finitude. For no death, no kenosis, no exteriority, no negativity, and no depths of our finitude could separate us from God, who is greater than our heart and hence than our chaos, greater than anything that can be thought. God himself, at least if one recognizes his trinitarian dimensions—the distance between the Father and the Son, which is crossed and unified by the Spirit—in advance surpasses and definitively recapitulates any death, any kenosis, any exteriority, any negativity, and any depth of our finitude that we could ever experience or even less one that we could imagine in our entire heart and in the worst of our chaos.

In this way the "death of God" attests to the destruction and the twilight of the metaphysical idol of God (to speak like Nietzsche), but, far from closing down the field of the divine and the question of God, they open it on a grand scale, without ensuring more mediation, in this way provoking the great trial and the "educating thought" of a naked, raw encounter of the human with a nonmediated divine. The twilight of the idol causes the sun of God to rise and requires managing the distance between the divine and the human, the very distance of the trinitarian God (*via eminentiae*).

Therefore, I tried to set out the modalities of this distance: metaphysical atheism and its equivalence with metaphysical theism, the retreat of the gods and the immediate advance of the divine according to Nietzsche, the question of the measure of the divine and Christ as the measure of God by himself in Hölderlin, God's anonymity and the unlimited plurality of the divine names, the transition from predication to praise according to Dionysius. I concluded by opening the link between distance defined in this way and the different meanings of difference in contemporary philosophy: ontological difference, ethical difference (if I can put it like this, thinking of Levinas), différ*a*nce (in Derrida's sense). I thus began a kind of destructive approach (in the sense of a deconstruction of the question of God), an approach that had to be continued in 1982 with *God Without Being*.[2]

This latter book resulted precisely from discussions that followed *Idol and Distance*, and more directly it resulted from a conference held in June 1979, which was afterward published under the title *Heidegger et la question de Dieu* [*Heidegger and the Question of God*], edited by Richard Kearney and Joseph O'Leary.[3] These two young and brilliant Irish (what followed bore this out), who were just finishing their theses in Paris, had gathered some strict Heideggerians (among them Jean Beaufret and François Fédier), Emmanuel Levinas, Stanislas Breton, Paul Ricoeur, Jean Greisch, and

2. [*Dieu sans l'être* (Paris: Fayard, 1982). Translated as *God Without Being*, trans. Thomas A. Carlson (Chicago: University of Chicago Press, 1991).]

3. *Heidegger et la question de Dieu* (Paris: Grasset, 1980); recently republished (Paris: Presses Universitaires de France, 2009) with an illuminating foreword by Jean-Yves Lacoste.

some free electrons (Maria Villela-Petit, Odette Laffoucrière, Bernard Dupuy . . .) in order to discuss, among other things, the thesis already implied by *Idol and Distance*—to the effect that the question of Being not only is not identified with the question of God but that this very question of God evades the a priori of being. What I called Heidegger's "double idolatry" on that occasion clearly announced *God Without Being*.

In fact (and the parallel work on Descartes's white theology proved this to me sufficiently), in assuming its metaphysical shape philosophy has finally very quickly come to consider that even or especially the authority of God is a matter of general metaphysics; that is to say, it falls under the science of being as being (*ontologia*). Within this framework God himself could be deemed a being, albeit most probably a being that is particular, exceptional, supreme, an object of the *theologia rationalis*. In this way even his transcendence in relation to created beings (the material and the spiritual world) must still appear at the inside of the question of being. Certainly, there were several ways of conceiving of this inscription: God could be a supreme *being* [*un étant*] or, rather, the act of *Being* [*d'être*], but he is no less obligated, in any case, *to be* [*être*] and to be thought within the common horizon of beingness. One understands that, in this case and solely in this case, the first question in regard to God consists in asking whether he is, whether he exists, and finally whether this existence can be demonstrated. One also understands that in the case in which one would have to respond to this in the negative—admitting that one cannot demonstrate God's existence—one would have been led either to God's inaccessibility (what we call agnosticism) or, more bluntly, to what one calls the "death of God" (what we call atheism).

*Proving God's existence or refuting the proofs of his existence would thus imply equally to repatriate God within the question of Being [*l'être*], to consider him as a being [*un étant*] that "has to be [*a à être*]"?*

Absolutely. The starting hypothesis remains the same. The theists, the deists, and the atheists are in agreement on the fact that the question of Being is posed in regard to God as a priority, that God is supposed to be, and that God's transcendence must be able to be laid open on the inside of the horizon of Being. This point of view by rights characterizes metaphysics, with all the variants one would like. But, in a rather surprising manner from the point of view of reflection, one must note that even a thinker as radical as Heidegger, who placed in question the enterprise of metaphysics and its onto-theo-logical constitution, nevertheless maintains that the question of

God can only be tackled from within the horizon of Being, which determines the horizon of the sacred, which itself determines the horizon of the divine, starting from which the question of the gods is raised and potentially that of the one God. If God is, Heidegger says, he will be a being.

But that's exactly the point: Does God have to be? In this sense, Heidegger retains the choice of metaphysics: There is a more essential question than the question of God, and that is precisely the question of Being. The terms have changed, but the result still remains the same: God must allow for a presupposition, the question of Being. This is the way in which I encountered what I called "double idolatry." The first idolatry consists in enlisting God as being the supreme founder of all other beings—that is the metaphysical idolatry; the second idolatry, characteristic of the Heideggerian position, gives up on reducing God to such a primacy of grounding and maintains that at least his manifestation depends on the conditions of the manifestation of being, namely the opening of Being. The common law of phenomenality, the disclosing in retreat, the essence of truth would hence also be applied to God, whatever status one admits for him.

Before going back to God Without Being, *could you take up precisely this main difference between icon and idol, a difference that some have analyzed as absolutely decisive in your work?*

Idol and icon offer two figures of phenomenality, of visibility. The idol can and must be seen; it is even defined as the maximum of visibility that can be borne by this or that gaze, the maximum of intensity, of light, before it is blinded by bedazzlement. In this sense, an idol defines the maximal range of a gaze and constitutes the mirror (low-water mark) of this gaze. Why do we all have idols? Because we all allow for a maximum of endurance, of resistance to the radiance of the phenomenon, to the degree of phenomenality. And this maximum in some way teaches us our own proper measure. It is not right to say that humans have a prize, but they certainly have their idols and identify with them; the idol becomes a mirror for them. Very often, the idol does not appear as such a mirror: It remains a mirror invisible to the gaze, yet I realize retrospectively that nevertheless it is the idol that allows me to know who I am. The idol shows me my ideal, my model, what I would like to reach, the maximum of what I covet or imagine. As Baudelaire says, any idol functions as a form of self-idolatry. Thus, if the term must be applied to God, the idol will indicate the "God" who resembles me, who serves as my ideal. Modern and vulgar uses of idols, the idols among the celebrities that one *sees*, each time mark the measure of an age that, as one rightly says, recognizes itself in them, *identifies itself* with them, as one recognizes oneself in some singer, in some athlete, even in some politician. These individuals assume the function of idols for a society and for an age. Let me stress that this use of *idol* does not necessarily imply a negative judgment: It is only a matter of describing and of noting that everyone takes the measure of the maximum of what one's gaze bears, of what one's will desires, and what one strives after in one's history. Consequently, the idol accomplishes as mirror what the gaze of the spectator sees.

The icon is defined in the opposite sense: We understand quite well that it remains visible, that it still belongs to the visible. Yet this image, which is not first of all or only made for seeing it, demands that one venerate it, sometimes that one pray before it, always that one consider it as bearing, if not the face of God, at least the features of gods, of the divine, in short, a form of the sacred. (Possibly, at the bottom of the scale, it carries the form of the political sacred, which is the most uncertain one.) Accordingly, it is a property of the icon that one must bow before it, almost lower one's eyes before it, *not* gaze at it. Why? Because *it gazes at us*; we do not gaze at it. It convokes us so that we invoke it. That gives rise to the following ambivalence: The same image can become an idol or an icon—depending on whether it is found in the shop of an antique dealer or erected in a Christian church, a Greek temple, even some ancient synagogue. The same image can remain something that I see or can become something that gazes at me [and is of concern to me]. When the icon leaves the church and becomes objectified by an antique dealer or is displayed in a museum, it becomes an idol. Reciprocally, assuming that some statue of an ancient god were to become anew an object of veneration, once more in a temple with sincere believers, it would function again as an icon. It is not the death of the Great Pan that forbids the restoration of pagan cults but the absolute lack of anyone praying—unless the death of the Great Pan would precisely consist in this final lack. In this way, the icon opens the experience of a counterintentionality, of a countergaze, of a face, as Levinas says. Of course, the idol, like the icon, is also a matter of a saturated phenomenon. We have already called to mind the four fundamental types: the event, the flesh, and then the idol and the icon. The idol is defined as the maximum of phenomenality that the gaze can bear. The icon is defined as the gaze of the other, which weighs on me and settles on me, contemplates me and summons me. But what is unique to the face is that it actually offers nothing to see, that it remains invisible, as Levinas also shows: It looks at me and concerns me, but I do not see it because in a sense it is not my job to see but to allow myself to be seen.

Yet, in *God Without Being*, I tried to show that Being itself can function as an idol. Because it constitutes the final horizon for metaphysics (and beyond it for Heidegger), the most fundamental and the largest horizon for all beings, God must be subjugated to it. Accordingly, God is found cut down to size, reduced to the dimensions of the maximum of what my gaze can see. But it is possible that God does not allow himself to be included in the idolatrous horizon of Being, that God not only is not the supreme being but that he does not have to be, that he reveals himself as *without being*. Obviously it is not a matter of going back to a Neo-Platonic position and to move to the One beyond being. For, if the horizon of the One or even that of the Good is found beyond Being, one finds oneself again in exactly the same situation, simply shifted from the transcendental of Being to the transcendental of the One, or the True, or the Beautiful, or even the Good. In such a configuration, one does not leave the idolatrous position, which always consists in allocating a horizon to God. I have tried to show instead that the question of God is not raised first of all in terms of Being. "To be or not to be" might constitute the first question *for us* (though not in the erotic reduction!), but we have no conclusive reason for thinking that it is also the first question *for God*, neither from his point of view nor from ours in his place. Everything points to the contrary.

This position appears to be polemical, without doubt rightly so. First because it is directly opposed to the common neo-Thomist position, for which God is identified with being. One should also point out that Thomas Aquinas's God is identified with the act of being [*l'acte d'être*], not with *a* being [*l'étant*], so that the distinction, which is found in all other beings between act of being and essence, is not found in God; the act of being absorbs the essence of God or exempts it from having an essence. In some way God is without essence, as certain texts of Aquinas say, for his only essence is to act. Yet, the act of being for Aquinas precisely remains completely unknown to us, *penitus incognitum*—as Gilson had already underlined. In this way, the fact that God is determined as an act of being means precisely that he has nothing in common with what we experience and understand by the name of "the common concept of being." That God is defined as an act of being does not include him but to the contrary *excludes* him from what *we* conceive as Being, namely the beingness of being. Even in Aquinas, one could almost say that God is without being, in the sense of common being, of the *ens commune*. Despite the appearances and simplifications of his successors it is then not self-evident that God *is* in Aquinas or that he is subject to the horizon of the concept of Being [*d'être*]—or, more precisely, of being [*d'étant*]—such as metaphysics understands it.

Besides these debates with the Thomists, you also had to face the Heideggerians?

Yes, and they were quite right to think that the thrust of the polemic was aimed at Heidegger. While writing *God Without Being*, I was not first of all thinking of the Thomists but rather of the Heideggerians, of Jean Beaufret and his friends (who incidentally were also my friends). They had the audacity, insufferable in my view, of asserting that the question of God comes second compared with a much more essential question, one that would possibly be able to determine the question of God, namely the question of the ontological difference, that is to say, that of the difference between Being [*l'être*] and being [*l'étant*], the *Seinsfrage*. Certainly, Heidegger's position is without doubt not a vulgar, metaphysical, atheist position (obviously it is also not Christian), but in some sense that makes it all the more dangerous for theological thought inasmuch as it regionalizes the theological question entirely by subjugating it to the question of Being. Incidentally, the same thing happens to the Beautiful. The authority of the Beautiful, when Heidegger takes it up, for example in "The Origin of the Work of Art," is interpreted, in an almost Hegelian manner, as a prolegomenon or a base for the truth of Being [*de l'être*] in a being [*un étant*]: as the truth of Being, which decides the possibility of the Beautiful, the beautiful being [*étant*] obviously a privileged case but nevertheless specific to the truth of Being [*de l'être*]. In the same way, for example in the "Letter on Humanism," the question of monotheism, of atheism, of the existence of God and others are all held to depend on the inquiry about Being as such.

I objected to raising this condition of ontological possibility and imposing it on the opening of the question of God, arguing that God does not admit of conditions (not even those that *we* would assess as standard for the *divine* condition, as the letter to the Philippians warns). The ontological conditions for the manifestation of God, for the revelation of God, do not precede it, because those conditions will not be found and are never found joined together anyway: God does not reveal himself at once—how would that ever be possible?—with all the conditions (the divine, the holy, the sacred, the hale, the open, the truth of Being, etc.) joined together; they never were and never will be unified. He reveals himself (and this is how Revelation is distinguished from simple manifestation) even when he *cannot* be manifested; he only reveals himself by having to *contradict* the real conditions of the unfolding of Being, of the open, the holy, the divine, the gods, and so forth. Come unto his own (and Being also counts, like the beings, among his own, because it comes with creation), God was not received, neither greeted nor welcomed. To the point of letting himself be killed. The unfolding of Being is not, was not, and will never be the measure of God. Thus, according to good theologians, any Revelation of God at bottom consists in a self-manifestation of God, which means that Revelation does not happen in order to make up for the lack of or the expectations of conditions of phenomenality ruled by Being (as the conciliatory theologians persist in claiming) but in order to *contradict* these conditions. And it is particular to Revelation never to find the ways already prepared, the hills already made low, and the rough places already made plain: The voice, which commands them, preaches in the desert, *vox clamans in deserto*. Revelation does not make up for expectations any more than it satisfies conditions; rather, it causes an upsurge. The reign of God causes violence because it withstands a violence that is first of all a phenomenal violence.

But how can God without *Being be heard positively?*

In order to show that actually the question of God is posed before and without the question of Being, I have maintained that it can itself be disconnected, as one disconnects or unplugs an electric grid (*ausschalten*), or, in Husserlian terms, that one can bracket it. In what case? In the test of boredom, here in opposition to that of anxiety. According to Heidegger's celebrated analysis, this boredom enables the test of Being by putting beings into parentheses. Reversing Heidegger's later analyses after *Being and Time* (for they reinstate boredom into anxiety), I attempted to show that what is particular to boredom is that it suspends not only being [*l'étant*] in totality (as anxiety does) but the question of Being itself. Boredom, in fact, renders the question of Being indifferent by confronting it with the question "So what?"—the *umsonst* of nihilism, according to Nietzsche. In the test of boredom, of spiritual weariness, and of the sadness of the soul, Being becomes in some way indifferent. I obviously used Heidegger, but above all, going back also to Pascal, the thematic of the three orders: the order of the body; the order of the mind, of science, of philosophy, and of Being; and the order of charity. For boredom intervenes, obviously negatively, at the level of charity, when it makes us weary of it (this is how *tristitia spiritualis*, acedia, functions), but it intervenes also positively, when charity makes us indifferent to vanity both in the first and equally in the second order. The order of charity defines the place where through boredom one can undergo the test of the vanity of vanities, of the vanity of everything that is not a matter of charity. From this point of view especially, the question of Being is not the first but is vain, struck with vanity. To the questions: "What is there as a being? What is Being?" one can respond positively, thus metaphysically, without that equating to a "movement of charity" for us, as Pascal says.

As regards the rest, if you wish, nihilism consists in considering that even a positive response to the question of Being, by evaluation, by the great *amen* of Zarathustra, that even this falls under the blow of the vanity of Being. Thus *God Without Being* ends by suggesting that the question of Being finds itself demoted because it is bracketed by the superior authority of vanity, which actually operates starting from or in the name of the question of charity or the third order. Vanity as the projected shadow of charity on what does not love. This new step directly reinforces calling metaphysics into question, which I attempted within the history of philosophy, but a calling into question of what, according to Heidegger, allows us to get out of metaphysics—if it is possible to get out of it—namely, the renewed question of Being. Henceforth, the proper place of theology appears very clearly: It is called charity, the question of love, which reduces, which suspends (one should not say "annihilates" because annihilating [*anéantir*], like the nothing [*néant*], still falls under the language of Being), and which demotes the metaphysical questioning about Being. Even so, these two texts (*Idol and Distance* and *God Without Being*) remained two negative moments, and I was fully conscious of this. Obviously, love already pierces through vanity, but more by simple opposition to the question of Being. Also, at the end of *God Without Being*, anticipating work still to come, namely that of a description of the logic of love that would appear twenty years later under the title *The Erotic Phenomenon*, I tried to describe a phenomenon free from any ontological determination and in this sense properly theological: eucharistic presence. This description hence remained outside the text [*hors texte*].

What is interesting about the question of the Eucharist has to do with what it questions, this time from theology's point of view, namely presence. A presence that is not directly linked to the subsistence of what persists in its Being from the fact of its essence (*ousia*), neither through objectness constituted by an ego, nor even to a self-showing of a being in virtue of the self, but to the process of givenness, here of the gift in the eucharistic sense of the term. For in this case the gift alone makes presence, the *present gives presence*. Obviously, for me, as a Roman Catholic, this sacrament had a particular force and perfectly corresponded to the experience of eucharistic adoration of which we have already spoken, a very vibrant and determining experience in my life. But doing this, I also thought ahead to a theoretical development that had not been begun, that of phenomenology. All the same, the collection of articles that appeared a little while later under the (obviously Kantian) title of *Prolegomena to Charity* to my eyes constituted a starting point, where I only described examples of what would finally permit a more positive thought of charity or of love. Clearly, theology required me to begin again in philosophy, this time outside of metaphysics, as much as it is possible to do so.

This thought was unfolded twenty years later in 2003 in The Erotic Phenomenon,[4] *which as a result one would hesitate to include either in the purely theological works or in the purely phenomenological ones because in it the two lines converge toward a point, namely that of love. Why this long delay?*

The delay had to do with the fact that, in order to attempt a positive description of love, I had to have a method of description available that would be able not to treat love starting from the ego or the subject of metaphysics, as a simple *affectus* or as a derivation of beingness. Thus a phenomenology was needed here, but even more a phenomenology limited neither to the phenomenality of objects nor to that of beings. In a word, one had to be able to achieve practicing the third reduction, that is to say, the reduction to givenness and from givenness. Once this description was developed, I could finally pose the question that becomes the conclusion of *Being Given*: What would happen if an *adonné* [a given self or a devoted] finds itself put in question not by a simple given but by the phenomenon of another given self giving itself and manifesting itself? This is what begins the erotic phenomenon. The phenomenon I had described in *Being Given* still remained a phenomenon within the world, but what would happen if we were to suppose that another *adonné* were at stake? It took me almost ten years to pass from one—the given in the world—to the other, the givenness of another *adonné*, from *Being Given* to *The Erotic Phenomenon*. At that moment, I could hope to have the phenomenological means to conduct a description of the link of one *adonné* to another *adonné*. Only this phenomenology, radicalized and pushed further than its own truth, would allow me to describe the beloved or, better, erotic phenomenon. Consequently, I was able to give real content to what appears only negatively, against the God of metaphysics in *Idol and Distance* or against Being's divine in *God Without Being*. Phenomenology thus *also* permitted me to resolve a theological question that so far I had treated only negatively. And in this sense *The Erotic Phenomenon* constitutes the culmination of a journey,

4. [*Le phénomène érotique* (Paris: Grasset, 2003). Translated as *The Erotic Phenomenon*, trans. Stephen E. Lewis (Chicago: University of Chicago Press, 2007).]

the moment where the phenomenological line meets up with the theological line. Contrary to Dominique Janicaud's objection, *Being Given* was not yet able to accomplish or even fully see this. Of course, the meeting of these two lines presupposes an essential point: It requires that the erotic logic stay univocal, that is to say, what is valid of the erotic phenomenon in human experience remains valid for the love with which God loves.

Then you refuse the opposition Nygren introduces between eros *and* agape?[5]

Absolutely! I made myself clear a bit later, in *In the Self's Place: The Approach of Saint Augustine*, published in 2008.[6] Luckily for me, there are two or three fairly important authors who go in this direction: Saint Augustine, for whom love, tender care, and charity are said in one word; but also Saint Bonaventure, Saint Bernard de Clairvaux, or Saint François de Sales. Other authors from the most ancient tradition confirm these views: the notion of *eros*, for example, is applied to God as the first and most venerable of the divine names by Dionysius the Areopagite. Actually the distinction that Nygren underlines in the first half of the last century relies on a recent distinction that has no true biblical basis. It even lacks any Christian sense. For, if love is not displayed in the same sense and univocally between humans and God, we cannot hope to love as God loves (by the grace of the Spirit), and, as nothing is divinized that is not assumed, deification becomes impossible (without doubt, that's even the case from a Jewish point of view).

On the contrary, that Being or the manner of Being does not stay univocal between humans and God should not pose any theological difficulty, if just in virtue of creation: Creation by definition separates, and anyway maybe we are separated from God only by Being. But what would it mean if we were to discover ourselves separated from God *by love*? How could one imagine a greater heresy, if not to say indecency? For in the end God wants us to be holy as he is holy. Yet we cannot find holiness in ontic perfections or ones arising from Being, because Being and its modes (finite/infinite, eternal/temporal, possible/impossible, etc.) separate us from God. But we can love him as he loves us—at least he took the trouble of making

5. Anders Nygren, *Eros and Agape: The Christian Notion of Love and Its Transformations*, trans. Philip S. Watson (Philadelphia: Westminster, 1953).

6. [*Au lieu de soi. L'approche de saint Augustine* (Paris: Presses Universitaires de France, 2008). Translated as *In the Self's Place: The Approach of Saint Augustine*, trans. Jeffrey L. Kosky (Stanford, Calif.: Stanford University Press, 2012).]

this known to us. One can suppose, above all if God becomes incarnate and if he lives with us, that he loves us all the way to death and resurrection and that he loves as we should love. In this case, one can understand that we share the ability to love and also, let's hope, one gracious day, that we have the same manner of loving. There is only one way of loving, the right way, that of the divine, and one must learn to love as he who knows how to love loves.

"God is the best lover," as you said?

That is the final line of *The Erotic Phenomenon*: What distinguishes us most from God is that, although he loves like us, he loves infinitely better than we ourselves love. The greatest musician plays to perfection on the worst instrument. For our part, we do not know how to play our instrument well; anyway, we have damaged or maybe almost destroyed it. He alone can come to play perfectly on our instrument because univocal love can do everything, namely love even in the worst circumstances. That is the thesis. Obviously, it does not mean that we really love as God loves but that there is only a single correct manner of loving, the one God teaches us. I have hence tried to describe the figures of consciousness (if I can take up this Hegelian expression) starting from the situation where the ego defines itself fundamentally as loving, *ego amans* and not *ego cogitans*.

You thus contradict this general position of metaphysics—according to which, when love manages to secure itself a place, it is a secondary, derivative place, in some way a subsidiary—in order to say that love is the central place where we recognize ourselves and the most decisive question. What happens when we love?

Why can we not be exempted from loving or hating, even if, first of all, we ask ourselves if someone or other really loves us? Actually, there is no contradiction here. For our first link to love consists in discovering that we are first lacking in love. It is for this reason that we demand with all our strength that someone love us. A first question arises from this: "Does anyone love me?" Such a questioning must appear entirely strange to us: Why do we have such need for someone to love us? Because autonomy, which we are nevertheless constantly told constitutes our profoundest (moral and political) ambition, to the point where self-love would define us from top to bottom, is doubtlessly precisely not what we truly want because on a deep level we cannot accomplish it (and know that to be the case). The standard idea according to which the modern human being desires autonomy more than anything else appears false to me: Maybe the market wants people to desire this, but they desire the love of the other.

In short, we want someone else to love us because we ourselves do not love ourselves. The thesis that turns self-love into our strongest passion nevertheless retains a meaning: We want the whole world to love us. But we want it in an unjust, exaggerated, unmerited manner, and we want it precisely because we are quite incapable of loving ourselves. We are incapable of it because we know ourselves to be totally insufficient, because we know perfectly that we are not worthy of love. Nobody gives me as honestly disappointed a look as I give myself. Thus, I hate myself much more than I love or than I love myself, and I want others to love me in my place in order to make up for this. From this results the crazy kind of logic we all know: Because I don't love myself, I want to make up for it through the love of others. But I find the others truly disgraceful because they love themselves or other things more than they love me (which is obviously exactly the way I proceed myself). In this way, I want to be loved by the same people that, incidentally, I find unjust and worthy of hatred, and I use all the means to make myself loved by force or even by constraint. Yet, to make oneself loved by force is precisely not to make oneself loved: We are here not only led to self-hatred but to the hatred of everyone by everyone. In short, I report an immense failure of everyone to become loved by others. This "Does anyone love me?" is the first phase of the experience of the erotic phenomenon.

A second experience follows this, that of the lover. The question is reversed and becomes: Can I love without requiring that one first love me? Can I, myself, love first? This is an absolutely central question, which actually decides the entire positive implementation of the erotic phenomenon. If I wait for the other to love me before I myself undertake the tiniest movement for loving him or her in turn, I will just keep waiting continually, and the other will never come. The lover takes the risk that one does not love him back; that is to say, he wrests away from reciprocity. The same is true of the phenomenon of the gift reduced to givenness, where the gift leaves the logic of exchange and of reciprocity. The lover leaves the logic of exchange and takes the risk of loving without return. That is Don Juan's position but also the position of God, who loves those who do not love him and, potentially, loves what is not yet, what he draws out of nothing (*ex nihilo*—after all, God's transcendence in regard to Being is also tied to the fact that God *loves* already what is not, what does not yet exist). In this case, one loves without return because there simply is no possibility for return. Love is hence not based on a being in order to become loved by it.

To the contrary, love loves and, possibly, in its unilateral love, it gives rise to a being. There is an advance of the lover, the lover makes advances, puts him- or herself in advance and takes the risk of an advance without cover.

How does he proceed? He makes love, in the ancient sense of speaking to the other. That is to say, he gives rise to the loving situation through the word. He says to the other: "This is me." This "this is me" gives rise to a countermovement that does not belong to exchange but to the crossing of gazes. From then on the erotic phenomenon properly speaking is put into place: a single poor, universal, and empty signification, namely "this is me," which begins to fill two irreducibly different living events of consciousness, which yet validate the same signification. The erotic phenomenon then emerges, but in no case does it come from a sharing of lived experiences of consciousness, as one very often imagines it. In fact, that would be completely impossible because the consciousnesses cannot merge without disappearing, and the actors cannot be reduced to a unity without losing their identities. In turn, there is truly the same signification for the two lovers, with two contents of consciousness, which yet remain irreducibly different. That is called the oath.

It is important that one acknowledge that within the erotic phenomenon the oath must in some way be validated anew at each moment; it creates a temporality of repetition, which includes the requirement of eternity within it. From this arises the paradox that one cannot say "I love you" and add a temporal restriction. To say "I love you for a month or for a year" simply means "I do not love you," for one cannot love on a contract of predetermined length. One can conclude a contract with a temporal restriction, even that of a marriage in the sense of an exchange of (sentimental, sexual, or economic) services, but one cannot say "I love you" in this way; it sounds like a performative or logical contradiction. Thus a very particular temporality is established here, that of the erotic phenomenon. It is a temporality that aims at eternity in a repetition that is itself always different and hence deferred, in other words, an eschatological temporality.

Erotic Relation and Sexual Relation

And the flesh?

It precisely comes in right here. We have already spoken of the flesh, of this gap between the physical bodies of the world and my own flesh, which remains, in a sense, a body in connection with physical bodies but which, in a different sense, senses these bodies because it has the privilege of sensing itself sensing. Yet, it turns out that this gap between body and flesh is further doubled in the case of the erotic phenomenon. In this encounter, my flesh can at times change nature and status when it enters into the presence of the other's flesh. The eroticization of the flesh is produced in this way, which can be explained phenomenologically quite simply. I have the experience of my flesh the most often and first of all via contact with a thing of the world: I sense this thing of the world at the same time as I sense myself sensing, but, in this case, which is not yet erotic, my flesh senses the thing of the world by remaining affected by the principal characteristic of this material extended thing, namely that it resists my flesh. It is its impenetrability that resists me. This is why my flesh draws back and experiences itself wounded or at least bruised. The flesh, and it alone, experiences itself passively as being pushed back by the resistance of the body, which itself does not sense anything and smashes into me. In this habitual case, the flesh is then itself experienced in the mode of nonreciprocal pain: sometimes very little pain, sometimes violent pain, but always the pain of a unilateral resistance.

To the contrary, when my flesh enters into contact with another flesh, it experiences for the first time something that does *not* resist it. The unilateral pain that enters into me without my entering into it is therefore followed by the caress, where the other allows me to enter into him, as I also permit him to enter into me, without pain and with pleasure. In this way, what opposes no obstacle to my flesh by not resisting me itself permits the flesh to experience itself as not pushed back, as received, as authorized to stretch out. What one vaguely calls pleasure is born from this. In contrast to what one often says, the caress does not consist in experiencing an indefinitely repeated limit (that of the other's skin) but of an indefinitely repeated nonresistance of the limit. What is strange here lies in the fact that both of them desire that the caress of the other enter more profoundly. From this results a third state of the body: neither the physical body nor the flesh but also the eroticized flesh. The descriptions of the eroticized flesh then allow those of sexuality, of excitement, of orgasm, and so forth.

What link is there between the erotic phenomenon and sexuality?

Although the erotic phenomenon leads to sexuality and to orgasm, it does not lead there necessarily: Erotization always consists in an erotization of the flesh and by the flesh, but this does not always consist, if I may say so, in meat [*la viande*]. The flesh can *also* be eroticized by the word and as word, *also*, or even *first*, because there is practically no eroticization without word, but there can be a nonsexualized eroticization. For example, there is an erotic phenomenon, with a certain erotization of the flesh without exercise of sexuality, in the case of friendship or of the relation between mother and child. The characteristics of the erotic phenomenon are discovered here again (for example, an absolutely individualized relation, without substitution, unable to be multiplied, unconditioned), and nevertheless it does not become sexualized properly speaking. We do not understand this because we are an *erotically very poor* civilization. In order to experience the erotic, we must therefore sexualize ourselves right away and too quickly, leaving aside what is not sexual in the erotic. This is a mistake because the erotic phenomenon appears large enough to encompass all the forms of love, including certain forms that are not sexualized and do not have to be. Certainly there are friendships, as described by Aristotle, which derive from exchange, from services rendered, from shared interests; while reasonable, they are no longer a matter of an erotic phenomenon but instead of a pure and simple exchange of sexual services (with a price or not). Our hypersexualization bears witness to a collapse of the erotic phenomenon that is continually marginalized or minimized (to the advantage, if one can put it like that, of pornography and of prostitution, under a thousand names).

Does the erotic relationship set up a role for the third?

The crucial question becomes that of the limitation of the erotic phenomenon. For there is a fundamental instability in this phenomenon, which is linked to finitude and to temporality. On the one hand, the erotization of the flesh, when it goes all the way to its sexual exercise, brings about a test of finitude because sexualization cannot last permanently. According to Kant, we experience finitude in sensibility in general and toward the intuitive given, but, in my opinion, we experience it much more when sensibility plays between two given selves [*deux adonnés*] and when the question of the sexualization of the erotic phenomenon becomes necessary. At that moment, we experience finitude in a clearer and very brutal manner. On the other hand, the erotic phenomenon, whether sexualized or not, always remains subjugated to the demand of repetition: The oath itself only endures, if it endures at all, by being repeated; the erotic phenomenon is only created by the duration of the repetition—what one calls *faithfulness*. Faithfulness is the name of erotic time. Without faithfulness the erotic phenomenon vanishes, for it lacks time, as one suffocates from a lack of air. Finitude and temporality therefore imply that the erotic phenomenon can never go without an external assurance and hence needs the third.

What is the third? There are two obvious faces of it: the child and God. I say the child, but one must also hear the possibility of the child, a possibility almost as strong as the real child. In fact, the child presents a witness because it results directly and in person from the erotic phenomenon. An erotic phenomenon that would not have the hope or the possibility of such a third would turn out to be even more fragile. That is why one must take the desire of homosexual couples for a child very seriously, despite the fact that the conceivable replies often miss the gravity of this possibility, which one wants to make effective by taking recourse to all the mechanisms of objectness (biological and legal). In this way, the erotic phenomenon disappears one more time into the (metaphysical) mastery of the object.

A verse in the book of Genesis says in regard to Adam and Eve: "Therefore a man leaves his father and his mother and clings to his wife, and they become one flesh." Actually the Hebrew adds a dative: "and they will be for *a single flesh." The rabbis interpreted this as indicating that man and woman will be* for the child. *The child here becomes the horizon of the erotic relation. I believe you quote this Rabbinic commentary in* In Excess *in 2001.*

Absolutely. The child raises a twofold problem. First, although it provides the witness because it can assure them that the erotic phenomenon has really taken place, it can also become a witness for the opposite, which shows that the erotic phenomenon comes undone. Moreover, the child will in any case leave; it will thus never give what it has received. Under these conditions, the child either accuses as a witness for the opposing side or drops its testimony. Consequently, this is a very ambiguous, unstable, and provisional witness. Yet, the erotic phenomenon demands eternity; an absolute third is hence necessary, a third who can thus only come from God considered as final horizon. The erotic phenomenon therefore necessarily has an eschatological dimension—not being able to assure itself permanently, it must be repeated, and the repetition can finally not be accomplished other than by access to eternity in accordance with history—which exactly defines eschatology. Eschatology means the passage and the transition between temporality and eternity because time itself follows an arrow, not a circle. We recover here again this major fact that the oath, which alone brings about the erotic phenomenon, from the beginning imposes a requirement of eternity at least implicitly. The question of the absolute witness is intrinsically posed by this phenomenon.

All the same, does one still need a third in the relationship with God, the best lover?

Here the question whether God has a trinitarian form becomes decisive because God plays all the roles in a trinitarian fashion. I do not want to venture into this properly theological domain, but one must in fact wonder whether the erotic phenomenon can finally become comprehensible without the relation to a Trinity itself. Obviously, we would have to pose this question; it is not added to the erotic phenomenon from the outside. God alone opens, in trinitarian fashion, the theater of the erotic phenomenon in all its dimensions, and reciprocally the question of God is posed first as an erotic question: The question of God does not ask (at least not at first) whether he exists or not but whether one can love without him or outside of him—if I can love anyone else than God without God. Maybe it is actually not even possible to make the advance, of becoming a lover, without God. Maybe it is actually not possible to repeat the erotic phenomenon without God. At least, for all the operations, one must imitate many of the attitudes particular to God. It seems strange to me that great thinkers or great theologians have missed this: Blondel or Rahner have chosen the reference either to being or to action as privileged experience, although a different, far more obvious, maybe more paradoxical but more appropriate experience exists: the fact of loving.

What constraints did The Erotic Phenomenon *impose on you?*

The Erotic Phenomenon logically completes a phenomenology of the given and of the saturated phenomenon, for the other *adonné* accomplishes the saturated phenomenon par excellence, obviously, because one absolutely cannot come to grips with it in terms of an object or describe it as a being. Only the thought of givenness can really lead to a phenomenology of the erotic phenomenon because it mobilizes the four types of the saturated phenomenon: event, idol, flesh, and icon. That is also why I was able to write *The Erotic Phenomenon* without quotations, without philosophical or theological references, only with the means of perfectly rational arguments and pure descriptions, all of it formulated in the first person, because one can only speak of love from the place that one occupies oneself. Speaking from myself therefore became an epistemological requirement, one I accepted without too many hesitations, despite the difficulty of attitude.

Of course, this didn't concern my empirical me, and it is not my love life that I wrote about, but, if you have no love life at all, you cannot describe the logic of the erotic phenomenon itself. If this was certainly not my empirical me, it was also not my transcendental me, who would not have known how to enter into the erotic situation; thus it was neither the one nor the other. That did not get me out of paying the price of experimentation: After all, the people who discovered radium readily accepted being exposed to radium. I thus spoke really in the first person, hoping to describe universalizable forms of consciousness, and I had in mind the avowed ambition, like Proust for *In Search of Lost Time*, that the readers reading *The Erotic Phenomenon* would be able to recognize their own experience behind mine.

What reception did The Erotic Phenomenon *have?*

For the first time the reception by the general public was very large, without noteworthy reservations, neither from the right nor the left. Even so, it seemed to me very clear that for the philosophical public the book raised some inevitable and almost desirable discomfort. A certain audacity and the absence of notes disconcerted readers. (Obviously there are any number of references in *The Erotic Phenomenon*, but they are implicit, for I wanted to avoid clouding the description.) If some philosophers found me too crude or even radical, some theologians did not appreciate the univocity of love. But, really, one often objects, what do they know of it? It is possible that they do not know much more than the average mortal. Is it not because one imagines the ordinary, for example, that pleasure and orgasm are a matter of sexuality itself? And what if sexuality remains a diminished and feeble form of infinitely stronger erotic pleasures without sexuality? I have not written that, but I think that this is the most probable hypothesis, and, in principle, one must not exclude any hypothesis, especially not in this domain, and above all not the most excessive ones! If there is excess even in sexuality, so repetitive, so unsubtle, and finally quite ridiculous, how must it be in other places, when the erotic phenomenon disposes of such superior means! It seems hardly probable under the circumstances that the Trinity is reserved for the uptight. Finally, I have a higher vision of love than that of the objectors, who have an extremely low vision of love, boiling it down to the most sinister sexuality.

A Theological Turn?

Does phenomenology not assume a role here that does not belong to it? Does it not become an ancilla theologiae*?*

No, for the theological unfolding of phenomenology is included without clash into the logic of its very powerful development over a century. Phenomenology began with formal problems: theories of judgment, of mathematical ideality, of the status of logic. But from Husserl onward the fields have become broader and, with Heidegger, Scheler, Levinas, Merleau-Ponty, Gadamer, Ricoeur, or Henry, phenomenology has conquered fields into which philosophy had hardly entered: hermeneutics, which metaphysics had barely skimmed; intersubjectivity, about which the same metaphysics keeps a wholly astonishing silence; aesthetics, or rather the artistic phenomenon—phenomenology has done extraordinary work on painting, for example, even if art historians without philosophical training still have a hard time taking it into account; certain painters have in some way been imposed upon by the phenomenologists. Similarly, it was very normal for phenomenology to seize the domain that philosophy had described as "mystical"—a vague, modern term for these domains. One cannot deny that they have a reality and a logic, but they escape the prevailing rationalism. Phenomenology wanted to go there to observe—there as elsewhere. There was no theological turn for phenomenology: phenomenology simply unfolded.

Here you allude to Dominique Janicaud's grand polemic in The Theological Turn of French Phenomenology *(1991),*[7] *where he accused Levinas of being the initiator of a movement that included Michel Henry, Jean-Louis Chrétien, and yourself. According to Janicaud, this movement misused Husserl's method for the benefit of theological aims or religious presuppositions. Could you go back to this polemic?*

As I have said, my sense is that there never was a "theological turn of phenomenology" because phenomenology treated theological subjects from the beginning, whether in Husserl (as Emmanuel Housset's recent

7. [*Le tournant théologique de la phénoménologie française* (Paris: Éditions de l'Éclat, 1991). Translated in *Phenomenology and the "Theological Turn": The French Debate*, trans. Bernard G. Prusak (New York: Fordham University Press, 2000).]

work, *Husserl and the Idea of God*,[8] has established), Heidegger, Scheler, to strict contemporaries. All the phenomenologists have dealt with subjects that fall under theology, from a disciplinary point of view, and there are no reasons why one should forbid it. Once more, it is not a matter of a "turn" but of a development and of an extension of phenomenology's field of intervention.

To go back to this polemic: I must admit that I did not respond to Dominique Janicaud until *Being Given*. We certainly talked to each other a bit, and I merely said to him that in my view he had completely missed the point. But I did not have any public dialogues with him; we only saw each other again when he had finished his study on the reception of Heidegger in France.[9] It was not a personal quarrel. I just think he was wrong, for this simple reason: He set himself up as a defender of Husserlian orthodoxy even though he did not actually know that much about Husserl himself but was a Hegelian and a Heideggerian who was close to Beaufret. His reading of Husserl was thus partial, quite superficial, and in any case recent.

Anyway, what is strange is that the generation before us was composed either of Husserl experts reticent in regard to Heidegger or, instead, of Heidegger partisans who were reticent about Husserl, while our generation—without doubt also thanks to the reestablishment of the Husserl Archives in Paris—endeavored to understand both of them. Yet Janicaud precisely never participated in that movement, and because he was a Heideggerian, he was not in a good position to know who showed the most respect for Husserlian orthodoxy. For Levinas really did not need to be taught anything from anyone about Husserl: He had taken Husserl's courses in Freiburg in 1929 and had been the first to translate the 1930 *Cartesian Meditations*, Michel Henry and Paul Ricoeur knew Husserl by heart, and Jean-Louis Chrétien and I had at least a smattering of knowledge about him. This polemic hence from the very beginning set off on the wrong foot.

Strangely enough, its result for French phenomenology was positive: In the entire world, first of all in the United States, then in Italy and in Germany, a new philosophical generation has been discovered in this way. At the end of the 1980s, French phenomenology was limited to Ricoeur, Derrida, Levinas, and Merleau-Ponty; today, foreign works (for example,

8. Emmanuel Housset, *Husserl et l'idée de Dieu* (Paris: Cerf, 2010).

9. [Dominique Janicaud, *Heidegger in France*, trans. François Raffoul and David Pettigrew (Bloomington: Indiana University Press, 2015).]

recently that of Hans Dieter Gondek and Lázsló Tengélyi, *Neue Phänomenologie in Frankreich* [*New Phenomenology in France*][10]) mention Henry, Levinas "in the latest fashion," Marc Richir, Chrétien, and myself, along with many others. Internationally, French phenomenology's supposed entry into theology was heralded as good news and as a sign of development, not at all as a corruption or a misappropriation. Let us give thanks for the just results of a misinterpretation.

In what capacity exactly is phenomenology interested in theological questions?

As a teaching about the phenomenon, phenomenology could only with difficulty avoid, much less forbid, taking an interest in all phenomena possible. Painting gives a phenomenon, literature presents a phenomenon, music presents a phenomenon, history presents a phenomenon, the other presents a phenomenon, the flesh and the eroticized flesh present phenomena, and so forth. Accordingly, the revelation or the manifestation of God also presents a phenomenon, at least a possible phenomenon, and actually a phenomenon of first rank within human experience. Metaphysics itself ends in philosophies of religion and of revelation: Schelling, Hegel, Feuerbach, Kierkegaard, and Nietzsche. If even metaphysics was obligated to end up there, how could phenomenology not face up to these questions?

One must only wonder about the conditions, about the how, and about which complications of method should be followed. These questions cannot be avoided, and they were not avoided. Yet the idea that a certain phenomenological purity would impose exceptions on investigation and description is infantile: As a philosopher, I do not have to decide whether I am a believer, but I must elucidate the things themselves, things that can take the face of Revelation, of revealed phenomena, of everything that rational and religious minds can take seriously. The phenomenological access to Revelation has the same legitimacy as others in terms of religious science, religious sociology, the comparative study of religions. It has the additional privilege that religions most frequently are given as a matter of manifestation, hence of phenomena and of visibility. The question is not *whether* phenomenology can be applied to the question of God or of religions but how it does so and especially *up to what point*.

10. Hans Dieter Gondek and Lázsló Tengélyi, *Neue Phänomenologie in Frankreich* (Berlin: Suhrkamp, 2011).

But you still play a tight game, situated as you are between the phenomenologists on the one side and the theologians on the other. How do you situate yourself vis-à-vis the discipline of theology?

I have indeed played a tight game. But theology raises several preliminary questions and requires much prudence. First, the very term "theology" became established only very late: namely, *grosso modo* in the twelfth century, when Abelard, not without polemics, began to say that he was practicing *theologia*. For beforehand, during the entire great period of what we now retrospectively but very imprecisely call the theology of the Patristic era and of the high Middle Ages, no one used that word—except to link it with paganism, as in Augustine. One should also pay attention to the fact that for twelve centuries Christian thinkers were very careful not to construct a science *concerning* God in the way in which the philosophers spoke without embarrassment *concerning* the world, the soul, the sky, the elements, being, and so forth. This submission of God to logical authority, which turns him into an *object* (or a *subject*, which is not much better) of knowledge seems to coincide approximately with the founding of the universities. Although certain (great) historians of theology were very happy that in the twelfth and thirteenth centuries theology succeeded in laying claim to the title of science (rigorous science, of course!), specialists of the seventeenth century doubt that this was good news for God and for knowledge about him. This suspicion was shared from Saint Bernard to Pascal, via Luther and Rabelais, all the way to Barth and Balthasar. The constitution of a *theology* (or, what amounts to the same, of theology as science) hence raises intrinsic problems of method. It seems prudent to return to them: Does God constitute an object of knowledge like any other, or almost so? What is hidden behind this *almost*? For the case of God, what does knowledge mean, and *who* knows in this matter? What does the saying *noverim me, noverim te* mean?[11]

Furthermore, even the theologians who escaped neo-Scholasticism or neo-Thomism and who do not think of theology as a science have at times only renounced the supposedly Aristotelian framework in order to surround themselves with a transcendental framework. There was a transcendental turn in theology in the modern era, in the form of transcendental Thomism or a kind of neo-Kantianism. The best example of this is Karl

11. [First line of a letter/poem by St. Augustine, which translated means roughly "let me know myself, let me know you."]

Rahner—whatever his greatness, one can all the same argue against his project. But many other theologies made similar choices, some relying on Hegel, some on Marx, some on Russell and Wittgenstein, some on Ernst Bloch and Hans Jonas . . . Every hypothesis was tried out, above all in Germany and in France during the last century. The question does not so much concern an assessment of these choices, which are probably all very interesting, at least within certain limits. Rather it concerns the inevitable suspicion that these renewals of theology all remain profoundly marked by a metaphysical posture where God would emerge as the object of a discourse determined from the outset by a priori conditions of possibility. These are endless variations adopted from a "religion within the limits of reason alone," that is to say, from the metaphysical a priori, whatever form it may take. Maybe the moment has finally come when, since we have to have a philosophical method in theology, we can ask whether one should not at least take it up consciously. Certainly, without conscious philosophical method in theology we either lose our way or we make the most dangerous unconscious assumptions, because in that case we cannot control them. But it is essential for theologians to know to which philosophy they appeal, to be conscious of its limits, and to critique it according to the scope of what is at stake—God.

In this context, phenomenology does not offer the worst solution, not only because for a century it has proven to constitute one of the most fruitful paths; not only because it has already obtained acknowledged results in philosophy of religion (Jean Greisch's assessments relieve me of the need for commentary); but above all because it does not apply any a priori method, indeed only works from and to the benefit of the a posteriori—more like a countermethod than a method. Professional theologians have admittedly so far employed it very sparingly (Balthasar himself was not a hardened philosopher, and, surprisingly, phenomenology had no direct influence on his theology of the *Gestalt*, despite its phenomenal character). But many professional theologians place their hopes in analytical philosophy, although it is full of foolhardiness and approximations. Why leave phenomenology idle when it seems, after all, more highly qualified to speak about revelation and manifestation? This is what I try to suggest, modestly and prudently (for I do not want to leave my role), because there is urgency. I remain patient and optimistic, for the needs of the thing itself always end up enforcing their rigor.

Was it in order to show the relevance of phenomenology for theology that you recently suggested a rereading of Saint Augustine?

Yes. I was granted the responsibility and the honor of giving the Gilson Chair Lectures at the Institut catholique de Paris in December 2004. Instead of repeating myself, I tried to undertake a crucial experiment: What would be the results of a reading of Augustine following the guiding thread of what has been established by the phenomenology of givenness? The point was to compare such a phenomenological reading with the more common readings, whether neo-Thomist, metaphysical, or purely historical. In my opinion, the result was that Augustine, read according to the logic of givenness, becomes more intelligible and more coherent. For although Augustinian studies have developed amazingly in the past fifty years, all the same, since Gilson's great (1928!) book, we have finally read very little of the global ways of approaching him, which attempt to restore the entire coherence of Augustine's thought. I tried my hand at this obviously by turning to the existential analytic of *Being and Time* (and earlier texts), to certain results of the history of philosophy (obviously Descartes and Pascal), to the insights of French phenomenology (Levinas, Ricoeur, Henry), but also to those of the phenomenology of givenness. In short, I made use of everything available to me.

The reaction of Augustine specialists, which was rather positive, was a happy surprise (I am still waiting for those that will follow the American translation). And, as my work continues to be that of a historian of philosophy, I also dissected the secondary literature sufficiently. Consequently, there was no massive rejection on the grounds that I had arrived at absurd results contradicting the work of scholars. The entire thing could be improved, but all in all the experiment has confirmed that, thanks to the hermeneutic tools derived from a phenomenology of the erotic phenomenon or of givenness, there really are possibilities of rereading the history of theology, which would allow us to restore abandoned or underestimated theses and texts.

Moreover, I'm still working on this: At the moment, I am trying to understand the Patristic apologists, Justin and all the second-century authors, who spoke to the emperor during a time of persecution—at an instant when the emperor, for example Marcus Aurelius, assumed the title of philosopher. As a professional philosopher and as a Christian, Justin argues with these emperors who claim to be philosophers in order to prove to them the injustice, but especially the irrationality, of persecuting the Christians. This shape of theology (if one must retain a term that was completely foreign to Justin) is not addressed to Christians or even to Jews but to pagans. It appeals only to rational arguments—because rationality remained the only common link between Christians and pagans—and consists in saying things in Greek that are not Greek, to speak like Levinas. In this case as well, it is a matter of Christian authors who have been entirely marginalized and in some way swallowed up by the theology of the universities from the thirteenth century onward but who today suddenly appear surprisingly powerful, provided that one reads them in all their rigor.

Accordingly, since Idol and Distance, *which devoted important pages to Dionysius, all the way to your current work on Saint Augustine and the Fathers, you continually labor to challenge metaphysical speech about God?*

Yes. The hypothesis can be summarized as follows: The Fathers found themselves in a premetaphysical position, hence not yet in the (metaphysical) situation, in which we probably really are no longer. At the time of the Fathers, metaphysics was not yet constituted as a system; one can reasonably say today that this constitution is accomplished, historically, with Duns Scotus and extends all the way to Nietzsche. The Fathers, for the most part, obviously thought before this system of metaphysics and even without knowing its medieval basis, with Aristotle's corpus and its various successive introductions. We ourselves are beginning to enter into a postmetaphysical situation. Not that we have already freed ourselves from metaphysics or that we really would have overcome it, but at least we can no longer limit ourselves to it and survive by repeating the system and the language of metaphysics. Maybe that allows us to enter into a privileged relationship with the Fathers, providing that the Fathers of the Church are no longer devalued in and by theory.

For there are any number of ways of devaluing the Fathers. For example, by deeming them merely insufficient and imprecise approximations of what will later become metaphysical theology. On this point, I "highly recommend" reading Father Van Steenberghen's preface to the entire work, *Œuvres de saint Augustin*,[12] in the Augustinian Library, who was a pure and hard-lined neo-Thomist of the Louvain School. For him, Augustine obviously remains rather inferior compared to the Scholastics in their precision of terms and in the rigor of concepts; Augustine would even be entirely childish but for his great rhetorical talent, emotion, and literary creativeness, and his writings could even, after all, do some good to souls once they are "corrected" by a good Scholastic annotation. To appropriate

12. *Œuvres de saint Augustin. Première série: opuscules II. L'ascétisme chrétien*, ed. and trans. J. Saint-Martin AA. *Introduction générale à l'édition complète*, ed. F. Cayré and F. Van Steenberghen (Paris: Desclée de Brouwer, 1949).

Léon Brunschvicg's expression concerning Aristotle, Saint Augustine has the mentality of a saint of eight or nine years of age.

First underestimation: to think of the Fathers as vague (even a bit crazy or excessive), as drafts of a truth that the great Scholastics will establish in all its splendor. Hence the second underestimation: The Fathers of the Church only provide Christian variations of neo-Platonism or even of ancient insights. Accordingly, one evokes Christianity's hellenization as common knowledge and self-evident. (The "ignorance" [of this "fact"] by Endre von Ivánka in *Plato christianus* or that of the works of Jean Daniélou or W. Völker is to be highly recommended on this point.) The third underestimation is obviously that of clinging to a purely positivist and historical reading of literary style, of the history of ideas or of dogmas, of psychology, and so forth.

Yet a different hypothesis remains possible: that the Fathers obey an extremely rigorous logic, but one that owes nothing even to Aristotle's *Categories* and that does not speak the language of metaphysics. It is our responsibility to restore it and to find under the apparently neutral, innocent, or surprising terms the operative concepts we lack. That is a project to which I try to contribute today, for it establishes the conditions for reading them seriously. All this reminds me of one of Emmanuel Levinas's comments, who often said that Christians think they are "dialoguing" with Judaism simply by being interested in the Old Testament, yet they completely miss the fact that Judaism does not rely on the Old Testament but on the Talmud. Christians thus do not understand anything because without Talmud there is no Judaism or any Jewish theological thought. Someone asked him why he then "dialogued" with me and he answered: "Marion has his Talmud, namely the Fathers of the Church!"

5. A Matter of Method

History of Philosophy, Philosophy of History

You have said that one can do history of philosophy without doing philosophy at the same time. In what sense can the history of philosophy itself be "philosophizing"?

That's a huge question to which I should return in a more explicit manner some day. Without waiting for that, one can at least point out that, while one can easily write a history of philosophy as a simple appendix to the history of ideas (a thing that is entirely possible; many do it), this raises at least one difficulty: When the history of philosophy is turned into the history of *philosophical ideas*, it loses the distinction between concept and idea, and thus it is no longer a matter of philosophy at all but at best of sociological history. One would then no longer be able to raise the question whether there was a philosophy (or a combination of philosophies) at a particular point in history that displayed the ranges of rationality of the time and described phenomena previously unknown. In the best of cases, one would be able to wonder whether, among the manifold ideas that are passed around like commodities in such a social space, so-called philosophical ideas had more or less influence than ideas identified as theological or just as political opinions, economic claims, artistic polemics, and so forth. But under these circumstances it is a matter of mere history, no longer of the history of philosophy, and, because the focus is on the spread of ideas, the pamphlets against Richelieu matter as much as Descartes's earliest writings or Mersenne's translations of Galileo. I conclude that one can only do history of philosophy by holding on to an appreciation and a living experience of what belongs to philosophy or does not, what it consists of or does not—if just to recognize its presence when it allows itself to be encountered. Just as, in order to study the history of music or of painting, one must know how to pick out those who produce *true* music from among the people who make audible noise and from among those who do visible things those who paint what can be *truly* recognized as a painting.

The choice of a philosophical criterion hence imposes itself for recognizing what is philosophical within history, for pinpointing what in history falls under philosophy. And no one can make this choice except someone who has really practiced philosophy by a sure exercise. Furthermore, the history of philosophy does not dissolve into the history of ideas for another reason: It is used to look for and to identify philosophical theorems (if I can put it this way), in order to reconstruct genuine historical proofs from them, to follow its demonstrations or public and private receptions. This research is decisive because it alone allows the speculative philosopher, who thinks within present reality, to know which historical arguments he still has available, those he must note as established without further discussion, those his personal technique must master. If he does not know the arguments that have already been developed, if he has not gone through the basics, the contemporary philosopher not only will not have available the necessary personal technique for being able to read the ancient texts, but above all he will believe that he is thinking up new arguments and accomplishing great progress while he is actually often just repeating the ancient arguments without knowing it.

There is certainly a classic objection often advanced against the practice of the history of philosophy: A real philosopher is interested in the things themselves and thus has no need for doing history of philosophy, no more so (at least that's the claim) than the mathematician needs to do history of mathematics or the physicist do history of physics. Yet this thesis suffers from several weaknesses. First, every concept a science uses has a history; thus, ignoring this history leads to repeating it blindly, hence potentially to repeating its aporias or omitting desirable corrections from it. Accordingly, one must learn the history of philosophy, if only, I repeat, like a chess player learns the great games played by the great historical masters: One gains time when one can immediately identify a typical situation, foresee far-off consequences of a particular opportunity, know where some kind of attack might lead, what endgame is on the horizon. When there is only one way of playing well, one might as well know it in advance. Many philosophers do not do history of philosophy, because they believe thereby to be doing *more* philosophy, but actually they are doing *less* of it. This is so because not having the map available that would keep them from losing their way, they either get lost or wear themselves out by groping about in some vague fashion. Accordingly, the history of philosophy remains an indispensable education in the spelling, grammar, and especially the semantics of philosophy as such.

Finally and above all, philosophy cannot be constituted like a regional science because there is no single field that would be the region of philosophy as there is a field for molecular biology, for the physics of fluids, or for the banking economy—the genre of a science, Aristotle says. Philosophy must create that of which it speaks because it cannot presuppose it as a field, a region, or a genre already available. Aristotle frequently reminds us that being is not a genre. There is certainly a science that considers being *as being*, but it discusses this being as a being no one has ever seen, for there is no being as being; there are only beings as other things, as *one* thing, for example as a tree, as a living being, as a stone, as a god. But never being as being. There is nothing surprising about this; being as being is not about a state of fact but results from the effect of a gaze, of an act of interpretation, of a kind of vision, which causes it to appear. Being as being results from Aristotle's interpretation, just as the object as a known thing certainly results from Descartes's intention or as the phenomenon as a synthesis of the manifold of intuition under the a priori unity of the concept via apperception belongs to Kant's design. If philosophy hence arises from what it makes manifest and from what it discusses by means of a preparatory operation launching everything else, then to declare that philosophy has nothing preparatory and that it has no need for its history is consequently to act as if that of which philosophy speaks would naturally be found in easy reach, spread out before us, accessible at every step.

Yet that is never the case: In philosophy, the early stages are decisive (and decide almost everything). To pay no heed to this not only means to sink into the one-sided positivism of "common sense," which is all of a sudden regarded as sacred, but above all it leads to a loss of the right, the need, and the meaning of philosophy. If there is no working angle or some way of seeing that would allow philosophy's appointed task to emerge, then philosophy as a whole disappears. It evaporates into the history of ideas, it disappears into the euthanasia of questions supposedly badly asked, it disappears in the boredom of trivial obvious facts without knowing it. For example, one begins to think that there is nothing more innocent and nothing simpler than doing an ontology of the object, without realizing the considerable historical burden of *ontology* and of *object*. Therefore, far from surpassing the common aporias of metaphysics, one repeats them all the more strongly and seriously because one does not even see them.

Yet beyond this primarily methodological function of the history of philosophy, can one not also introduce history into philosophy, as Hegel or Heidegger did, by showing that philosophy itself is unfolded as history?

Definitely. One can and must take the history of philosophy as a proof of the historical nature of philosophy itself. Some people who were not great philosophers (Cicero, Voltaire, and some others) have claimed repeatedly, as a reproach against philosophy, that there is no foolishness that has not been upheld by a philosopher. For in fact, one can always blame philosophy for being delusional or for contradicting itself. Why are there many philosophies, if not because not one of them is true? One can respond to this quite commonsensical objection that philosophy is historical and hence that the succession of teachings itself follows a logical but historically determined order. The history of teachings does not give a simple reduction ratio or a contradictory dissipation of philosophy but an organic development of one philosophy after another. A philosophy is not so much contradicted by the one following it than it is *made possible* by the one preceding it, or it is highlighted by the contrast with an alternative theoretical possibility.

It is therefore right to maintain that philosophy develops intrinsically and essentially as a history. The historicity of philosophy remains a thesis about philosophy. Nevertheless, this historicity itself can be philosophically extended in various ways. Hegel's version (historicity of being completed) coincides neither with Nietzsche's (or Gilson's: historicity of waning away) nor with that of Heidegger (historicity of destiny, coming from a sending, *Geschichte* via *Geschick*). One can cite other views about the development of philosophy, which are more facile because they are derived from others: Kant's view and that of the Enlightenment thinkers about a limited but continuous progress of philosophy toward abstract rationality. Or, in contrast, the pretension of a sacrosanct and eternal philosophy, the *philosophia perennis*. (One should point out that even this supposedly eternal philosophy had a historical situation: The *De perenni philosophia* was published in Lyon in 1540 by a Catholic bishop, Agostino Steuco, who had come from

Crete to Rome, where he ran the Vatican library.) But what is in my opinion most important is the fact that a philosophical practice without history of philosophy induces an ignorance of previous arguments in such a way that it makes us blind to the path we are following or, rather, that it causes us to follow no path at all and even has as a result that we do not know that we are lost. I have often noticed this when teaching in the United States.

Is this a critique of "analytic philosophy"?

I'm not criticizing analytic philosophy (which, besides, itself practices the history of *its* philosophy and of *its* concepts but deals with too short a historical period, or else, when it goes back to Locke or Aristotle, without assuming long-term continuities; anyway, I don't really criticize it as much as I prefer a different, more powerful, and more coherent option). Instead I mean the way of teaching philosophy in the Anglo-Saxon world, which, besides, is spreading everywhere like an epidemic: working with translations, with select extracts, and not with the original texts; not trying to understand what the author wanted to show or possibly what his opponents wanted to resist but amusing oneself by messing about and making up arbitrary arguments for blocking those of one's neighbor; then, once one takes one's argument to be personal and portable, removing it from the text and the context, parading it, using it everywhere, triumphing recklessly, reestablishing philosophy from square one, and so on, one after the other. The consequences are obviously disastrous: In particular, in order to assure the polemical victory, one cheats by attributing positions to the respective authors that they never held, one transforms them into simple labels for identifying contemporary positions, and so forth. Great confusion ensues, where very quickly one no longer knows exactly what one is speaking about. Actually, one no longer speaks of anything at all.

But then, to what do you think you owe the important success of your books in the Anglo-Saxon world?

The Anglo-Saxon world, as one says, obeys the laws of the market, and that has at least one positive consequence: Those who really work (and many truly work) are interested in what they do not spontaneously produce themselves; thus they do not hesitate to import what they cannot make locally, such as philosophers who do the history of philosophy or do philosophy that is not typically American, obviously provided that they respect the customs, take the trouble of erecting debatable arguments, and speak

English. Certainly, it is still correct that said Anglo-Saxon world is the privileged place where what we call somewhat simplistically analytical philosophy is developed (there are actually several by now quite diverse analytical philosoph*ies*), but it is also the place where what the Anglo-Saxons call continental philosophy is practiced on a large scale, notably the history of philosophy as we conceive it and French phenomenology. Too often we retain a reductive and narrow view of the Anglo-Saxon world: In truth, all the great universities include "continental" philosophers, though certainly often not very many of them. Finally, experience has convinced me that Americans, even when one is before a public unfamiliar with phenomenology or the history of philosophy, will be ready to debate, as long as one has the patience to construct an argument without settling for the authority of citations or for seductive vaticination (which often serves as proof for some Europeans). Nothing is forbidden or unable to be heard, as long as it is demonstrated. In this sense, America censures much less than France.

As regards "analytical philosophy," I do not have the reservations on principle toward it that are in vogue in some parts of the French philosophical community. Admittedly, there is more bad than good in what I know of this immense and often repetitive field, but every now and then some excellent things emerge that one must immediately try to salvage. I don't hesitate to appeal to it when I find solid arguments there, even including some for interpreting Descartes's texts. For example, the theory of speech acts obviously constitutes an asset indispensable for phenomenology or the history of philosophy. In any case, the recent history of philosophy has shown that phenomenology and analytical philosophy share the same origin: the debates within neo-Kantianism around, in, and after the Marburg school, at the end of the nineteenth century and at the beginning of the twentieth. The origin remains shared despite the oppositions of persons or of institutions, and, by right, we should be able to move about from one extreme to the other.

*What can be the contribution of phenomenology for the historian of philosophy? I recall having heard you say one day: "In the history of philosophy, one is Heideggerian or anti-Heideggerian, which is to say, still Heideggerian; the others just take notes [*font des fiches*]!" What exactly did you want to say?*

That was exaggerated, as usual, but I'll take it on! The history of philosophy is indispensable—namely, for doing philosophy: If it is not for doing philosophy, it is not worth an hour of trouble, in contrast to the history of ideas. Only the philosophical intention justifies the interest in the history of philosophy. We can obviously occupy ourselves with reconstituting the systems, with studying a historical period, with taking notes: There is certainly nothing more legitimate or even more necessary, and I always spend some time there, but this only becomes completely enjoyable when there are speculative stakes.

One must aim for the accuracy of information—we can even dream about exhaustiveness—but, as to the truth of the thing itself, knowing Kepler's years of training in detail or Mersenne's development in his monumental correspondence does not provide anything in itself if you are not guided by a question. Therefore, to do history of philosophy, one must have, I don't want to say a philosophical *position*, but a *horizon* or a *question* concerned with philosophy; after all, one can reconstitute the great chess games very precisely without ever comprehending why the players chose this move rather than that one. This is what happens to certain historians of philosophy or to some historians of science: They can reconstitute what the protagonists in the debate say without really seeing what they were in the process of discovering. Thus, one should always have some stake in mind, some question not yet resolved; in other words, we cannot do without philosophy if we want to do the history of philosophy. Yet the questions raised by phenomenology are the ones currently giving life to research. Hegel was able to read the preceding philosophy from a metaphysical point of view, for that was the philosophy for him that made thought come to life, but we cannot reread philosophy as if a Hegelian, hence metaphysical, point of view defines our present. One can obviously celebrate Waterloo or Austerlitz by dressing up once a year as Austrian, French, Russian, or English soldiers, but that remains a historical reconstruction; in the same way, one can always write philosophy from a Kantian, Hegelian, or even Marburgian point of view, but today that has mere documentary interest. The history of philosophy does not need to open a wax museum of concepts.

Yet it is a fact that very often we raise philosophical questions—obviously not exclusively—thanks to contemporary phenomenologists. The questions raised by phenomenology (What is a phenomenon? How can such a phenomenon be manifested?) can perfectly well be discovered to be operative in the ancient texts; one can even definitely show that these ancient texts already confront them in their own way. It is obviously no coincidence that the scholarly inquiries regarding the emergence of the word and the concept of "metaphysics," its link with first philosophy or the imposition of the notion of "ontology," for example, led to the moment when a new global model of interpretation of philosophy as metaphysics was speculatively put in place by Heidegger. The latter raised the theoretical question of metaphysics by overinterpreting the Kantian concept of onto-theo-logy, and this theoretical question reflected back on investigations that the history of philosophy henceforth found itself in a position to consider. For, most frequently, we owe it to a theoretical rupture to be able to reread the history of philosophy in a new light and with new stakes. It is no insult to Aristotle to say that he gained a lot from *Being and Time* (and from other German critics, of whom Heidegger was heir) because the reading of the *Metaphysics* has benefited from the Heideggerian radicalization of the question of Being. Henry, via his surprising teaching of auto-affection, has made possible a completely remarkable rereading of Descartes but also of Malebranche, of Kant, or of Nietzsche, just as he also renewed the reading of Marx. In some way, Levinas has made us rediscover and reevaluate the idea of the infinite as it was suggested by Descartes in still an enigmatic form, almost like an aporia. In the same way, we can (or we could, for the undertaking is barely sketched so far) have a history of philosophy starting from the early and certainly the later Wittgenstein.

In this way, the history of philosophy finds itself ceaselessly raised up [*suscitée*], even resurrected [*resuscitée*], by the gaze, guided by a present philosophical inquiry, resting on ancient texts, which suddenly themselves become again philosophical and no longer documentary. It is then starting from living philosophy such as it is unfolded with its unanswerable questions that the texts recover their profundity and breathe anew. Otherwise, the history of philosophy exhausts itself in a history of ideas, for no conceptual breath still wafts across it. The history of philosophy does not belong to the department of history but to the department of philosophy.

Certainly, phenomenology gives philosophy its stakes and its questions, but, conversely, is there not some paradox in including the history of philosophy into phenomenology because the latter claims to describe the things themselves? When you describe the erotic phenomenon, you yourself announce that you will not work from the authors of the philosophical tradition and that the description of the erotic phenomenon can in some way do without an investigation of the history of philosophy. Would the phenomenological description not have to do without the history of philosophy?

I do not believe so. I do not think that there is a break between phenomenological description, which would remain ahistorical and synchronic, and the history of philosophy, which would be exclusively diachronic. One of the ways of performing a phenomenological reduction, that is to say, of distinguishing between what is truly given and what remains inferred, added on, or reconstructed, consists precisely in using all the conceptual distinctions *already* elaborated by the tradition; in fact, they allow us to refine the reduction: I can make reductions because I know already where to apply the blade in order to cut correctly; if not, I do not even see that there is a possibility of a reduction. To display the teaching of the reduction, even Husserl undertakes a historical trajectory in *First Philosophy* in order to discover that the reduction was already in some way present in Cartesian doubt, in Hume, in Fichte. There is always a moment where the reduction is found in outline, in anticipation, and we can—by acknowledging it or not—summon up sketches of the reduction that we have to do.

In the case of *The Erotic Phenomenon*, for example, when I described the aporia of the first question "Does anyone love me?" and when I showed that the desire to become loved by the other admits that we do not love ourselves, I summoned Hobbes and Spinoza, the principle of persistence in one's being (*conatus in suo esse perseverandi*), hatred, and the classic seventeenth-century debates about the status of self-love or pride [*amour-propre*]. Although my distinctions and my arguments were formulated without historical references, they really belonged already to the history of philosophy even if they were not at all organized deliberately.

Another example: To support that the erotic phenomenon allows one to think the origin of the ego, we must take up again the Cartesian doctrine of the ego as *res cogitans* and distinguish between its different modalities. Otherwise we would not be able to understand the potentially radical nature of a loving ego, equivalent to a cogitating ego, yet taking place according to a different modality. The historical exercise thus makes the reductions much more effective, precise, and radical. To remain imprecise or perfunctory in phenomenological decisions is never a good solution, and the history of philosophy helps prevent us from thinking that we have gone to the very end of a reduction when we in fact only cursorily sketched it. There is, then, an exchange: The history of philosophy gives concepts to phenomenology that are ready for use for the distinctions that require the reduction, but the concepts and the descriptions of phenomenology can perfectly well reflect back on our reading of the ancient texts.

What do you say to the critics who reproach you with proposing too forceful an interpretation of Descartes or even one that begins to lose Descartes himself from view?

To understand a philosopher does not mean only or even probably first of all to try to reconstitute what question he strictly had in mind, whether consciously or explicitly: "He said this and he said it well because a great philosopher thinks what he says and says what he thinks." In principle, we should be able to understand without too much difficulty what he has already made explicit. Understanding him (according to the hermeneutic principle that the interpreter must understand what is interpreted *better* than the author understood it and himself) means instead to pose questions to him that were not *exactly* his. For, often, in trying to respond to a question he believed to have clearly in mind, the philosopher has found the response to a *different* question that maybe he did not see. That is why it can become very pertinent to take a philosopher a little bit the wrong way, at a tangent. I fully accept the idea that questionings or rereadings of a philosopher can come from problems entirely foreign to him because they are contemporary to us.

Who would dispute that Kant has very frequently been read starting from entirely contemporary epistemological questions, just as we still read Hegel to the extent that we think that notions of dialectic, of negativity, or of historicity still retain a crucial validity today? Does this insult Kant or Hegel, or does it pay them tribute? Certainly, these retrospective questions always impose a displacement in regard to the ideal point of view that the author himself had—supposing that one could reconstitute this point of view. Is this displacement illegitimate? Once again, a generally admitted hermeneutic principle posits that a good interpretation allows us to understand the author *better* than he understood himself, which is the reason why hermeneutics remains a serious endeavor; if it were on principle not possible to understand the author better than he understood himself, then we would in all honesty have to stop interpreting authors and instead learn them by heart. Otherwise, it is left for us to effect knowingly a reevaluation or an overestimation of an author, either by addressing a question to him that was maybe not his (is that not, after all, the definition of a true question?) but to which we think he could respond (overestimation) or by maintaining that, if we have something to learn from him, he himself also gains from hearing our question (reevaluation). This is what we think when we read an author philosophically.

The question is then no longer about the displacement of supposedly authentic questions of the author by our own questions but about knowing how far is too far. The answer to this excellent question appears relatively straightforward to me: It is enough to see whether this new question addressed to the author does or does not allow us to *reinforce* our understanding of the text in detail, to ask oneself whether the elements or the passages of the text that have so far remained incomprehensible or of an appalling triviality suddenly become clear and crucial. *On Descartes' Metaphysical Prism* precisely presents the example of one of the books where I enter into the text in the most detail: I explain, for example, why Descartes was really right to prefer the title *Meditations on First Philosophy* rather than that of *Metaphysical Meditations* (as the [French] translation says). Or also, by bringing to light an onto-theo-logy of the cause and an onto-theo-logy of cogitation, which has at times been denounced as an arbitrary construction imposed on the text but actually manages to explain a lexical fact that the entire world could have noticed beforehand but that no one had picked up on or understood: the textual fact that Descartes never uses the word "cause" in the *Meditations* before the first proof of the existence of God, no more than the word "substance." These two words appear together for the first time on page 40 in the seventh volume of the collected works,[1] indicating, among other results, the introduction of a new vocabulary, thus of a new beginning and a revival of the order of reasons, henceforth intelligible and justified by the overlapping of the first onto-theo-logy (without cause) by the second (with cause) on this precise page. These are obvious philological facts, which had all the same not been noticed. Why? Not at all because we did not have the concordance (the passage is so brief that one passes over it, and, anyway, one can read without a concordance) but because one did not ask oneself the question. Why did one not ask oneself the question? Because one did not have the general schema, in this case that of a double onto-theo-logy. In the same way, the classical question whether the Cartesian ego is like a substance or not only appeared after Kant's, Husserl's, and Heidegger's analyses; it is no accident that it is on this occasion that *On Descartes' Metaphysical Prism* remarks that the existence of the ego in the "Second Meditation" does not (yet) resort to the word "substance" because the first onto-theo-logy, that of cogitation, still has no need for it. When apparently arbitrary models allow us to unshackle a more precise meaning of a detail of the text, they are no longer arbitrary but intelligent.

Starting Off from Far Away in Order to See More Closely

But what, then, is the right distance for reading a text?

My experience is that, paradoxically, the further away the hypotheses arise, the more profoundly they can go into the text. For example, in Descartes's

1. AT VII = Charles Adam and Paul Tannery, *Oeuvres de Descartes*, rev. ed., ed. P. Costable and B. Rochot (Paris: Vrin/CNRS, 1966).

Rules for the Direction of the Mind, it is crucial not to translate *mathesis universalis* by "universal mathematics": It is not enough that Descartes himself points this out explicitly; one must also know more generally the role of mathematics according to Plato and their ontic status according to Aristotle. The study of long-term references often justifies the interpretation of the details of the text. If, jumping from a running start, you manage to land on the detail of the text more precisely than if you had strolled into it without seeing anything, you know that it was a good idea to jump. Very often, one must come from afar because a completely immanent reading of an author by definition cannot reach the *hapax*, or the displacement, which only makes sense compared to another author or to another case come from afar. Furthermore, that is why the history of philosophy only becomes possible by comparison. Without comparisons between one philosopher and another, one cannot see what new thing one brings and what he displaces in regard to another. In short, to understand Descartes, one must compare him to his successors and to his predecessors.

One can then not reconstitute Descartes from the inside by speaking from Descartes's own point of view?

The commentator's problem stems from the fact that he is never anywhere near as good a philosopher as the one on whom he is commenting. He thus constantly needs to maintain the principle that the interpreted thinker thinks more deeply and more correctly than his interpreter, and, paradoxically, this is especially the case if the interpreter has the ambition of understanding the author better than the author understood himself. One should thus always assume that the person interpreted knows far more things than the commentators believe; by dint of working on Descartes, I have become convinced that he knew medieval thought far better than the majority of his modern readers. One keeps repeating of Saint Augustine that he did not know any Greek . . . Let us not exaggerate. He certainly knew more of it than many Augustine specialists themselves know; besides, he makes all the necessary distinctions in Greek and in Hebrew as they seem necessary. A little modesty never hurt.

One can put it differently, too: We still today read such and such an ancient thinker because we admit his speculative genius, his innovative inventiveness. What can the commentator hope for before this superior force of the interpreted thinker? Above all, he or she must continually apply what the analytical thinkers call the "principle of charity": Not to reduce an author to the limit of his own understanding, not to attribute to him an obscurity, a contradiction, or an inconsistency every time that one does not grasp his argument. Then, one must ask for help, first of the author himself (by searching for parallels to an obscure passage), then of philology (by verifying the text in question, pinpointing whether it is a matter of an implicit citation from another author, etc.), and, finally, by searching how other philosophers, they also apparently brilliant and hence more qualified than the perplexed commentator, have understood the accused text. For they must know at least a little better than we do on what it turns. When Spinoza or Leibniz criticize or approve of Descartes, maybe they are wrong or maybe they are right, but in any case they merit our paying great attention to their remarks. On principle, until proof to the contrary has been given, they are worth more than the commentators on philosophy. Even if the philosopher exaggerates, as one says (Heidegger, for example), or is not necessarily right (Husserl, for example), at the end of the day his analysis illuminates more than a supposedly erudite platitude.

To return to an example already cited, I have never found anything better for understanding Descartes's doctrine of substance than this admirable remark by Nietzsche: "The concept of substance is a consequence of the concept of the subject: not the reverse!"[2] This is exactly what happens in Descartes, and it is the best way to respond to Kant's critique of him. This is a phrase that Nietzsche wrote maybe without thinking in particular of Descartes but which even so in one go helps us understand the Cartesian transformation of the concept of substance, which anticipates Kant's (which Kant himself does not see). Thus, there is much more to this phrase, tossed out in passing by Nietzsche, than in all the conventional books that condemn the supposed substantialization of the Cartesian ego. We can derive from this the final principle for the practice of the history of philosophy: The great philosophers who follow on another great philosopher are the first and often the best historians of philosophy. One could go even further and recover Jean Beaufret's paradox: One must not only read the successors of a philosopher as his commentators but almost read his predecessors as so many commentators. Let's not forget it: Aristotle had read Descartes, and Descartes had read Kant, *obviously, obviously.*

In On Descartes' Metaphysical Prism *you use the concept of onto-theo-logy not as a thesis but as a model that you can put to work by applying it to the text so as to measure what enters into this framework or what is excluded from it. Is that not a somewhat structural or structuralist approach to the texts?*

2. Nietzsche, *Will to Power*, §162; Marion's translation.

Why not? In fact, it does not seem useless to me to remain a little structuralist, on the condition that it is a matter of models employed with the reservation of an *as if*, not a matter of structures imposed ideologically. Besides, onto-theo-logy remains practically a model employed *as if* by Heidegger. He borrows the term from Schopenhauer and especially from Kant in order to redirect and utilize it, so as to show the articulation of two senses of the principle in metaphysics: On the one hand, the founding principle (reason, sometimes cause) of all beings, as the mode of Being of all the beings as beings by a privileged being (theo-logy); on the other hand, the logical principle by which all the beings, here including the privileged founding being, illustrate and depend on a universal definition of beingness of being (onto-logy). This doubled foundation, in the manner of a self-sufficient circle, characterizes the systematic closure of metaphysics on itself. This closure itself constitutes the power of metaphysics but also its flaw: The question of the *Being* [*l'être*] of being [*l'étant*], taken in onto-logy, taken up again in theo-logy, will always have a response, but a response that will still say only *being* [*l'étant*]. To the question "What is Being [*l'être*]?" metaphysics responds that "Being is the being that causes it—the supreme being" or rather and also that "Being is what logically grounds all the beings, that is, the definition of being." In any case, *being* decides the truth of *Being*—the forgetting of Being. Heidegger wanted to think this closure of metaphysics, which is forgetful of Being, in the unity of a concept of being: Little by little he establishes this model and uses it with caution, above all starting from Hegel, without entering into the details and without measuring the violence of his approach. He applies it to Nietzsche and to Leibniz without going much further or determining to which point to make it revert. Obviously, he keeps in mind the debate (launched by Werner Jaeger) about the two rival definitions of philosophy in Aristotle: a theology or a doctrine of being as being. He appreciates the ambiguity of titles of philosophy: *prima philosophia*, metaphysics, ontology, science of being as being, science of problems and of principles, and so forth. Nevertheless, very prudently, he does not decide whether Aristotle already accomplishes an onto-theo-logy. His use of the term hence remains close enough to what you understand by model.

As concerns me, I had not considered onto-theo-logy as a thesis, for I did not use this concept in order to unify metaphysics but for testing its model. I wondered how far back in history this model of onto-theo-logy could function. Can it be modified in order to make intelligible not Descartes's supposed incoherence but just simply his nonmonolithic character, in short, the absence of a system in Descartes according to the order of reasons—or is it then a matter of reason*s*, really in the plural, which change and must be articulated one after the other? For the double onto-theo-logy certainly does not constitute a new system of Descartes but exactly the opposite: It consists in explaining, by the doubling of the model, what otherwise would remain an incoherence. Let's go back to the massive difficulty evoked above: In the name of natural light, Descartes introduces new reasons into the "Third Meditation" (the principle of causality and the hierarchy between accident and substance, then between finite substance and infinite substance) without having them validated by the test of doubt, as if the natural light validated itself. How should we understand this new beginning? Two choices seem possible: Either it is a matter of an incoherence that one will conceal by imagining a homogenous order of reasons, or one admits a cut that is explained by the move from one onto-theo-logy to another, and according to this hypothesis one understands why there is a competition of the two first principles possible in Descartes, something the history of post-Cartesian philosophy has validated to a great extent. And onto-theo-logy then becomes an operative model that one modifies and complicates as necessary but that, in the end, produces more intelligibility in the detail of Descartes's text.

As you yourself have recognized you thus privilege the lectio difficilior *compared to the* lectio facilior, *that is to say, a reading that does not try to silence the difficulties of the text.*

This is in fact a crucial rule because, quite obviously, the more an interpretation can help us understand a textual difficulty that seems at first glance insoluble, the more it proves its power. One must also begin by acknowledging the difficulties and above all not erase them by straight out correcting the text: Alquié insisted on this and practiced this rule more than others. More than Derrida, who was a very fine reader but not always enough of a historian of philosophy. He had a propensity for seeing difficulties where the text did not present them and to skip over those that were present (during the debate about the supposedly "negative theology," he clearly did not have the texts in mind very well). More than Heidegger, for whom the relevance depended on the authors and on the dignity he granted them. It is really Alquié who taught me to see the contradictions of an author and to try to make positive use of them. I think of his making explicit the discrepancies inside the *Ethics*, or between the *Ethics* and the *Short Treatise*, or between the different editions of the *Short Treatise*. I also meet up again with Beaufret, who warned: "If one understands everything, it means that one has not understood anything."

Philosophy, Literature, and Painting

You said that philosophy does not have its own proper object but that it must be fed by other disciplines. What are those disciplines, and what kind of link must philosophy establish with them?

Since the Greeks and all the way to Husserl (and Russell), philosophy seems to have been inspired and captivated by another way of knowing, namely mathematics. The idea of rigorous science modeled on mathematics has lived on through its entire history and has shaped its fate especially: The fact that philosophy had essentially tied its project to a different discipline no longer needs to be demonstrated. The real problem is a different one (and one must acknowledge that we owe this reversal also to Heidegger more than to Bergson): Has not the authority and weight of the mathematical paradigm—that is, the paradigm of the sciences, of *the* science—in philosophy had as a repercussion that it turned philosophy into metaphysics? Or, conversely, has not the innate tendency of philosophy to turn to metaphysics provoked its mimicking of mathematics? The two hypotheses can also strengthen each other. Consequently, the question could be modified to ask whether there would not be other disciplines that could lay claim to an essential, historical, and documented link with philosophy, which would then all of a sudden help free it from the fascination with the mathematical paradigm of rigorous science. In this way, the principle formulated by many philosophers, especially philosophers of science, according to which philosophy must always know and work on something other than philosophy, seems perfectly accurate. Even so, must this principle go all the way to turning philosophy into the *ancilla* of the sciences and the commentator on their results? Some of the best philosophers have let us think this. I am not convinced of it because it seems to me that the real problem consists in determining *what* the philosopher must profitably learn elsewhere and then *from which* disciplines he can expect it.

For my part, I would insist on three areas: theology, painting, and, more broadly, language. I think of theology, whose link with philosophy goes very far back and which also faces up to the question of manifestation, under the name of Revelation. Thus, it shares the same ordeal with philosophy and especially with phenomenology: to say and to explain what it observes appearing. Yet the conflict between the faculties, which is itself also very ancient, and the difference in territories, a difference that has not yet been much clarified, makes the alliance too ambiguous and, as we have seen, full of polemics.

Second, I think of painting, which today finds itself, sometimes reluctantly, loaded with the weight of visibility—not with the visibility of what shows itself by itself spontaneously but with a visibility, one might say, stirred up although not produced, provoked in the erotic sense but not manufactured by a production. The difficulty here has to do with the reluctance of painters to speak about what they are seeing (except to speak in order to get out of seeing and making visible), one that has no equal except the philosophers' bad sight. In both cases, the cause of visibility becomes badly defended or, rather, becomes too much the prisoner of its defenders.

Finally, we must think of language [*au langage*] or, rather, of tongues [*à la langue*].[3] First, because its link with literature defines the history of philosophy essentially, because philosophy only forms its vocabulary by redirecting so-called natural language [*langue*], that of work and life, that of the poets, toward a formalized vocabulary. This question of redirection increases all the more today as we treat language [*langage*] increasingly as simply a means of transmitting information, means that in the end would have to control (and submerge) artificial tongues [*langues*]. Finally, at the same time, philosophy notices that it can no longer limit itself to speaking the language of metaphysics, which is powerless to permit an ever larger portion of phenomenality to be said (and hence to be manifested)—namely, the most decisive or fascinating portion. But at the same time philosophy either does not own up to the disqualification of the language of metaphysics or remains unable to speak a different language.

Do all these symptoms concern a crisis of language [*langage*]? In fact, they concern a deeper crisis, a crisis of tongues [*langue*]—or rather the crisis created by the decisions of linguists to separate, for the needs of objectness, *langage* (object of a theory and which no one speaks or reads or writes) from *langue* (which itself also remains an abstraction because actually there are only *plural* tongues [*des langues*], which are alone really practiced) and speech [*la parole*] (which alone resounds and is audible, alone refers to voice, alone becomes flesh and alone is real). The influence of logic has broken up these three aspects of a single word [*verbe*]. One must hence

3. [Both *langage* and *langue* mean language. I use the less common "tongue"—as in the "tongue" of a people—here in order to distinguish them in the text. Marion comments on the French distinction in the next couple of paragraphs.]

become able to question this dismantling by beginning to doubt language [*langage*], to the effect that the word should be interpreted as a predicative act that does not say anything other than something about something and does not say it to anyone, by no one, in no tongue [*langue*]. What good is this supposed language? Can it be used for saying something about something or saying it from someone to someone? And can one not, when one speaks to *someone*, precisely *not* speak to him or her of something, even less predicate him something of something? Finally, can we not speak to someone *about nothing* and when doing so speak to him much more successfully because, in that case, we direct ourselves directly to him?

Pragmatics has begun to describe this play on words, but philosophy is still above all preoccupied with the prediction and the homage it always pays to objectness. It only barely suspects that the fundamental function of what should no longer be called *le langage* or even *la langue* but word [*le verbe*] is practiced in speech [*la parole*] as an act of address.[4] The address or the word is directed to the other, not loaded down with any object. It can therefore do what it is saying by saying it, which coincides sufficiently with the self to be confirmed by itself. But we are still students of Saussure and of his strange operation, linguistics, which chooses to distinguish between speech (and the truly natural tongues) and language. The characteristic of language consists in not existing, in not being said or heard, but in producing an object for linguistics: language *in itself*, universal structures that are not connected to any natural tongue or to any exercise of speech at all. Obviously, one can formalize such an artifact via computers and transmit information in this way, but it no longer has anything of the power of the word: It does not say anything (in the sense that it does not give rise to anything); it is not addressed to anyone (it can thus "inform" everyone). Furthermore, the revolution in information technology, the manufacturing of automatic languages, the flood of pieces of information are about an extremely reduced layer of the phenomenon of the *logos*. And they uniquely bear witness to the metaphysical disappearance of the word.

What *logos* remains a *logos* without being mobilized into the service of predication? Aristotle responded to this question in the treatise *On Interpretation*: A *logos* that does not say anything of anything but still declares is called a prayer. For, de facto, prayer is addressed, addresses a call to someone. Prayer is the *addressed logos*.

4. [Both *le verbe* and *la parole* mean "word" in English, although *parole* often refers to spoken word or speech. *L'acte de l'adresse* could also be translated as "act of speech."]

What resources can literature or poetry recover for philosophy? For example, must we say that poetry shows the world better than we see it?

Let's avoid talking hot air! I've read many poets who neither saw nor showed anything at all. The majority of poets remain average poets who don't show a whole lot; even the greatest don't always succeed in showing. Each poem gives it a shot, but only some, in fact, have the capacity to help us see, while others show nothing. Recently, I was interpreting a poem by Baudelaire, "To a Passer-By" ["*À une passante*"]: The event actually unfolds in it, in the movement of the woman passing by, which is shown and even actualized by the poem. But Char himself does not always show; sometimes he even shuts the horizon. Rimbaud, Mallarmé, or Claudel are able to allow us to see better and more, provided that one makes the effort to *realize* what the words suggest, for when the poet speaks there is no need for what one *sees* to be what he or she sees. Very often, one does not see anything at all because one does not listen carefully enough or does not *realize* what one reads. A labor of reading is thus required, for which the philosophers are not the least gifted.

That being said, I'll make several obvious remarks. First, left to itself philosophy dies from the narrowness of its own formalized and thus repetitive and exhausted language, as the language of metaphysics inevitably tends to become. This expression, "language of metaphysics," is neither vague nor polemical. For the language of metaphysics, this kind of cancerous outgrowth of Aristotle's categories, encoded and redundant, finds its way all the better as the thinkers try saying something about it that so far has been silenced by the tradition—and, like Bergson or Husserl, fail at it. Therefore, only poetry, especially when it comes from a bit further away or sounds a bit old-fashioned, has sufficiently powerful and rich lexical resources available to shatter the metaphysical vault of the philosophers. To read Ronsard or Rabelais, Montaigne or Scevius thus becomes a measure for linguistic health. It is enough to compare the (double) language of Descartes to that of Malebranche to see immediately who speaks freely and who thinks inside of the box.

You alluded to the importance of painting in philosophical practice. You yourself were interested in it very early on. In your opinion, what is its contribution to philosophical work?

Painting obviously helps the philosopher do his or her work. Philosophers don't have to become art historians, except in a minor way and on an ad hoc

Gustave Courbet, *The Painter's Studio: An Allegory* (1854–1855). Oil on canvas, 361 × 598 cm. Photo: Hervé Lewandowski. Musée d'Orsee, Paris, France, © RMN–Grand Palais/Art Resource, NY.

basis. And it is not necessary that they claim to become art historians, especially as it is not always art historians or museographers who best speak of art. To know everything about the conditions of the composition of a painting, about its history, its sociological significance, its codes, tells us a lot, but it does not help us see it.

Let's take the case of a well-known and frequently interpreted painting: Gustave Courbet's *The Painter's Studio*. We have admirable scholarly investigations available that allow us to identify with near certainty all the persons in it, reconstructing their symbolic role, their mutual relationships and political background, and so forth. An impressive result. But what this painting wants and manages to show in the clearest manner is that all these characters actually stay pure phantoms, unreal, except in the painter's imagination. In contrast, the only thing that is real in the painting is not even identified with the model, because this woman looks at a painting that the painter in the picture paints. The model looks at the painting in the painting. Similarly, the painter, who should look at the model, looks at his painting, and the child (of the painter? of the model?) does not look at its little white cat but also gazes at the painting of the painting. And what does that painting show? Neither the model, nor anything of what the real painting depicts in the studio, but a landscape—a landscape that itself comes out of nowhere because it is always found in the studio, where no river flows in any valley. In this way, the landscape without model remains the only real thing, the only "thinglike" thing, appearing from itself. The landscape, the painting in the painting, albeit purely imaginary, has invalidated everything else. The painting thus functions by withdrawing by and for the painting in the painting. What one knows about the central painting has finally no importance at all: The only real thing of the great painting is what disappears faced with the only reality of the painting, the painting within the painting. Under these conditions, one sees quite well what must be understood and what Courbet wants to show. He himself speaks of a "real allegory," and one couldn't put it any better. The landscape, that is, the little painting in the bigger one, engulfs the big one, even though in principle the little painting should be contained within the big one. And that's the sole thing the painting wants to show! To proceed in this way amounts to unfolding a kind of reduction because we think we see what seems given to us while actually what is really given to us is the heart of the Loue valley: the landscape is more real than the society.

But, more generally, why do you have this passion for Courbet?

Most probably because I have a personal account to settle with him: He is my hometown painter, and for a long time I did not understand him, thinking him a minor painter. For me, he was a painter of villages, actually of the village that is about eleven kilometers [about seven miles] from mine. It took me forty years and a great number of visits to American and Japanese museums to notice that he was really not at all a second-rate painter. At that point, I took an interest in the matter, almost out of courtesy, and I very quickly discovered that the commentary on Courbet offered the typical example of a complete disconnect between a painter and what one says about him, between the analysis of an oeuvre and what its author truly desired and made. And this misunderstanding struck me all the more as he himself had fostered it by accepting everything that was said about him, by allowing (and encouraging) people to say, for example, that he was a realist painter, while repeating that this did not mean anything at all. But being not at all inclined to theory, he was never in a position to make distinctions. He thus seemed to me the exemplary case of an artist whom one would have to try to put back on his feet via means that do not come only under the jurisdiction of the history of art or the history of ideas but also fall under a philosophical approach, in this case a phenomenological one.

From Saint Augustine to Lacan

I would like to go back to the Bible. At the beginning of our discussions you said that very early on you felt the need to acquire a solid theological education. Do you think that philosophers have suffered from a lack of theological knowledge?

I am fully convinced of that. Let's take Descartes: It is astonishing that no one realized that the 1630 letters to Mersenne are based on literal citations from Suárez and Vásquez. Certainly, a couple of people noted it a bit in some corners (Gilson, Geneviève Rodis-Lewis) but without appreciating the stakes. Indeed, in order to get there, one would have to handle very important material, but, in short, Descartes knew this literature perfectly, as his interpreters could have known. In truth, no one really saw it. Likewise, when one asks Descartes Scholastic questions, he knows perfectly well how to distinguish between formal distinction, modal distinction, and real distinction; thus he knew Scotus. In the discussions about the Trinity, he distinguishes the language of the Greek Fathers from that of the Latin Fathers: thus he knew his theology (from where he got it is another matter, but he certainly knew it). And further, when Gisbertus Voetius dumps biblical citations on him in order to accuse him of atheism, he responds by citing Saint Paul and the Beatitudes: he knew his Bible. As regards his appeal to the divine names, maybe he had not directly read the authors of the apophatic tradition, but he had at least read Lessius's *Treatise on the Divine Names*, which appeared in 1640. And when he speaks of God's incomprehensible power or upholds that the formal reason of the infinite consists in incomprehensibility, he cites classical authors and positions and without doubt is thinking of Benoît de Canfeld. All this was well known to him and well known to his readers.

We have thus refused to accept the resources of theology for interpretation and inflicted our own ignorance on the author because we ourselves know nothing of theology. Recently, I tried to pick out the quotations from Saint Augustine in Montaigne: Obviously, Montaigne knew Augustine—admittedly not his entire work, but at least he knew *The City of God* quite well, for example, because it was being discussed a lot during the religious wars. On the other hand, he never cites the *Confessions*: but is that really because he did not know them? That's not very likely. Maybe the whole world knew them too well, and therefore there was no need to cite them? One would have to examine this more closely because Montaigne's theological learning was considerable: He knew Bernard de Clairvaux better than Pascal, for when Pascal cites Bernard, they are—what a coincidence—the same citations as in Montaigne. We thus have a retrospective outlook on the authors who appear to us as we understand them, yet we understand them only within the scope of our ignorance, which is considerable.

How do you explain this paucity in the philosophical environment?

It obviously has to do with ideology: Progressivism joined with Enlightenment thinkers, and for them the history of theology appeared to be a matter of the obscurantism of another age. Yet the Enlightenment is also a bit of a retrospective invention of the Third Republic, and this concept [of *Lumières*] under the name *Aufklärung*, *Enlightenment*, or *Illuminismo* only became necessary in the nineteenth century. Our view of the eighteenth century was obviously entirely peculiar, and it reconstructed a distorted century. The eighteenth century was in reality much more complex than what *Lagarde et Michard* says about it.[5] What's more, the department of

5. [Marion is referring to a well-known and widely used series of schoolbooks describing a period of literary history through illustrations, historical notes, and extracts from literary works.]

theology at the Sorbonne was shut down in the 1880s.[6] And, as the theologians, who resisted this development for a long time, nevertheless held on to a view of theology that was itself metaphysical, thinking Christian theology after all as a countermetaphysics, things did not work out too well. On an optimistic view, the contemporary situation could appear as that of a rediscovery of theology, especially thanks to the publication of pre-Scholastic theology, but it can only be a matter of a phenomenon to be unfolded in the long term. My generation knows much more about theology than the preceding generation, and I hope that your generation will know still more. We are in a situation of slow and progressive reappropriation of theology within the cultural field.

That being said, does not this reappropriation of theology risk weakening the foundations on which the Republic was constructed?

I think the opposite is the case. Nothing weakens the Republican ideal as much as the dismissal of so many elements of religious culture into irrationality, for this rejection itself feeds the worst declines and frustrations. It is when the essential elements, which are potentially rational or could establish rationality, are excluded from public debate that one abandons them like an underground culture to those who transform them into irrationality and ideology. Then, indeed, one weakens the ideal of the Republic. If the latter does not prove itself capable of integrating some of the religious phenomena, as seems to be the case today, it will no longer be able to manage it, and the extremists will take care of it. And at that point I am not at all certain that the Republic would have the force to resist. If secularism in the French style [*laïcité «à la française»*][7] has held up so far, it owes it precisely to the fact that one did not stay with the 1905 law. Briand redid things in 1924; there were compromises; a great part of what had been excluded was tacitly reintegrated. That was the best way of proceeding for relieving this external pressure on the Republic.

6. [Since that time there have been no departments of theology in French universities, which are public secular institutions. Departments of theology are found in separate, private institutions, such as the Institut catholique or the Protestant Faculty of Theology in Paris.]

7. [*Laïcité* is the French term for the rigorous separation of church and state dating back to the French Revolution. The principle of *laïcité* is one of the ideals of French public education and culture.]

All the same, can one not confirm the anxiety of some "Republicans" faced with the rise in power of the history of medieval philosophy?

I find these fears ridiculous, first because medieval philosophy, to a large extent, is presently done with a profound disinterest in theology. Specialists in medieval philosophy are not obsessed with speculative Christian theology, to say the least! Moreover, paradoxically, the distinction between theology and philosophy proves to be recent because it dates to the second Middle Ages: One could almost say that the Enlightenment began in the Middle Ages! We owe the notions of the lay person and of secular education [*laïcité*], the opportunity for nonclerics to study philosophy, to this historical period. If one wants to defend the ideal of secularism [*laïcité*] and the Enlightenment thinkers, one should instead give preferential treatment to the study of the thirteenth century, when the founding of the universities and the debates between the faculty of arts and the faculty of theology took place. The eighteenth century was a century of heirs—the serious debates had taken place four centuries earlier. Anyway, it is this point, and not speculative theology, in which specialists in the Middle Ages are interested. To forget this implies staying dependent on distorted and perfectly ridiculous pictures, imported by nineteenth-century English gothic novels or by *Notre-Dame de Paris*. In contrast, the Middle Ages is the place of the invention of secularism—which is really born in the Old Testament with the separation between God and king.

In any case, this question of the borders between philosophy and theology seems strange, fragile, and completely modern. Fragile because currently it still appears strongly ideological: While politically powerful, it lacks any serious basis. For it only holds up if one keeps philosophy in the position of an a priori and transcendental science, which would govern all the other kinds of knowledge by establishing their conditions of possibility. But what philosopher still seriously thinks today that philosophy has the rank of a transcendental science establishing a priori the conditions of possibility for any object of experience? I don't know of any, either in phenomenology or in the doctrines deriving from the analytical movement. This distinction has thus become greatly weakened, precisely on account of the situation resulting from the end of metaphysics. That is why those who speak of *the* philosophy, of *the* secularism, or of *the* rationality are actually intellectually behind, supposing the existence of a situation that has not been maintained for a century; in short, it is a reactionary, ideological, and hence profoundly irrational position. A certain kind of defense of the clear distinction between a universal and a priori philosophy and a regional and empirical theology is a matter of pure ideology and of a now very weak ideology. Today, the real distinction would rest on fields of inquiry, on the kind of text one privileges, on the kind of experience one records or in regard to which one extends a hermeneutic. This work is barely sketched.

There is very little psychoanalysis present in your work, although it occupies a strong place in your generation. You cite Lacan in a footnote in your book on Saint Augustine but criticize the reductive dimension of psychoanalysis in The Erotic Phenomenon. *In what estimation do you hold this discipline?*

I do not have a unified and clear opinion on this subject. I can risk some comments that are maybe contradictory and incoherent. At first, I went a bit to the psychoanalysts for my personal needs, but very quickly—that's at least what two of them said to me—despite my declarations of good will, I was totally not a good subject for analysis: I was told that everything in me refused analysis. Absolute resistance. I was incapable of speaking, I always immediately proceeded to interpretation of what I had not yet said, and I could not give the brute facts of the psyche. The first reason maybe had to do with the fact that I understood that I was lucky to have high-functioning neuroses and that it was important to keep them. I have always thought that good neuroses, fully identified and well channeled, lead to very good results and that there is no reason at all for spending lots of energy, time, and money to get rid of one's work tool. I wanted to remain master and possessor of my means of production. The second reason is that during my time psychoanalysis really functioned essentially like an ideology—and as an ideology of denial: Anything one did not want to or could not understand became a matter of analytic treatment; the treatment became the simplest way of fleeing from the real. I had also been struck by the effect that not only treatment but Lacan's charisma produced on individuals. To become "Lacanized" became for me a synonym for becoming lobotomized. One saw people in such a strange situation that it almost produced terror in me.

All the same I've read enough of Freud, because that was indispensable at the time, but I could never make myself be really interested. I was always surprised by the determinism, the positivism, the scientism that emerged in it. Obviously, Lacan interested me far more inasmuch as he seemed to me actually Augustinian, light-years away from Freud's scientism. All of Freud's epistemological and methodological presuppositions were cancelled, it seemed to me, by the so loudly proclaimed "return to Freud." I have never understood how one could believe in this return or how Lacan was able to make people believe it. A tour de force for which I have the greatest admiration. On the other hand, one must take seriously what Lacan says, even if his rhetoric sounded a bit like that of [the cartoon character] Achille Talon (but Achille Talon has always had a heuristic and completely serious Socratic function for me): after all, one deconstructs metaphysics as one can. But, if one wants to take his gesture seriously, one must make several steps backward toward Saint Teresa of Avila, whom he really did read, toward Saint Augustine, whom he knew well. What he said hence came from elsewhere. That is why I went to look directly at the source.

What matters in psychoanalysis are the circumstances of its birth, which, retrospectively, seem very significant to me. The end of metaphysics is not an opinion or an option we could refuse: It is the fact that, once metaphysics had entirely succeeded, had constituted its system, had accomplished its entire program, namely to think being as an object, at that very moment, its four privileged questions were found to be without answer. First, being as being comes down to the concept of being, that is to say, to what is simply thinkable: being had disappeared under the *cogitable*, and, in the concept of being, the concept has regained being. And, as the concept itself does not and *must* not have any content, everything became a being, including what is not, what cannot be. The question of ontology settled in this way, the three principal objects of *metaphysica specialis* follow: God, the world, and the soul. Everything that metaphysics says of God turns him into an idol, and that is why "God is dead": because there are only idols, we know how to construct them, to deconstruct them, and to reconstruct them. The question of God becomes settled in this way. Similarly, the question of the world, because the world is summed up in the totality of extension and of objects that technology permits setting up there: the question of the world disappears, recovered by generalized objectivation that encompasses the whole. Thus the question of the soul, of the *mens*, of rational psychology, is left. On the one side, there is the transcendental subject that does not truly exist and that anybody can or must be; on the other side, empirical egos who end up as technical objects not yet totally identified. In this configuration, there is no place for a rational psychology.

How does one admit that there is no place for a rational psychology? One calls the vanished soul the unconscious, which becomes the loanword for rational psychology in the era of the culmination of metaphysics. Psychoanalysis offers symptomatically in rational psychology the equivalent of the death of God in rational theology. The death of God, technology, and the unconscious articulate the three ways in which metaphysics emerges at the same time as totally accomplished and as totally destroyed. Psychoanalysis, in this sense, cannot envisage the real stakes of rational psychology except in the mode of the unconscious because speaking of the unconscious is strictly equivalent to saying that God means the death of God: Because one cannot say anything of him, God equals the death of God, and the world equals technology. In this sense, psychoanalysis appears as one of the clearest signs of the end of metaphysics. That is why I take it very seriously.

One can say that Freud is situated exactly at the border: On the one hand, he shares the positions of metaphysics (positivism, determinism, objectivism, etc.); on the other, like a magician, he opens his hand and out leap fire, the flowers of desire, and the nightmares of impulses, all kinds of things he himself maybe does not know what to do with and that he can only treat as vague myths. Psychoanalysis tries to give names to these things, without feeling itself entirely qualified to do so. Who can have the strength and the courage to go into this world of elves, of demons, of phantasms where one must not be squeamish in order to remain more or less rational? Psychoanalysts seem to me like very courageous people, who leave themselves exposed a lot—may their proprietary antidote against radiation protect them! I have for them the greatest admiration, but I do not feel myself obligated—or cut out—to go see it.

This link simultaneously of profound sympathy and nonintervention is probably a good idea, for I have seen with pleasure that both *The Erotic Phenomenon* and *Being Given*, or beforehand *God Without Being*, aroused the interest of psychoanalysts, who often invite me to their seminars. When I ask: "What should I talk about, I don't speak about psychoanalysis?" they answer me: "We talk psychoanalysis among ourselves, and we don't need you to speak about it to us. We want you to tell us what you are talking about because what you say gives us concepts for psychoanalysis such as we understand it." For example: the lover who makes advances in *The Erotic Phenomenon*; similarly, the given taking the place of the real and the object; or also the idea of desire without object, and so forth. Psychoanalysts tell me that my work sometimes allows them to have concepts available to them adapted to their own practice. It is not up to me to judge this; I am content to tell them what I have found, and they can make use of it as they wish. I practice the system of lend-lease.

6. The World as It Runs—and as It Doesn't

God Is Not a Value

You stayed comparatively discreet in the media for your entire career, until you started appearing in it, especially when you were elected to the Académie française. Was this discretion deliberate, calculated, or completely unintentional?

Did I stay discreet enough? At least I hope so, but hearing journalists or interviewers point this out to me at the start of every published or broadcast interview, I start to doubt it. If there was discretion, it was in fact voluntary because I had the luck (if one can call it that) to engage the media very early, on the occasion of the publication of *Idol and Distance* and in the flurry caused by the so-called New Philosophers. This flurry did not spare me; I was on the television and radio, heard lots of stupidities said about me and the others, most probably saying quite a few myself; in short, I noted the devastating effect the media has on young authors and even on older ones. One is quickly borne away by the temptation to write only in order to prove one exists, the writing itself becoming finally just a pretext for television exposure and radio polemicizing. So much so that the opinion of the media (return, repeat, as one says) became a ridiculous parody of the Final

Judgment, such as fantasized by any writer—a final judgment every day! Some never recovered. I understood very quickly that it would be better not to insist and to remain cautious.

I really came to understand this comedy one day in Rio de Janeiro. The Brazilian media, which was in fact continually talking about the New Philosophers without understanding anything about them, asked my opinion about it. I said to them: "It's just a joke, a simple hoax." The next morning, all the daily papers, starting with *O Globo*, announced: "The new philosopher declares that the movement of the New Philosophers does not exist." Immediately, at the crack of dawn, journalists rushed to my hotel, pestering me: "Do you confirm it? Do you deny it? What is the political import of your declaration?" (I should say that the military was still in power, for a little while longer, and that the political situation was tense.) Explanations, corrections, commentaries—still more mental confusion. But the next day students invited me quasi-secretly into the basement of their university to ask me very seriously whether, as a Parisian "intellectual," I would advise them to move to armed battle. Taking permission from Clavel and Glucksmann, who had been confronted with the very same question by the ex-Maoists, I argued in favor of a, let's say more diplomatic, choice. To crown it all, a bit later, after giving a lecture to explain that the death of God means the death of the death of God, that God therefore was *not* dead, I got a double page in color in the local equivalent of the *Paris-Match*, with the big title: "The New Philosopher Says 'God Is Dead.'"

This type of farce happened to me often enough to teach me caution: First, as Kant says, critique does not have to be popular; second, there are no reasons why philosophy should be able, I don't even say to be appreciated, but only to be heard in the time of the media (which lasts on average twenty-four hours) because the real criterion—true judgment—takes much more time. Besides, a thought that does not last any longer simply is no thought. I have even come to conclude that only books that are reprinted are books that have found an audience, that one does not have to read books until their second or third edition or until they survive their author. There is a time of reception that does the sifting, and the more the work deals with essentials the longer this time lasts.

Then you don't think of yourself as an intellectual?

No, not at all. I am far too busy doing philosophy and writing books to play at being an intellectual. When it comes down to it, an intellectual is defined as someone who sincerely believes truly to have a brilliant or decisive idea about the state of the world two or three times per week and above all feels the moral duty to make it known as widely as possible, arguing from his scientific authority, which, whether slim or large, was often obtained in a *different* field than the one he wants to discuss that particular week. Current developments can certainly bring several thoughts to my mind, but not to the point of spending my time commenting on them; all the more because what is current one day is by definition no longer current the next. The time I have left for serious things is more important than losing it in such a brief present. Actually, the books that are judged to be unreadable last much longer than journal articles or press declarations; thus, they reach far more true readers—namely, slow readers (just as true authors, who are sometimes the same).

Our era is characterized by nihilism. From Nietzsche to Heidegger, from Valéry to Husserl, everyone saw it, at least among those who think about what they are saying. But surprisingly (unless that itself *is* nihilism) the category of nihilism does not seem to be used by current commentators and observers of society. This is a grave mistake, because if for example we wanted to establish a link between the economization of society and the technologization of industry or the production of knowing (because technology becomes the engine of knowing and knowledge one of the products of the technological enterprise), if we wanted to understand ideologies and their equivalence or understand the motives for the famous "return of the religions" (as if they had left—where to?), if we wanted to provide a serious account of the ecological crisis, the demographic question, or the ethical situation of our societies, then we would have to consider all these phenomena as symptoms of the same situation, which finds its logic and its setting solely in nihilism.

Nihilism is defined as the situation where the highest values are devalued. The highest values are devalued not only because one can destroy them and knock them down but also because one wants to establish other values at will, by the will to power. Whether it is opposed or defended, in fact, value always is intrinsically a matter of nihilism: To describe a reality with the *sinister* qualification of value consists in saying that being, which has already been reduced to its representation and its cogitability by triumphant metaphysics, must in the last analysis be reduced to the judgment of value that affirms or denies it, that is to say, to the will to power. One could radicalize Nietzsche's definition by deeming all beings to be values, depending from beginning to end on the power of affirmation or negation of the will to power—which is instituted by its unique guarantee and unique authority. In the end, nihilism lies as much—in some way maybe more—in defending or affirming these values ("Let's fight over our values!" wails the right and the left, without having any clue what they are saying) because in the best of cases it actually amounts to pushing them even further into the servile function of value. Value, as the slave of the one who evaluates it, eliminates the thing, is alienated.

And thus, those who claim to defend God as a value "blaspheme," as Heidegger said very well. For if God had the rank of a value then he would only exist because we exist. If God had need of us, we who only barely exist, if God had need of us to *defend* him (and with what weapons?), then this "God" would be even *less than us*. Some Catholics and other conservative believers often give the impression that they think that God is very lucky that they are there to defend him and that, if one were to allow God to defend his cause alone, he obviously wouldn't manage to do so, not being really on top of things or very informed about the functioning of the media, in any case unable to communicate correctly, and so forth. Thus, to help him, one must mount demonstrations with banners and slogans. To defend God as a value, one would have to have a theological May Day parade, a well-broadcast "God pride"; or instead establish sites, cover oneself like a fanatic, invade the social networks, twitter like a chaffinch or a soccer player, be a dedicated collector of "friends."

To tell the truth, a believer is defined obviously as someone who is ready to uphold what he is, what he believes, what he hopes especially, not because he would defend God like a value but because he knows himself to be defended by God: "The Lord is my shepherd," "my God is a rock," "I know that my redeemer liveth." God defends us, and first of all against ourselves, against fear—for, as Baudelaire says, the "*good news* causes inexplicable fear in everyone." If the believer must potentially be prepared for confrontation, this is because he knows himself defended by the truth, by the power of God himself, not by his own will, by his own power, by (and for) his own will to power. Thus, God is not a value at all; the believer is valued by God, not God by the believer. It is nihilism when we pull God down to the level of one of the masks of the self-affirmation of our collective or individual identity. A believer believes in God more than in himself, and that is because he has much more confidence in God than in himself and knows that, whatever happens to him, nothing can happen to him. One does not (and will not) get out of nihilism by reaffirming the ancient values more strongly but by freeing oneself from evaluation and by relying on the fact that God goes beyond nihilism by freeing us from the will to power. In deciding on this as a rule: "That *your* will be done on earth as in heaven." But this rule is first of all the trinitarian logic revealed by God himself: "Not my will but *yours*."

Thus, to go back to the initial question, I think that nihilism defines the horizon of the totality of phenomena we must investigate and maybe at times bemoan. In this sense, nihilism must also be understood positively because it de facto explains contemporary rationality. Nihilism accomplishes the objectification of the world by the imposition of calculability as the criterion of being, which leads to profitability and finally to a judgment of value. Not only Hegel's law that "everything that is real is rational; all that is rational is real" but Nietzsche's law: "The human is the evaluating animal par excellence." In other words, to be is to be evaluated or to make oneself be evaluated. Or rather: Only what is profitable really exists; only what is worth one's while has value. We close a factory and open another by *reason* of its value; we move from one moral code to another by *reason* of its greater value (efficiency, reactivity), and so forth. In this way nihilism unfolds the rationality that is left to us for thinking ahead to the future: The entire future henceforth will result from an evaluation (from this comes the determination of any future exclusively from and as a perspective on, forecasting of, or projection of potentially negative growth). But the possible disappears, for the future is always what is seen from the now because it will always result from a calculus of value and will only cause a reproducing of the present, in a close variation: an eternal return of the same. What makes nihilism simultaneously fascinating, reassuring, and at the same time terrifying relies on the fact that it accomplishes to perfection a certain (metaphysical) mode of rationality: We can plan the future as an outgrowth of the present because we know through the will to power that it will obey the rules of evaluation. In some way, the future is emptied of anything possible because it is exhausted in its foreseeability. This is the situation that provokes the crisis because the more one claims—in some manner justifiably—to be able to foresee and evaluate in advance, the more the event appears as a contradiction of all rationality.

The Crisis and the Event

Are you saying that the contemporary crisis is the same thing as nihilism?

I would say that in the situation of nihilism every event becomes a crisis for nihilism itself because the event goes beyond the possible by definition, that is to say beyond what can be foreseen and evaluated. The event, far from remaining stuck in the development of the flow of this temporality, intervenes then as a crisis that interrupts, thus provokes a crisis of foundations. Let's note the ambiguity of our comprehension of crisis. We live our time as a succession of radical crises, even though strangely the recent era (let's say since 1968) numbers fewer deaths and fewer wars than all the preceding centuries, has seen poverty and famine recede and the production of wealth grow as probably never before in human history. Objectively speaking, comparing our situation to that of the sixteenth or eighteenth century, we are immersed in unparalleled bliss and peacefulness. Even so, we feel as if we are going toward the end of a world, and at rapid speed. Why? Because we have such powers of projection, of prediction, and of evaluation that the smallest gap between what we forecast and what comes about appears as a crisis challenging the foundations of rationality itself: That is the explanation for the prevailing pessimism, a profound pessimism terrified by the surprise of the next moment. Like a homeowner who, having covered his house with alarm systems out of precaution ("one never knows," everything is there), jumps every time one of them is triggered and is worried about whether they are functioning correctly when they don't go off. In fact, rationality has never been unfurled so efficiently, but what will we think when it gets caught out by reality? How should we avoid the terrifying suspicion that actually *this* rationality maybe has no bearing on reality? It is the suspicion of this silent and massive discrepancy that worries us, to the point that public opinion from now on has become convinced (quite rightly in my opinion) not only that political power no longer has any real power but that the people economically in charge who think they hold real wealth don't have much left, that even the financiers who at least seem to exercise (obviously secret) power no longer know what they are doing or even whether they are really doing something other than running after their devices and deregulations. Finally and above all, even the discourse of the "scientists" (what a strange expression, one should study it!) no longer dares to claim to be able to speak the truth.

The so far undecided polemics about the warming of the planet provide an astonishing symptom of this. Does one record a warming of the planet? Does it constitute a danger? Does it result from human activity? For none of these three questions do we have a unanimous and clear scientific answer available despite the scores of people whose job consists precisely in trying to respond to it. Actually, they cannot really respond because of a conflict of authority that opposes them. It is as if, short of tumbling into ideology (of submitting truth to a will to truth, hence to a will to power), one could not affirm one or the other thesis. This means that nihilism invalidates even scientific discourse—not at all because it would be false or feeble but, more seriously, because we know that it only becomes and remains completely pertinent to *objects*, while we are confronted with *events*. Yet, climate change, like peace, war, poverty, and social justice, cannot be reduced to objects; they come to us as events. The specialist of a science can speak of the object (of its field of objectness) that he has defined and on which his method has been used; he can hope to know what he says about this object. But the question remains whether this object has any connection with reality.

The old Kantian division between the object phenomenon and the thing in itself reappears today as an extremely concrete question of political decision. It asks whether the object of science, an object of experience instructed and constructed by the scientist in his or her research institute, recovers things such as they are (if there still are any). Yet it has been a long time since the scientist gave up knowing things such as they are in order to replace them with the construction of an object: since Descartes and Galileo. To start with, this objectification was a liberation, allowing finite knowledge to become comfortable and to imagine itself creator. But the problem remains that we do not live exclusively or even first among objects—despite the fact that we produce lots of them and they cover the whole Earth with a mantle that very quickly thickens and even already spills out into space—but in the final analysis we live toward things such as they are (if there are any left), and our access to these things disappears.

The evolution of the economy and the new problems it raises present a good example. Until the time of Malthus and probably a bit further, economy was ruled by the hypothesis of scarcity because the production and the circulation of wealth were linked to natural resources. Then the problematic of scarcity seemed disputable, when it was seen that the production of wealth itself increases wealth and, so one hopes, indefinitely. Under these conditions the economy no longer has any direct link with the earth, ground rent, and so forth but with the development of credit. Marx thematizes the time of the bourgeoisie: Bracketing the hypothesis of the scarcity of resources begins the great development of economy, whether capitalist or socialist—this other face of capitalist economy. Yet, today, the question of scarcity is raised anew, this time no longer because of the exhaustion of resources but because of the exponential growth of pollution. Scarcity is now reversed into the excess of pollution regarding the possibility of reducing waste and of returning it to the natural cycle. The irreducibility of the world of the object to that of nature stands out in the fact that the evaluation no longer concerns the thing that it overwhelms with waste (what is left over from the object). This irreducibility can be seen empirically by the excess of the mass of nonrecyclable trash over the spatial reserves of nature. What does it really mean to say "nonrecyclable"? It means that the objects produce a leftover and that this leftover cannot come back into the thing in itself. One must take ecology very seriously, but first because of trash. Like the pretence to reduce reality through valuation universally, that is to say *without leftover*, to the object, trash proves *in a filthy way* that nihilism allows the in-itself of things to escape, in short the phenomenon happening by itself. In the ecological crisis understood in this way (and to which the official ecological movements hardly pay any attention, mowed down as they are by the most reactionary ideology), we have the most concrete symptom of this discrepancy between object and thing in itself, the indication that nihilism lets loose the world.

By describing the event can phenomenology describe what science cannot foresee and what is impossible to it?

In fact. For I have increasingly come to think that the most determinative of all the saturated phenomena is found in the event, and thus that all the other types of saturated phenomena turn out to be governed each in their own way by eventness [*événementialité*]. How should we define the event? As the impossible, as what was not possible or thinkable before really appearing, thus as what is made real without, for all that, ever having been thinkable. But, on the other hand, the reality held to be impossible will open a new horizon of possibility for it. Let's take the example of political events: When a real political change endures (which remains rare enough and in any case has not happened in France for a long time), no one knows exactly what happens, even less what has ended, but everyone knows all the same that from now on things will be no longer as before, that "a new era begins at this moment," that all the cards are dealt again, that there is a "new deal," and that not only the real but the possible will be different. When the Estates-General decided the common vote for the three estates,[1] when the war of 1914 broke out, when de Gaulle came back as head of state, one saw right away that a new game was being played, with new, unexpected, but normative rules. The fall of the Berlin Wall and the end of the Bolshevik empire to some extent remain mysterious to us, but

1. [The *états généraux* is the prerevolutionary assembly of representatives from the clergy, the nobility, and the "third estate"; the event to which Marion refers is often identified with the beginning of the French Revolution.]

we know that they have redefined everything; the same is true for 9/11. The event redistributes what is possible to the very extent that it remains inconceivable—I would say impossible, in the sense where the onlooker goes around repeating: "But this sort of thing is impossible!" even though he has it right in front of him. The impossible and the real are reversed, at least in their metaphysical definition: The possible, having already ruled out the impossible, no longer precedes the real. But the real, which arises from the impossible and even remains impossible, which goes directly into becoming effective and without asking permission from cogitability, will stir up new possibilities, which thus deserve their name. This reversal of modalities defines the event; it is the impossible really taking place without ever having been possible.

We then find ourselves always late with respect to the event because we can here no longer play the role of the transcendental subject: The event cannot be foreseen a priori because, if it were to be foreseen a priori, it would quite simply not happen at all. Also, the majority of things that one calls events (those that the media announce each day) are precisely not events. These supposed events that are completely anticipated strictly speaking change nothing at all. They only offer news about the never-interrupted flow of expectations. The same is true for technological advances. One *predicts* that they will change everything, yet they are characterized by the fact that they don't change anything: The computer hasn't changed a whole lot; it has just magnified the networks of calculation and of communication already underway. And politics itself, its events and its regular terms (elections, presidential changeovers, murders or deaths of presidents and the vanishing of quasi-elected candidates) do not change anything. Thus, they are not events. The place of the event is neither political nor technological but historical; in other words, it is one of destiny.

Could the phenomenology of the event replace nihilism that way?

Eventness most probably represents precisely what nihilism would like to erase and de facto cover up. The event contradicts the principle of identity because it differs from the state of affairs that preceded it. It contradicts the principle of sufficient reason because there is no conceivable reason that triggers it: The event is not foreseeable, it has no a priori, it is not repeatable, in contrast to the technical object, which in principle always is all of those things. It is also no longer measurable but immeasurable, incomprehensible, and irreducible to metaphysics in general as to its final form of nihilism. What philosophy can thus have some sort of hold on the event?

In either case, not one that would wonder for instance about the reasons we have for acting, as many moral philosophies do today, for the event does not result from a more or less rational calculus or deliberation: The event comes without reason and, as concerns our action, without our reasons for acting. If it holds onto the principle that everything that shows itself first gives itself, and if it manages to think this given, phenomenology can find itself in a position where it obviously does not foresee the event but is able to make it out when it arrives, to face up to it and to receive it, in short to see it, to *go see* it.

Philosophy belongs to matters of destiny, that is to say, it has the capacity to receive a sending, a bringing into play, a departure. In contrast, nihilism establishes a situation where no new sending can occur: In nihilism there is no new dealing of cards because the cards were dealt and the contracts settled at the time of the metaphysical dispatch, and, since then, all the metaphysicians have made predictable moves without error. (As Nizan comments: "One must take philosophies as events."[2]) From this stems the security of nihilism, which assures that nothing ever happens, which defines precisely the *nothing*. Once something happens, nihilism becomes unseated. It is also possible—and Heidegger is right also on this point—to turn nihilism itself into a salvation: It clearly expresses what one cannot do and shows that salvation will grow thanks to it, by the event that contradicts it.

Are you content to take note of nihilism, or do you instead fight against it?

I think of myself as essentially *nonreactionary*—if I can express it like this. I start from the situation such as it gives itself, without dreaming of a golden age, which, besides, I've never known, and I cannot stand those who are nostalgic or complain about decadence. Decadence, they say, but in regard to what? Compared to some supposedly blessed state of French society, of the republic, the kingdom, of Christendom? Someone conjures up decadence? To show him at a loss, just ask him for a date, a period, or a century where he would place the golden age or to which he would date the beginning of the fall. One does not need great historical erudition to prove that all the dates one could propose correspond to catastrophic periods in some field or other. The question is then not whether it was better before and when that *before* took place; the real question would ask what model of interpretation of society and history we have available after the two world

2. Paul Nizan, *Les chiens de garde* (1932; Marseille: Agone, 2012), 81.

wars. Nietzsche announced in 1888 that nihilism must cover two centuries; thus we still have to go through a century of ideology. On this point, philosophers have done their job well: Nietzsche, just like Marx and Heidegger, drew the map and outlined the route through the area we are trying to cross: It is enough to have bought a tour map to not be too surprised at the strangeness of the landscape passed through.

The Withdrawal of God

In your view what sort of talk about God does nihilism make possible?

Born in Nablus, Greece, Justin, was a philosopher and martyr during the second half of the second century after Christ. He established himself as a professional philosopher and was condemned to be devoured by the lions in Rome under the very pious, gentle, and humanist Marcus Aurelius. Justin argued with the emperor (who claimed to be a philosopher) in this way: We are being accused of atheism, but we are not atheists except in regard to the gods the City honors erroneously instead of the true God. This strongly resembles Socrates' precise stance: He also acknowledged that he did not honor the gods the City honored but the true gods. Yet philosophy, in its metaphysical and hence modern form, constructed figures of God that were all, little by little, invalidated by the philosophers themselves and in detail. This went on until the moment when the final figure, that of the moral God, emerged as the outcome of German philosophy and Kant's second *Critique*. It was disqualified by the hypothesis—which was, after all, sensible and quite close to contemporary reality—that it is possible for humans to evaluate beyond Good and Evil. Since then, as the status of morality reverts to us, at our own risk, we do not have any other [figure of God]. We are thus in the situation where all the metaphysical definitions of God are pure and simple idols; in other words, God is dead. In some sense, we know quite well how we have killed him: We have killed him with our incapacity to have a concept, an image, or a definition of him; all the definitions of God have followed on one another, and all have ended up as idols (Nietzsche said this before me). One can then, with a good dose of naïveté, conclude from this that one must close down the question of God.

Matters are not that simple. Admittedly, we no longer have the means for reaching God with a concept adequate to him, but all the religions worthy of the name have always said precisely: "No one has ever seen God." Far from this being an argument for the absence of God or his nonexistence, we can derive from it a positive observation of a divine property—God transcends any immediate presence, and this absence indicates his privilege. Consequently, I simply wondered whether our powerlessness in regard to the concept of God would justify that we conclude the "death of God" from it or whether this death of God finally has no other meaning than the destruction of an idol, namely that of the final *conceivable* "God." Instead, it might be possible that knowing God without concept implies knowing him as unknown, incomprehensibility being part of his definition, because, if he were comprehensible to us, it would no longer be a matter of God. If you understand it, it is not God, as Saint Augustine warned. The fact that society produces false gods for us and above all recognizes them as pure and simple idols suits me very well. Provided that they remain false, I put up with them, but I will become an atheist in regard to them as soon as one asks me to take them seriously. For the case of the true God everything is obviously quite different: The fact that we do not have any concept of God available emerges as the first and most basic condition of knowledge of him. In short, one can make good use of nihilism, and I have drawn from it a consequence of, if I may say, *biblical* simplicity.

But then what speech can one maintain before this event or about God? If we are never worthy of God, must we then conclude that we must shut up or, on the contrary, that any proliferation of talk is allowed or even legitimate?

Neither one nor the other. As Claudel says: "To keep the secret we know, it is not enough merely to keep quiet." The alternative you point out remains too close to the conclusion of the *Tractatus Logico-Philosophicus*: "What we cannot speak about we must pass over in silence." Maybe it is there that one best sees the limits of any logical interpretation of language: Wittgenstein's saying in fact presupposes what it should demonstrate—that speaking means saying something about something. Certainly (as he says), the mystical cannot be spoken, but does that reduce us to silence? If and only if speaking does not mean anything other than saying something about something. But, at the end of the day, is speaking really only saying something about something? When one speaks of something, yes. But not when one speaks *to someone*, for what matters then is not first of all what one says but *the fact* that one says something *to someone*. When I want to remain in contact with someone who is far away from me, I don't have to tell him or her a great number of tales on the telephone or inform him about the type of tobacco I have smoked or the last course I have taught. All of this is only of interest because I am talking *to him* and because, by talking to him, I show to him that he has never stopped being present to my mind. Besides, that's what interests him: The other wants news of me not first of all because he wants to know what I have been doing but because he wants to assure himself that I think of him. Thus, the question is not whether I have nothing to say or have too much to say: Rather, the stakes are to know whether there is an answer to the explicit or implicit call of the other. This is why not speaking or talking in order to say nothing does not prevent talking in the sense of *speaking to*, of responding to a call or of sending it. Claudel is thus completely right: in view of the scope of the secret we have, it is not enough to be silent. One can even say: The more the secret remains by right unutterable, the more one must announce it, make a call, launch appeals, hope for responses, and so forth.

In your view the so-called negative theology then culminates in prayer?

Of course! If I understand it correctly, what one calls, albeit falsely, "negative theology" is defined as the exercise of the word by which we can affirm everything about God (God bears all the names) and, at the same time, we cannot affirm anything of God (God remains anonymous), and these two forms of predication—positive and negative—remain at the same time lawful and ineffective. A third path then opens up. The third path has been interpreted as a law of supereminence or as a law of causality (understood in a still nondogmatic manner), but I don't understand it in that way at all. I understand it as Dionysius practiced it: getting out of predication and, instead of and in place of predication (whether negative or affirmative), *praising* God *as*. When I say to a person that I love him or her *as* the sun of my days or *as* a little bird of the islands, I do not want to say to her that I think she *is* the sun or a parrot. Really, and that is how I am understood, I want to say that I relate to her according to a relationship that employs certain determinations without descriptive value, but I am also reporting a way of aiming at her, of sending me back to her, indeed of praising her. Prayer forms a particular case of praise, or the reverse (one can debate this, and I thrashed this out with Derrida in order to figure out which is the model of the other), but, be that as it may, it is a matter of passing from predication to address. And in address, praise, prayer, celebration, supplication, call, or appeal (in the sense in which one launches an appeal to someone or one calls on someone), one gives all the names to the other; literally, one calls him by all the names. When one gives him all the names, one certainly does not think that one of these names would be completely suitable for him, but on the contrary one gives him several names precisely because one knows that none of them is suitable. I call someone by all the names because he is not worthy of any of them or, rather, because none are worthy of him.

Thus, the fact that we cannot settle the concept *of* God does not imply that we have nothing to say *to* God. Moreover, the same is true of simple interpersonal relationships: We cannot finally define the people we love or whom we know. The more we are closely in relationship with them, the less we know who they are—and we can only continue to live with them on this negative condition. If we could foresee their attitude and their reactions, if we had a concept of them like that of an object, if they ceaselessly matched a definition, unfolding all their actions like one of Leibniz's monads, like the consequences of their definition in the manner of Spinoza, we would get tired of each other and would leave. It is obviously necessary that the other remains in a sense indefinable for us to stay with him or her. The unknowability of the other in no way forms an obstacle to the experience of the other but is its very condition. This is even more true in the case of God. I have always found it infantile and ridiculous when people say: "I do not know God; therefore I have no relationship with him." For if they were to "know" God (as they say without knowing what they are saying), they could not have any relations with him.

A Philosopher in the Church

Do you think that the world is being de-Christianized?

To be completely honest, I don't feel qualified to respond to that question. Just one comment: Sociologically speaking, de-Christianization has meaning on two or three conditions. First, one must have criteria of Christianization and of non-Christianization. Do sociologists and researchers have such criteria available? Obviously not. Do individuals actually know the stage of their personal Christianization or de-Christianization? It goes without saying that at the moments when people are born, when they get married, when they divorce, at the point when they have children, when they are sick, at the moment when they die, they cannot have exactly the same relation to the matter. Who can decide at what time *t* and according to what criteria? Who can do the investigation? For my part, I don't know at all where I would be in a different situation. All these analyses thus seem very abstract to me. Second, I would want to know to what other historical moment one compares the present situation, assuming one could know it: What would be the reference period of positive Christianization? That is difficult to indicate, all the more so as otherwise one spends one's time being suspicious of sociological, popular Christianity.

For a long time, a devout sociological literature has not stopped criticizing a Christianization that it calls too ritualistic, too exterior, too social, or too sanctimonious: Thus, one might suggest that even in an era of sociological Christianization the world would not have been as deeply Christianized as one imagines, and, now that it is no longer Christianized by ritual, the same people tell us that the world is no longer Christianized at all, while they should be pleased that one would have gone beyond an external and ritualized attachment to Christian faith. Reproaching me for my optimism Hans Küng one day lamented to me about the closing of country churches for want of priests: Had he not hoped that this would happen? It would be necessary to agree about the criteria of Christianization, their referents (external worship, the beliefs of the "anonymous Christian," regular or festal practice, etc.) and their hermeneutic validity in comparison to the content of faith (confessing Church, institutional Church, communion of saints, etc.). I think, for example, that there is probably more Christian culture in French society today than at the end of the time of the wars of religion.

I would like for historians or sociologists to have measuring instruments and serious concepts, yet there is no choice but to accept that we do not have them. After all, one of the fundamental principles of Revelation reserves to God alone the knowledge about people's state of Christianization or Judaization, the number of Israel's small remnant. If there were only ten righteous people left in the city, what would that prove, for or against? Not a whole lot. For Christians, there was a moment in sacred history where the people of Israel amounted to a single individual who was condemned to death. Should one interpret this moment when everything was accomplished as the low or the high point of Redemption? Thus, what good are quantitative criteria and polls here? I should like to think not a whole lot. If I judge by my own history since I have entered public life, I have not had the impression of a greater de-Christianization but, on the contrary, of an expansion and a deepening of questions linked to Christianity, hence to Judaism, which seem today much wider, more flexible, and richer than in the 1960s.

As to comparing our time to the 1920s, 1880s, 1810s, before the French Revolution, the wars of religion, the civil war against Mazarin and Louis XIV in the 1650s, the transition from Saint Louis to Philippe Auguste, I must admit that I am a little hazy on this. But, when I read the Fathers of the Church, when I consider the Cappadocian geniuses of the fourth-century I realize that these great bishops could not get into their cathedrals because they were being thrashed by brigands or by the Arians, who manipulated the police in order to forbid access to the place [of the council] of Nicaea. When one thinks of the great Saint Augustine, who, at the summit of his glory, could not go from Hippo to Thagaste without an escort because he ran the risk of being attacked by the Donatists, that really puts things into perspective. Maybe these times will return; that would be no worse. In short, in the meantime, let's have a little moderation.

What do you think of the diagnoses by journalists concerning what has come to be called the "crisis of the Church" or the "crisis of vocations"?

What does this expression "crisis of the Church" actually mean? There is only a single pope, which is already pretty good because there were times when there were two of them. Bishops are regularly appointed, which wasn't always the case under the kings of France or elsewhere. One can go to Mass without retaliation, which hasn't always been true. One might not be Catholic, but one knows for the most part what being Catholic means: The faith and the catechism are taught with one voice. There is certainly a crisis of vocations. But it can be explained simply enough; besides the fact that the standards for recruitment are being continually raised, the crisis of vocation is affecting all social institutions, the army and education, the law, the sciences and the crafts, and there is also not a big crowd of candidates for pastors. There is a general crisis of vocation; what is more normal than that the Catholic Church would not be exempt from it? It is one of the institutions with educational aspirations, and there are no reasons why it would avoid what is happening to the others. Even if we were to admit to a specific crisis of vocation in the Church, there are finally still more priests in France than there were after the Revolution, after the wars of religion, or in the fifth century; it is never impossible for a citizen, even in a very modest situation, to go to one Mass per week; it is just not true that there are no priests and no celebrations [of the Mass]. When a journalist tells me yet again that the churches are empty in France, I know at the very least that he does not go to Mass very often, in any case that he never attends Mass in Paris. Otherwise, he wouldn't say this. Under these conditions, I would settle for this sort of crisis of the Church for a couple of centuries!

But what do you think about the treatment given to the Catholic Church or to believers today?

It is true that there is a "soft" persecution that is unpleasant, insufferable, and of a nameless stupidity. It could still become much worse, but it is already nasty and hurtful. That being said, "if someone reviles you on my account, rejoice": so, I rejoice! But I am not surprised or terribly upset to hear someone say about me: "He is crazy, that one, with his good God, whom only he can see" (Baudelaire). I find this even unavoidable. It belongs to the normal pattern of situations that we have been familiar with since the beginning of the matter in question: The servant is not greater than the master; thus, if the master himself faced worse than that, a fortiori the servant! If Christians were constantly being praised to the skies, like soccer players or rock stars, were admired like shady bankers or questionable people, or were adored like political demagogues, I would look for error, I would suspect misunderstanding. When those who don't agree with you insult you, you can be sure there is no misunderstanding: the whole world knows quite well where the difference lies, and it belongs to the things one must bear. During my intellectual and university career, I have sometimes been criticized for being Catholic (albeit quite rarely), but after some time people just got used to it.

Does the phrase "Catholic philosopher" have meaning for you?

No. As Heidegger says, Catholic philosophy exists no more than Protestant mathematics. There are Catholics who do philosophy just as there are butchers who are Catholic. The real question is whether they are good butchers, good metalworkers, good firefighters, or good philosophers. I assume that, if one has allowed me to have had a not entirely disgraceful career, it is not because I did Catholic philosophy but because the philosophy wasn't too bad, and from that I get great satisfaction. And it so happens that moreover I try to be Catholic. I say that I try because I make an effort. I apply myself to it; I hope to improve, but slowly.

You were very close to a prominent personality in the French Catholic world, Cardinal Lustiger. How did you meet him? What role did you play for him? What role did he play for you?

Jean-Marie Lustiger was one of the most remarkable among the personalities I got to know before they became widely noticed, like Jean Beaufret,

Michel Henry, or even Emmanuel Levinas. At the moment when I made his acquaintance, the greater public knew hardly anything about him, but his readership was already quite large. It is always very instructive to encounter great people before the public acknowledges them as such: the people who know what is at stake certainly know a certain person to be great, but the people who don't know haven't yet figured this out. I encountered Lustiger in May 1968, as the director of CEP (Communauté des étudiants de Paris), at the Place de la Sorbonne, where he had taken over from Maxime Charles. In the reigning chaos, he seemed like one of the rare minds among the clergy and more generally to remain unmoved, not to be easily hoodwinked, like a true Maoist; he quickly decided that in a sense it was a nonevent—even though the whole world at the time used designations like "the events of May." Politically speaking, he was perfectly right.

Our initial relations were tense because I did not belong to his circle. Little by little he became one of the priests, then one of the friends, to whom I was closest. I followed him when he was named curate of Sainte-Jeanne-de-Chantal, at the Porte de Saint-Cloud, where I started doing little jobs for him. When he left Sainte-Jeanne, he wondered what appointment he would get. I had my own little opinion, and we made a bet, each putting our hypothesis in an envelope; his, as I saw later on, was to end up as chaplain at the monastery of Abou-Gosh near Jerusalem; mine said *literally*: to begin with, bishop in a province with problems. We made a bet of a hundred of the old francs [about $20] and a bottle of champagne; when he found out about his appointment to the see of Orléans (precisely a province with problems, which also reawakened very ambiguous memories for him because it was in Orléans that his mother was arrested and sent to Auschwitz, and he had also been baptized in Orléans), I won the bet "fair and square," and he brought us a bottle of champagne and a hundred-franc bill, which my wife obviously put into the collection plate on the following Sunday. I went to visit him several times in Orléans, and, a year and a half later, he was named archbishop of Paris.

He then gathered all the people he knew in order to assemble a team. I served him as an intermediary with the universities, especially the philosophers; I helped him prepare lectures, write texts, and so forth. Jean Duchesne and I also formed a kind of working group with some others, priests and laity, for inviting personalities from all sides and with all sorts of competencies to dialogue directly with him. And that was true all the way to the end. The last time that I saw him, very shortly before his death, he lectured me by saying: "You have written your books, that's good, but it's not enough; you must affect the public space! But what are you doing?" He thus gave me a good telling-off, on the final occasion as on the first. And it is maybe with this final admonishment in mind that, when I was urged to present a candidature for the Académie française, I said to myself: "Go ahead!" Because, if he had been there, he would have told me to go ahead. It concerned his chair, was a matter of doing his eulogy, quite a delicate undertaking: that's why I went forward with it.

To sum everything up, I think that Lustiger had an exceptional fate: He had been born Jewish; he always claimed, with good reason, to have remained so, although never within Judaism, a completely accurate distinction. He was an obviously exemplary figure because, for Catholics, he was in person—if I can say this—the absolute memory of their Jewish identity; that did not fail to stir up some difficulties from the—minimal—portion of Catholics that were unfortunately still a bit anti-Semitic. But two things in him seemed to me also or even more remarkable. On the one hand, the point to which he pushed the *imitatio Christi* in the tradition of the French school, with the figure of the priest understood as *persona Christi*: you only had to spend a week with him to understand this. He also saw everything from the point of view of charity, from Christ's point of view, if I may say so. When he encountered someone, especially someone who came to ask him serious questions—whether political or personal—he did not speak; he listened, he watched, and then one felt that he asked himself only a single question: "If I want to understand what this person says and possibly provide him with some sort of answer, I must reconstruct his spiritual situation as quickly as possible. Everything else will be clarified from there." He had this penetrating stare, which said: "Here is my diagnosis." I felt it almost physically. Certainly, this kind of charisma is found in other spiritual directors (in Charles or in Bouyer, for example), but in him it was particularly evident.

Furthermore, he thought and acted like a Father of the Church. First by the fact of not having quasi anything *written* himself directly; to my knowledge everything he published came first from sermons jotted down and preserved. Very early on, one started recording and transcribing them, to the point where he ended up having a secretary dedicated to that task. He would reread the transcriptions and correct them before they were retyped a final time. He thus worked exactly like Augustine, Gregory of Nyssa, and the others who, for the most part, published their sermons. Here, then, he was at his best: This form of theology owed everything to meditation in act and word, from the heart, before the public. This was not an academic theology or an amateur theology or a rhetorical theology but a liturgical and sacramental theology. Bossuet wrote his sermons; he did not write them himself, but he prepared them and he thought them; he had everything organized, but without accomplishing the literary act: He made a speech act, included in the eucharistic liturgy. The writings resulting from this had a very particular style, truly that of the Fathers of the Church.

Having lots of information available that was far superior than average, he understood very quickly how to touch where it hurts, at the center. I remember encounters between him and Derrida, where, after Derrida's talk, they had a conversation together about Saint Paul—and it was Derrida who was taking notes. In the private seminar, which Jean Duchesne (whom I mentioned a moment ago) led especially, we invited for him all the significant intellectuals, and thus lots of philosophers came: Luc Ferry, Emmanuel Levinas, Michel Serres, Jacques Bouveresse, Anne Fagot-Largeault, Luce Irigaray, and epistemologists, philosophers, feminists, even anticlerical individuals, indeed, the whole world. Everyone was delighted to come and speak, the session lasted two or three hours: the person invited chose his or her theme, and that allowed Lustiger to get to know people, to ask them questions, to hear them speak, to know them not just by hearsay but face to face. His capacity for absorption, discernment, judgment, and his clear-sightedness struck everyone, ourselves included. He proved himself to be very funny, very attentive, and at the same time extremely exacting. One either went with him or one did not go with him. When one marched, then one marched as if in the army; one could not say at the first gunshot: "Excuse me, I have other things to do." He would send me a request at seven o'clock at night for a lecture he had to do the next day and would need it for eight in the morning. No excuses.

Very respectful of university expertise, he said he didn't know philosophy, but he understood it very quickly. We spoke about my work, but he never read a single one of my manuscripts. I explained them to him, sometimes he would make comments about it to me, sometimes drawing very surprising conclusions, but I never submitted any hypotheses to him. After some time, I ended up understanding that he was not in disagreement with what I wrote.

Beyond this privileged friendship with an archbishop, what opinion do you have about the papacy of John Paul II or that of Benedict XVI, still unfinished [at the time of the interview]?

One can only respond to this question by making a kind of judgment about the papacies since the French Revolution. I hardly dare sketch it. After

Leo XIII a system was put in place that was composed of a theology and a political theology. The theology was characterized by an actually fairly indiscriminate return to Saint Thomas Aquinas, which was to bear very contrasting fruit, tending to form a kind of philosophico-theological ideology of the Catholic Church.

The political theology, in a sense, married modernity and thus democracy, the Republic, the laity. From then on, a sort of system was installed that was at the same time admirable and questionable, constituting a kind of countersociety with a state set apart, which for nineteenth-century Catholics was a bit like the same status as the state of Israel for a certain number of Jews: that of a second political identity. It was also a vast system of education, with the temptation of a supposedly unique system of thought, which was fortunately not realized (despite such derivatives as French Action) and finally a kind of militancy (Catholic Action; we underestimate today the importance it had at the beginning of the last century), an international activity (enormously successful missions), which responded in a sense to the Communist International. All of this functioned under Leo XIII, Pius X, Benedict XV, Pius XI, and Pius XII and allowed the Catholic Church to remain intact, to resist two world wars and the great totalitarian ideologies, so that at the end of the war the Catholic Church was still alive and *grosso modo* on the side of the democracies.

But this system—I was going to say of defense and emergency—was no longer adapted to the new world; it had to be modified. This modification began, for the most part, under Pius XII. Despite his reticence, he accomplished many extremely important things: He was the one who liberated exegesis. He was the one who freed the question of evolution from the hypothesis of Darwinism. He reformed the paschal liturgy, he increased Christianity's Jewish consciousness, and so forth. It was even under Pius XII, *volens nolens*, that we had the "Sources chrétiennes," Teilhard and Lubac, the historical Thomism of Chenu and Congar. In a sense, the council launched by John XXIII continued the work carried out under his predecessor. Thus, inevitably, if on the one hand you make possible an evolution in comparison with a somewhat militarized body (I was familiar with its leftovers when I was a child), if on the other hand the structure of society undergoes important modifications, the period of transition inevitably seems like a crisis: That's what happened.

This crisis takes a particular turn after the council, for it concerns the clergy, but it had begun before the council. France was a country where (Lustiger recalled this) there were *too many* priests, to the extent that during the entire nineteenth century, half the missionaries in Africa and Asia came from France. It was a completely exceptional period (my birthplace France-Comté was about three kilometers [less than two miles] away from a village, hardly any bigger, that counted among its children the first bishop of Saigon). But when the model of the priest—the classic model of Bernanos—underwent a crisis, this crisis reached the heart of the institution. All that happened in the 1960s and 1970s. When John Paul II arrived, he picked up the torch, he put things back in marching order. As his stakes correspond to his origin and to the history of Eastern Europe (which must return to becoming "Central Europe" again), the trials of communist (and Nazi) occupation, he undertook a political, spiritual, and pastoral battle in his own style. But his priorities were neither theological (which is why he called Joseph Ratzinger, a born theologian, to be near him) nor juridical (which is why he neglected reforming the internal administration).

Do you know the thought of Karol Wojtyła?

He knew Husserl and Scheler very well, whom he taught, trained in the German (and Roman) fashion. Before becoming pope, even when he was archbishop of Krakow, he was considered one of our most honorable colleagues specializing in these two authors in Poland. Fluent in all the languages, he sometimes came to conferences, where he had his own place. One knew, by reputation, the influence of his teaching as professor and bishop. He had published an article in one of the first issues of the Francophone *Communio* in 1976. I would say of his book *Person and Act* (which I have unfortunately only read in its American translation, which I have been told is quite bad) that it sounds like a rewriting of Blondel in a Husserlian but also Polish context, and I have to admit that it did not impress me much. But *Love and Responsibility* has a simultaneously pastoral, biological, and spiritual dimension, which is completely lacking in my *Erotic Phenomenon*. The common point, if I dare say it like this, lies in the desire really to speak of things and to call an *eros* by its name. But, having become John Paul II, he took on such an epic caliber of personality that like the whole world I found myself stunned.

Did Joseph Ratzinger evaluate God Without Being*?*

Indeed. I met with him when the book first came out, informing him about the objections and the reproaches that came from all directions; he reassured me. He had just been named to the Congregation for the Faith, having defended his thesis on Saint Bonaventure (not without encountering some reservations); he thus proved to be much more in agreement with *God Without Being* than Balthasar, who gave me a dig in a volume of the *Theologik*. With Ratzinger's approval I was much calmer. Moreover, the last time I saw John Paul II, sick and old, he was still able to say a word about *Being Given* to me. That outweighed all the decorations.

Do you regard the papacy of Benedict XVI as a stiffening or a contraction, or even a return to a preconciliar era?

There were polemics in regard to the Second Vatican Council, above all in France, which are now beginning to become watered down. Certainly there are still people who would like to oppose the application of the council to the development of the "conciliar spirit," that is to say, who demand a third council, a Vatican III, in order to draw out consequences that were still implicit in Vatican II or even censured by the curia. That does not make much sense: Church history shows that a council does not come into effect without, so to say, reinforcing the very crisis it wants to bring to an end, precisely because it has identified it. Years, a half-century, sometimes more, are required to implement it; we are still at it. As to the idea that Benedict XVI would threaten the council, it seems to me all the more strange as he was himself one of the most "progressive" actors in it (as one said at the time), and he was one of those who elected Wojtyła precisely because he represented the best intentions of the council. Besides, when I met him in 1975, he was a young professor in Tübingen, considered a liberal and very close to Rahner; I saw anything but a big bad wolf—for all intents and purposes the most courteous, most gentle, most modest man in the world. As concerns the traditionalists (rather badly named because often enough they know very little about the tradition), he had an obsession: Apart from being responsible for a schism, the worst thing for a sitting pope is to allow a schism to stiffen. Thus he tried everything that charity bears and truth permits, that is to say, a lot (I hope, not too much). In my opinion, a good number of the Ecône people will believe themselves obligated to say "no" again, and not all will return to communion, but everything will have been fairly tried.

The Judeo-Christian Revelation

Two personalities have played a very important role for you: Cardinal Lustiger and Emmanuel Levinas. Both were Jewish, each in his own way, and in absolutely different ways: one left Judaism while claiming that he remained Jewish; the other deepened his Judaism and went there to find elements for renewing philosophy. In a general fashion, what is your link to Judaism? And how do you understand Christianity's link—and that of Catholicism in particular—to Judaism?

Let me first pick up again in summary the position Lustiger had, among other things, developed in *The Promise*: The caesura does not pass between Jews and Christians but first among the Jews, among those who became Christian and those who did not. Those who did not become Christian reacted to the destruction of the Temple with the formation of Judaism, of the synagogue cult, of the Talmud, and so forth. Those who became Christian reacted with the formation of the Church. The Judaism organized in this way hence must be understood as one of two responses to the destruction of the Temple, when one does not admit the hypothesis that Jesus was the Messiah, the Christ. Christians chose a different response to the Temple: the Temple is the body of Christ. Appended to this, one could, following his own analysis and correcting your formulation, say that Lustiger did not *leave* Judaism because, although being born Jewish, he had never practiced it and had never entered it. Or instead that he assumed his Jewishness in Christianity and not in Judaism.

Furthermore, I hold invariably to an often-repeated position: There isn't Judaism on one side and Christianity on the other but one unique *Judeo-Christian Revelation* open to a double reception following a double interpretation, according to which Jesus is or is not recognized as the Messiah. Certainly, one cannot underestimate the difference or even the antagonism of these two manners of receiving, but one also cannot underestimate their common content and their common stakes. The difference has less to do with the revealed matter than with the modality of its accomplishment: already real or still possible? And also, this opposition still simplifies too much, for one must at the same time discuss the widely admitted thesis according to which the difference has to do with the fact that for the Jews the Messiah has not yet come, while for Christians he has already come. It is not up to me to confirm that, even for the Jews, the presence of God is already really accomplished among the people even before the coming of the Messiah, but I can stress that for Christians the coming of Jesus as Messiah does not eliminate the Messianic expectation but reinforces it to the point of a fevered pitch, under the form of the expectation of the second coming in glory of Christ. This second coming of the Messiah takes up in Christianity all the characteristics of waiting for his coming in Judaism; it raises the same questions. In a word, at the risk of simplifying and of appearing perfunctory or even brutal, my position can be summarized in this way: There is no deep difference between Jews and Christians, for we have to respond to the same election, even (and above all) if we do not want to (or *should* not) respond to it in the same way. In other words, the difference of answers does not forbid the identity of the election but presupposes it. We know very well that we speak of the same thing.

What you say assumes a Christian point of view, and a Jew would maybe have some difficulty adopting it. One has the feeling that Marcionism is certainly a Christian temptation but also a Jewish one: From each side one wants to form two religions, as watertight as possible, Christianity by challenging its origin and Judaism by challenging a posterity in which it does not recognize itself.

I completely agree. In the two cases, the worry about affirming one's identity by the exclusion of the other (who precedes or who follows) accomplishes the same mistake: utilizing the election God gives in order to reinforce humanely instead of responding to the call. But the most striking for me was to discover to what extent the Christian eucharistic liturgy remains unintelligible without the Jewish liturgy. Louis Bouyer has shown this in detail in his two admirable books *The Eucharist* and *The Paschal Mystery*. Christians can no longer be Christians unless they admit that they think and speak Hebrew, even without knowing it: Their dictionary and their theological grammar come from Jewish prayer. Otherwise, they can no longer speak of baptism, of sacrament, or of the Eucharist—they can no longer speak of anything at all!

To close these interviews, is there a question that you want to be asked that hasn't been raised?

There is indeed a question that I ask myself more and more: Why did all this happen to me? Actually, for a long time I have had the impression that without foreseeing it and without wanting it, I have followed a journey that could have a meaning, that in no way is it an absurd history told by a fool. I am surprised that these things have happened in this way and that they show such coherence. But I neither wanted nor foresaw this coherence; I was too preoccupied with staying on course and managing my efforts, advancing step by step, without lifting my eyes too much. Retrospectively, I come only to a single and final explanation: I must admit that I have received this coherence, which I could not have produced.

Did you then feel something like an election?

Yes, at several points, indisputably, I had the impression of being taken from the herd and put where I did not even know one could go. In these moments, I did not realize projects or ambitions coming from myself, but I received what happened to me. Often, my life as a whole seems to me like some of the years when I trained as a runner: During long and exhausting training sessions, one suffers enough to know oneself to be the one who makes the effort, but, once one is in form, on the day of competition, in the sun of spring or the overhead light of an autumn evening, when suddenly a state of grace causes one to accomplish the impossible (a victory, a personal record), one wonders who has done all that, or, rather, I wonder whether I have done it or even whether this has happened to me. From there stems this strange feeling that has never left me, of living with someone *bearing* (in all the senses of the word) my name, who does things without warning me and whom I had to accompany. At times I would almost have preferred that he leave me alone, but I have always lived with someone who . . .

. . . who is stronger than you and whom you follow?

Yes, and I cannot do otherwise. This gives me a real detachment. I hope so, all the way to the end.